Property and Trust Law in Cyprus

Property and Trust Law in Cyprus

Tatiana Eleni Synodinou

This book was originally published as a monograph in the International Encyclopaedia of Laws/Property and Trust Law.

Founding Editor: Roger Blanpain, Frank Hendrickx
General Editor: Alain Verbeke
Volume Editors: Alain Verbeke & Vincent Sagaert

Wolters Kluwer

Published by:
Kluwer Law International B.V.
PO Box 316
2400 AH Alphen aan den Rijn
The Netherlands
E-mail: international-sales@wolterskluwer.com
Website: lrus.wolterskluwer.com

Sold and distributed in North, Central and South America by:
Wolters Kluwer Legal & Regulatory U.S.
7201 McKinney Circle
Frederick, MD 21704
United States of America
Email: customer.service@wolterskluwer.com

Sold and distributed in all other countries by:
Air Business Subscriptions
Rockwood House
Haywards Heath
West Sussex
RH16 3DH
United Kingdom
Email: international-customerservice@wolterskluwer.com

ISBN 978-94-035-2730-7

e-Book: ISBN 978-94-035-2731-4
web-PDF: ISBN 978-94-035-2732-1

This title is available on www.kluwerlawonline.com

The Author

Tatiana Eleni Synodinou is an Associate Professor of Private and Commercial law at the Law Department of the University of Cyprus. She obtained her law degree from the Aristotle University of Thessaloniki. She completed her postgraduate studies at the University Aix-Marseille III and her doctoral and postdoctoral studies at the Aristotle University of Thessaloniki, receiving fellowships from the Greek Scholarship Foundation and the Committee of Research of the Aristotle University of Thessaloniki.

She is the author of numerous books, journal articles and chapters in edited books on copyright law, Internet law, private law and commercial law. She has participated as a speaker at numerous conferences and seminars and organized various national and international conferences and study days. She has been nominated as an expert in many projects and EU studies. She is the Chief Editor of the student law journal *Nomomacheia*. She is a Founding Member and President of the Union of Copyright Law of Cyprus (EDPI) that is the Cypriot affiliate of the International Literary and Artistic Association (ALAI) and Member of the European Copyright Society (ECS). She is a contributor to Kluwer Copyright Blog.

The Author

Table of Contents

List of Abbreviations

CJEU	Court of Justice of the European Union
CLR	Cyprus Law Reports
ECtHR	European Court of Human Rights
ESIS	European Standardised Information Sheet (EU)
EU	European Union
JSC	Judgments of the Supreme Court of Cyprus
UK	United Kingdom

List of Abbreviations

General Introduction

§1. General Background of the Country

I. Geography

1. Cyprus is the third largest island in the Mediterranean Sea, after Sicily and Sardinia. It is also the third smallest country of the European Union, after Malta and Luxembourg. It has an area of 9,251 square kilometres and a population of around 0.8 million inhabitants. The island is situated in the north-eastern corner of the Mediterranean, very near to Turkey and Syria, and north of Egypt. Cyprus takes its name from its copper mines, that were intensely exploited in antiquity. It possesses two mountain ranges, the Troodos Mountains and the Keryneia Mountains or Pentadaktylos. The island has a Mediterranean climate which is warm and rather dry.

2. Cyprus lies on the intersection of the thirty-fourth latitudinal and longitudinal parallels. Its strategic position in relation to the three continents of Europe, Asia and Africa made Cyprus an attractive target for its neighbours and for more distant foreign powers. The Mycenaeans, Achaeans, Phoenicians, Assyrians, Egyptians, Persians, Alexander the Great, the Romans, Byzantines, Crusaders, Franks (Lusignans), Venetians, Turks and British have all, in turn, exercised control and influence over the island and its inhabitants.[1]

II. Cultural Situation

3. The island is culturally and demographically divided into two. In 1878, the United Kingdom persuaded Turkey to cede Cyprus in exchange for the annual payment of a rent corresponding to an estimation of the taxation incomes of the island. The UK's occupation of the island was consolidated in 1914, as the United Kingdom annexed Cyprus after Turkey entered the World War I on the side of Germany. Under the Treaty of Lausanne in 1923, Turkey relinquished all its claims to Cyprus and the island became a Crown Colony in 1925. The colony was therefore comprised of Greek-Cypriot and by Turkish-Cypriot residents, forming two separate communities. However, the Greek Cypriots' political movement of 'enosis' (literally, 'union'), which sought not only independence from UK but also the political

1. Andreas Neocleous and David Bevir, *Legal History, Introduction to Cyprus law* §1, 1 (D. Campbell ed., Law Publishing 2000).

union of the island with Greece, gradually grew in fervour and finally took the shape of an insurrection. While the situation was nearing the proportions of a civil war, Greece and Turkey agreed, with the consent of Great Britain, to the creation of an independent state in Cyprus in 1960.[2]

4. In 1974, after years of civil unrest between the communities, Turkey sent its army and invaded the northern part of the island, in order, according to the Turkish government, to protect the interests of the Turkish Cypriots. The occupation led to the creation of the self-proclaimed 'Turkish Republic of Northern Cyprus', which is not recognized at international level (except, obviously, Turkey).

5. For the last forty years, the situation has remained the same, with various negotiations held by UN failing to solve what has become known as the 'Cypriot Problem'. Cyprus joined the European Union in 2004, but the application of European Union law on the northern side is suspended until the resolution of the Problem. Cyprus has also joined the monetary union. However, the country is not part of the Schengen Agreement.

III. Political System

6. The Republic of Cyprus is a unitary presidential representative republic, whereby the President of Cyprus is both the head of state and the head of government. The constitution possesses a complex system of checks and balances including a weighted power-sharing ratio designed to protect the interests of recognized minorities. However, after the Turkish invasion in 1974, the courts have made bold use of the international law principle of the 'law of necessity',[3] and all sections of the constitution that cannot be applied while the occupation exists are temporarily suspended.

7. The president is elected by popular vote (with two rounds) for a five-year term. The House of Representatives has 59 members elected for a five-year term: 56 Greek Cypriot members chosen by proportional representation and 3 observer members representing the Maronite, Roman Catholic and Armenian minorities.

2. For a detailed analysis of the historical and political situation until 1960, *see* Georges Tenekides, *La condition internationale de la République de Chypre*, Annuaire Français de Droit International, 6 pp. 133–168 (1960).
3. *See* Constantinos Kombos, *The Doctrine of Necessity in Constitutional Law* (Sakkoulas Publications 2015); Christos Papastylianos, *The Cypriot Doctrine of Necessity within the Context of Emergency Discourse: How a Unique Emergency Shaped a Peculiar Type of Emergency Law*, 30(1) Cyprus Review 113–144 (2018); Polyvios Polyviou, *The Case of Ibrahim, the Doctrine of Necessity and the Republic of Cyprus* (Chryssafinis & Polyviou Publications, 2015).

§2. Legal Background of the Country

I. Legal Family or Tradition

8. Because Cyprus' independence is the result of not so much a revolution as an agreement between foreign powers, the creation of the Republic of Cyprus did not lead to a rupture in the legal tradition. This means that Cyprus is mainly a country of the common law tradition. In principle, most of its laws are inherited from the time of British rule. Even though the common law's case law is used as a persuasive and not as binding precedent, English case law is still used on a daily basis by the courts. However, this influence concerns the interpretation of common law general principles, which existed before independence, and not British legislation, which has no effect in Cyprus. As regards the common law, this is applicable in Cyprus in virtue of section 29(1)(γ) of the Courts of Justice Law, 1960 (Law 14/60). As the Supreme Court held in the *Panayides* case,[4] what is applicable in Cyprus is the common law, not the common law as it came to be modified by statute in England. Section 29(1)(γ) incorporates the common law,[5] not English Law as applicable in England at any one time. The *Paikkos* case[6] considered that for common law to be valid in Cyprus, three criteria have to be met: (1) it conforms to the Constitution, (2) no other provision has been made by any law save under Article 188 of the Constitution, or enacted by the legislature of the Republic; 'other provisions' are made, if it is very clear from the enactment which is being relied on, that it is the intention of the legislature to exclude the common law, (3) it is compatible with the local specificities of the island, since the common law must be pruned by judicial decision to suit local conditions.[7]

9. Without underestimating the considerable effects of the dogma that Cyprus is a common law country, some elements have to be mentioned that render these concepts less absolute. According to Prof. Symeonides, 'Cyprus is too small a country (less than 5000 square miles) to have geographically dispersed legal diversity. However, Cyprus has a different type of legal diversity – by subject matter … in Cyprus one changes laws as often as one changes subject matter. Indeed, the law of Cyprus resembles the beautiful mosaics that adorn so many of its ancient Byzantine churches – it is a colorful plurilegal mosaic. It is so diverse in terms of sources, legal traditions, and applications as to be insusceptible of being neatly classified as a member of either the common law or the civil law legal families … it is an example of what is known as "mixed legal system". Nevertheless, it is a decidedly European legal system.'[8]

---

4. *Constantinou v. Panayides* (1984) 1 CLR 466.
5. *See* Law 14/60.
6. *Paikkos v. Kontemeniotis* (1989) 1 CLR 50.
7. The Common Law is now applicable in Cyprus in virtue of s. 29(1)(γ) of the Courts of Justice Law, 1960 (Law 14/60).
8. Symeon C. Symeonides, *The Mixed Legal System of the Republic of Cyprus*, 78 Tulane Law Review 442 (2003).

10. Cyprus has such a legal system that reflects its rich and diverse history. Specifically, four arguments can be advanced that show Cyprus has de facto a hybrid legal system.[9] First, the language used by the court changed in 1990 and since then legal practitioners have worked exclusively in Greek.[10] This shift in language was not just a formality. The legal way of thinking is closely related to the use of specific words and expressions, that are not strictly identical in all languages. Second, Cyprus does not use common law principles in the same way as the UK does. Most principles were codified at the end of the nineteenth century in legislation. In this context, common law rules were codified into a set of laws that strongly resembles a code. For instance, Cypriot contract law is quite similar to the Indian contract law (Indian Contract Act 1872), the primary differences between the two texts being mainly technical.[11] It is also noteworthy that for the interpretation of Cap. 149, for a long time Courts referred to the classic book 'Pollock & Mulla's Indian Contract and Specific Relief Acts'. The mere fact of this codification influences the way the principle is interpreted, as the judge is bound by the terminology and definition used by the law. Third, the legislative activity that is characteristic of all modern civilization means that with each new legislation voted Cyprus and Great Britain's legal systems depart a little bit more. Finally, the common law's influence is not equal in all fields of law. While its supremacy in private law and criminal law cannot be doubted, public law is the opposite, heavily influenced by general principles of Greek administrative law. Overall, private law, criminal law, civil/criminal procedural law and legal methodology follow the common law tradition, whereas public/constitutional/administrative law and family law[12] follow the civil law tradition.

II. Relation and Hierarchy Between the Sources of Law

11. The occupation of the north of Cyprus has had a substantial effect on land law. The real properties of Greek Cypriots in the northern part had been annexed by the Turkish government.[13] As this was illegal expropriation, it is not recognized. The protection of Greek Cypriot property in the occupied territories has been repeatedly brought before the European Court of Human Rights (ECtHR). In the landmark case *Loizidou v. Turkey*[14] and in a number of subsequent decisions,[15] the ECtHR held that the denial of access to property and the consequent loss of control is attributable to Turkey and not to the illegal *Turkish Republic of Northern Cyprus*

9. Dimitrios Koukiadis, *Legal Transplantation's Contribution to the Formation of Mixed Legal Systems, and the Paradigm of Cyprus' Legal System as a 'Polyjural' System*, 30(2) Cyprus Law Review 94 (2018).
10. The change was introduced with: Law 67/1988, Gazette, Section I, Appendix 2327, 27 May 1988, p. 2275 and Law 146/1989, Gazette, Section I, Appendix 2433, 11 August 1989, p. 3481.
11. Nikitas Hatzimihail, *Reconstructing Mixity: Sources of Law and Legal Method in Cyprus, Mixed Legal Systems, East and West* 81 (V. Palmer, M. Y. Mattar & A. Koppel eds., Routledge 2016).
12. For an analysis of family law in Cyprus, *see* Achilleas Emilianides, *Family and Succession Law in Cyprus* (2nd ed., Wolters Kluwer, 2019).
13. *See* Article 159(1)(b) of the 7 May 1985 Constitution of the 'Turkish Republic of Northern Cyprus' (the 'TRNC').
14. ECHR, *Loizidou v. Turkey*, (Preliminary Objections) No. 15318/89, 23 March 1995; ECHR, *Loizidou v. Turkey*, (Merits) No. 15318/89, 18 December 1996.

and that there is an infringement of Article 1 of the First Protocol of the European Convention on Human Rights due to the continued denial of access to the applicant's property and the loss of control and enjoyment of its property. The ability of Greek Cypriots to directly appeal to the ECtHR has emerged as the most appropriate and popular measure of protecting their property in the occupied territories for many years. However, the ECtHR's ruling in the *Demopoulos* case[16] on 1 March 2010 reversed the legal situation. In this case, the ECtHR accepted as a lawful means of judicial redress the Immovable Property Commission, which was set up by the occupying state in 2003 as Turkey's domestic legal remedy, to which Greek Cypriot property owners must first appeal. If they are not satisfied with the decision, they must then appeal to the 'Supreme Court' of the occupied territory and, if they still not satisfied, there is the possibility of appeal before the ECtHR.

12. Foreign occupiers of the land could also be held liable for the occupation of property belonging to Greek Cypriots and be obliged to render it to its legitimate owner, as the CJEU confirmed in the *Apostolides v. Orams* case, where it was held that the suspension of the application of the *acquis communautaire* in those areas of the Republic of Cyprus in which the Government of that Member State does not exercise effective control does not preclude the application of Council Regulation (EC) No. 44/2001 of 22 December 2000 on jurisdiction and the recognition and enforcement of judgments in civil and commercial matters to a judgment which is given by a Cypriot court concerning land situated in areas not so controlled. Furthermore, the CJEU held that Article 35(1) of Regulation No. 44/2001 does not authorize the court of a Member State to refuse recognition or enforcement of a judgment given by the courts of another Member State concerning land situated in an area of the latter State over which its Government does not exercise effective control and that the fact that a judgment given by Cypriot courts concerning land situated in an area of that State over which its Government does not exercise effective control, cannot, as a practical matter, be enforced where the land is situated does not constitute a ground for refusal of recognition or enforcement under Article 34(1) of Regulation No. 44/2001, and it does not mean that such a judgment is unenforceable for the purposes of Article 38(1) of that regulation.[17] Consequently, the recognition and enforcement of the judgments of the Cypriot court could not be refused in the United Kingdom on that ground.[18]

15. ECHR, *Cyprus v. Turkey [GC]*, No. 25781/94, 10 May 2001; ECHR, *Demades v. Turkey*, No. 16219/90, 31 July 2003; ECHR, *Eugenia Michaelidou Developments Ltd and Michael Tymvios v. Turkey*, No. 16163/90, 31 July 2003; ECHR, *Xenidis-Arestis v. Turkey*, No. 46347/99, 22 December 2005.
16. ECHR, *Demopoulos et al. v. Turkey [GC]*, Nos 46113/99, 3843/02, 13751/02, 13466/03, 10200/04, 14163/04, 19993/04, 21819/04, 1 March 2010.
17. Case C-420/07 *Meletios Apostolides v. David Charles Orams, Linda Elizabeth Orams*, Judgment of the Court (Grand Chamber) (2009).
18. *See* T. Synodinou, 'Protection de la propriété à Chypre: cadre légal et frontières de l'acquis communautaire', in *La singularité de Chypre dans l'Union Européenne, Diversité des droits et des statuts* 307–322 (J. Rosseto & K. Joséphides eds., Mare & Martin 2012).

13. On the Greek Cypriot side, the Turkish Cypriot real properties are de facto managed by the State under a legal framework of 'state guardianship' (*see* Chapter 7).

14. It has to be mentioned that in addition to the Cypriot Problem, Cyprus hosts British military bases that possess a very peculiar statute. They are under the sovereignty of the UK. While Great Britain, on the basis of the Constitution, is obliged to pay rent for the exploitation of these bases, the country considers that its obligation is forfeited while the Cypriot Problem remains. Specifically, according to the London-Zurich Treaties of February 1959, the United Kingdom holds sovereign overseas installations, the Sovereign Base Areas, which are divided into two sections (the western and the eastern), and they have their own legal system, distinct from the United Kingdom and the Republic of Cyprus, which consists of the laws of the Colony of Cyprus as of August 1960, amended as necessary,[19] while an independent court of the Sovereign Base Areas is concerned with non-military offences. The Supreme Court of Cyprus has repeatedly ruled that 'in accordance with the Treaty of Establishment and existing case law, the sovereign base areas are not part of the territory of the Republic of Cyprus. These regions, upon the establishment of the Republic of Cyprus, remained in the sovereignty or dominion of the United Kingdom and therefore the Cypriot courts do not have the necessary jurisdiction.'[20] Thus, when the areas were being established, the boundaries were deliberately drawn to avoid centres of population. At the moment, of approximately 15,700 people living in the areas, about 7,700 are native Cypriots who work in the areas themselves, or on farmland within the boundaries of the areas, and the rest of the population are British military and their families,[21] consisting of a considerable centre of social and economic activities. In this aspect and regarding the immovable property status of the relevant areas, it is of great importance that an agreement was signed on 15 January 2014 between the Government of the Republic of Cyprus and the Government of the United Kingdom of Great Britain and Northern Ireland to regulate property development within the British Bases.[22]

15. This political peculiarity has some consequences as regards the hierarchy between the sources of law. Indeed, while acceding to the European Union, Cyprus did not have political, cultural or societal oppositions to putting European Union law at the top of the hierarchy – that is, even above even the Constitution of the Republic of Cyprus. Specifically, the supremacy of EU law over the Constitution of

19. Sovereign Base Area, https://www.sbaadministration.org/ last visited on 23 December 2019.
20. *See, e.g., Preece v. 'Estia' Insurance & Reinsurance Corp.* (1991) 1 CLR 568 and *In relation to the application of Chimonas*, Civil Appeal No. 190/2015, 10 February 2016.
21. Policy Department External Policies, The status and location of the military installations of the Member States of the European Union and their potential role for the European Security and Defense Policy (ESPD), Briefing Paper in Security and Defense, February 2009, http://www.europarl.europa.eu/meetdocs/2004_2009/documents/dv/sede300309studype407004_/SEDE300309StudyPE407004_en.pdf, last visited on 09 October 2017. *See also* Akrotiri Population, http://www.indexmundi.com/akrotiri/population.html and Dhekelia Population, http://www.indexmundi.com/dhekelia/population.html.
22. Written statement by the President of the Republic (15 January 2014), http://www.mfa.gov.cy/mfa/mfa2016.nsf/All/D91DB7BC3BFBFEC3C2257FA000459773, last visited on 23 December 2019.

the Republic of Cyprus is safeguarded under the Constitution of the Republic of Cyprus, which was amended by the Law relating to the Fifth Amendment of the Constitution (Law 127(I)/2006) in order to clarify the supremacy and precedence of EU law over the Constitution. According to Article 1A of the Constitution, which is modelled loosely on the blanket EU clause of the Irish Constitution, 'No provision of this Constitution shall be considered as invalidating laws enacted, acts done or measures adopted by the Republic necessitated by its obligations as a Member State of the European Union or shall prevent Regulations, Directives or other acts or binding measures of a legislative character adopted by the European Union or by the European Communities or by their institutions or by their competent bodies under the provisions of the treaties founding the European Communities or the European Union, from having legal effect in the Republic.'[23]

16. Therefore, the hierarchy of the sources of law in Cyprus are: EU primary law, EU secondary law, the Constitution, International Conventions/Treaties/ Agreements,[24] domestic laws,[25] regulatory acts, Supreme Court case law, common law and equity principles, and customs.

17. Due to the lack of a Civil Code in Cyprus, property law is governed by a series of laws, the most important of them being the Immovable Property, Tenure and Valuation Law of 1946 – Cap. 224, which is the basic source for the regulation of property rights over land in Cyprus. Other important laws and regulations are: the Transfer and Mortgage of Immovable Property Law of 1965 (Law 9/1965), the Legal Entities (Registration of Immovable Property) Law (Cap. 218), the Sale of Property (Specific Performance) Law of 2011 (Law 81(I)/2011), the Immovable Property (Sales Restriction) Law of 2002 (Law 82(I)/2002), the Bankruptcy Law (Cap. 5), the Protection of Immovable Property Located in Areas Not Controlled by the Republic (Special Provisions) Law of 2014 (Law 137(I)/2014), the Tenancy Law of 1983 (Law 23/1983), the Civil Procedure Law (Cap. 6), the Regulations on Immovable Property (Tenure, Registration and Valuation) of 1956 (Law 622/1956), the Lands and Surveys Department (Fees and Rights) Law (Cap. 219), the Town and

23. According to Kombos and Shaelou, a serious substantive problem exists, since at the time of the enactment of the Fifth Amendment of the Constitution, the Republic of Cyprus gave a more extensive scope and effect to the principle of primacy of EU law than what the jurisprudence of the ECJ required, even though now the issue has lost its relevance since the entry into force of the Lisbon Treaty. *See* Constantinos Kombos & Stephanie Laulhé Shaelou, *The Cypriot Constitution Under the Impact of EU Law: An Asymmetrical Formation, National Constitutions in European and Global Governance: Democracy, Rights, the Rule of Law* (Al. Bardutzky ed., T.M.C. Asser Press 2019).
24. Under Art. 169 of the Constitution, once international conventions, treaties or agreements entered into by decision of the Council of Ministers, have been ratified by law and published in the Official Gazette of the Republic, they have supremacy over any national law (with the exception of the Constitution) and, in the event of conflict with such laws, they take precedence, provided that they are similarly applied by the counterparty.
25. Under the provisions of Art. 188 of the Constitution, the laws which apply in the Republic of Cyprus today are the laws which were on the statute book pursuant to that Article on the eve of Independence Day, unless some other provision has been or will be made pursuant to a law which applies or is passed pursuant to the Constitution and the laws passed by the House of Representatives after independence.

Country Planning Law of 1972 (Law 90/1972), the Regulation of Streets and Buildings Law (Cap. 96), the Preserved Buildings Law of 2002 (Law 240(I)/2002), the Consolidation and Redistribution of Agricultural Property Law of 1969 (Law 24/1969), the Turkish Cypriot Properties (Administration and Other Matters) (Temporary Provisions) Law of 1991 (Law 139/1991), the Turkish Cypriot Properties (Administration and Other Matters) (Temporary Provisions) Regulations of 1992, the Central Agency for Equal Distribution of Burdens (Establishment, Objectives, Functions and Other Related Matters) Law of 1989 (Law 141/1989), the Missing Persons (Temporary Provisions) Law of 1979 (Law 77/1979), the Acquisition of Immovable Property (Foreigners) Law (Cap. 109), the Taxation of Inheritance Law of 1962 (Law 67/1962), the Property of Deceased Persons (Taxing Provisions) Law of 2000 (Law 78(I)/2000), the Matrimonial Assets Law of 1991 (Law 232/1991), the Real Estate Agents Law of 2010 (Law 71(I)/2010), the Insolvency of Natural Persons (Personal Repayment Schemes and the Debt Relief Orders) Law of 2015 (Law 65(I)/2015), the Insolvency Advisors Law of 2015 (Law 64(I)/2015).

18. The way the legal mechanism of judicial precedent is applied in Cyprus was defined by the Supreme Court in a series of cases. In *Demetriades v. The Republic*, the Supreme Court affirmed that 'subordinate courts, and with it is meant District Courts and Assize Courts, are bound by the existing judicial precedent of superior courts, and as far as such subordinate courts are concerned, the Supreme Court whether sitting as a Full Bench or in Benches of three, should be deemed as a superior court'.[26] As regards matters of constitutional and administrative law, there is greater leeway for reversing a binding precedent. Specifically, as the highest court of the land, entrusted with both original and appellate jurisdictions, and concerned with the interpretation of the Constitution and having exclusive jurisdiction on administrative law matters, the Supreme Court is entitled to depart from precedent if it is of the opinion that precedent has been wrongly held or that changed political, economic and social developments call for a review of its previous approach. It should, however, be reluctant and cautious to depart from precedent and should always be guided by the fact that such a departure should not interfere retrospectively with contractual relations and fiscal arrangements.[27] Similarly, in criminal law cases, the doctrine of precedent does not apply with the same severity. Specifically, '[i]n its criminal jurisdiction, which it has inherited from the Court of Criminal Appeal, the Court of Appeal does not apply the doctrine of stare decisis with the same rigidity as in its civil jurisdiction … '.[28] Furthermore, the application of a principle of law to the facts of individual cases does not establish precedent in the sense of stare decisis. The only principle of law relevant to an award of damages is that damages should, on the whole, be fair and reasonable.[29] Previous awards do not give rise to binding precedent in the sense of stare decisis, but they offer guidance.

---

26. *Demetriades v. The Republic* (1974) 4 JSC 480 and *The Republic v. Demetriades* (1977) JSC 2102.
27. *Ibid.*
28. *Salem Ali A-Hamad et al., Appellants, v. The Police*, Criminal Appeals Nos 4974–4975 (1988) 2 CLR 164. *See also The Republic v. Sampson* (1977) 2 CLR 1.
29. *Ioannou and Paraskevaides (Overseas) Ltd., et al. v. C. P. Christophis* (1982) 1 CLR 789.

Foreign awards must be seen subject to the realities in this country.[30] In the event that there are conflicting rulings of the Supreme Court in plenary on an issue, the judges of the Supreme Court, in their jurisdiction, are bound to follow the latter decision if said decision has already examined the issue and has not accepted the former decision. Exceptions can only be made to any subsequent plenary decisions which are taken *per incuriam,* that is, unknowingly of a previous decision or decisions of the plenary on the same subject, or without the knowledge of a legislative provision. In such a case, the Court of First Instance is free to choose which one to follow, so it can follow the earlier decision if it considers that the subsequent one was taken *per incuriam.*[31]

§3. Introduction to the Law of Property and Trust

I. Historical Origins and Evolution

19. The importance of using immovable property as a means of financial transactions in Cyprus is clearly illustrated by the contract referring to immovable property, engraved above a bronze tablet, which was discovered near the area of the ancient city of Idalion and is written in the Cypriot syllabary. Above this tablet, which dates around the first quarter of 5th century BCE, is the contract which was concluded between the King of Idalion, Stacikipros and the doctor Onasilos, according to which, the King invited the doctor to come to Idalion and provide, along with his brothers, health services for the casualties, when the city was besieged by the Persians and the Kitions, in consideration of one silver talantum or alternatively, if the doctor preferred, part of a land with fruitful trees.[32]

20. Since Ottoman rule, the history of Cypriot land law has been characterized by three main landmarks, all of which have the functioning of the Land Registry as a focal point. These landmarks are the initial enactment of the Ottoman Land Code (discussed in section A below) and subsequently two other important legislative changes, which took place during British rule in Cyprus: Law 12/1907 and the Immovable Property Law (Cap. 224) (discussed in section B below).

A. The Ottoman Land Code

21. The Ottoman Land Code (1857) was an important chapter in the history of Cypriot land law. Later on, the functioning of the Land Registry (1858) was based upon its provisions. The Code provided for the specific categories of immovable

30. *P. A. Polycarpou, 2. A. Polycarpou, v. Adamou* (1988) 1 CLR 727.
31. *Iosifidis v. The Republic of Cyprus through The Public Service Commission (EDY),* (1998) 3 CLR 490, 24 June.
32. Ninos Koutas, *Real property in Cyprus, Studies on Cypriot Law* 3–4 (G. Shergides ed. 1992).

property and established specific provisions for the registration of immovable property, as well as the purchase and grants, the mortgage, the inheritance, etc. thereof.[33]

22. However, the concept of a title to property precedes even the enactment of the Ottoman Land Code. Even so, titles were granted under non-formalized procedures and were not registered anywhere. An institution of inspectors was recorded, with absolute rights and full jurisdiction (and discretion) to decide to grant to 'loyal' farmers agricultural land, which belonged to the State, after the payment of a symbolic fee, from which the State would collect taxes or tariffs. Upon this grant, the inspectors would give to some loyal farmers a rudimentary form of a title deed, known as 'Tapu Senedi or Tapu Sened'.[34] Thus, this form of deed was often uncertain, lacking information and registered nowhere.

23. Another form of title deeds was 'Hüccet' titles. These deeds were not issued by the inspectors, but by Muslim Religious Courts, and their subject matter was not the cultivatable land, but buildings, trees, water and plots. Neither Tapu Senedi nor Hüccet was registered anywhere.[35]

24. Nowadays, the knowledge of these categories of immovable property is important, since the existing legislative framework and especially Cap. 224, neither has retroactive effect nor refers to the legal relationships that were formed before its entry into force.[36]

25. In particular, the Ottoman categories have still some significance in immovable property disputes, especially in cases of acquisitive prescription.[37] These five categories of immovable property are listed as follows.[38]

---

33. *Ibid.*, 28.
34. As it is stated in *Papagheorghiou v. Komodromou* (1963) 2 CLR 221, 'Before the General Survey and the system of registration with reference to a survey plan was introduced in this country, transfers by kotchans or tapu seneds were in vogue. These kotchans and seneds as a rule did not relate to any survey plan and therefore where a dispute between two neighbouring land-owners in respect of a portion of land falling between their properties arose the only way of deciding the dispute was to find out which of the neighbouring land-owners had undisputed possession over the disputed portion and in such cases possession by transferor and by transferee of the disputed portion could be computed together.'
35. *Ibid.*, 7–8.
36. *Millington – Ward v. Roubina* (1970) 1 CLR 88 (with reference to s. 10 of the Explanatory Law): in relation to registrations that took place in 1937, Mejelle applies and not Cap. 224. For the retroactivity of Cap. 224, *see also Theodorou v. Hadjiantoni* (1961) CLR 203; *Papagheorgiou v. Komodromou* (1963) 2 CLR 221; *Kakkoulos et al. v. Kakkoulos* (1985) 1 CLR 209; *Hadjiloizi Stokkas v. Arghyrou*, Civil Appeal No. 4202, 20 December 1956; *Diplaros v. Nicola* (1974) 1 CLR 198; *Polydorou et al. v. Attorney General of the Republic*, Civil Appeal No. 10657 (2001) 1 CLR; *Fotiou v. Municipality of Larnaca* (1997) 4 CLR 2815; *Ellinas v. Hajisolomou* (1984) 1 CLR 225 *Savva v. Petrou* (1985) 1 CLR 12; *Agapiou v. Panayiotou* (1988) 1 CLR 257.
37. Ioannis Pogiatzis, *Immovable Property Law*, Cypriot Law Review 6404 (1993).
38. For these categories, *see also* Criton Tornaritis, *The Evolution of the Law Relating to Land in Cyprus* 7 et seq. (1982); Lefkios Tsikkinis, *Land Law, Neocleous's Introduction to Cyprus Law* (D. Campbell ed. 2009).

1. Category 'Mulk' or 'Arazi Memlouke'

26. This category corresponds to the fullest and most absolute ownership concept. It is said that the acquisition of this category of property was so absolute to 'reach up to the sky and deep enough to the bowels of the earth' (*usque ad coelum usque ad inferos*).[39] As regards the legal terminology of property interests and according to Cap. 224, this category corresponds to the term 'private ownership' or 'private property'.

27. The owner of a 'Mulk' land had the power to dispose of it freely, that is to grant, buy, sell, mortgage, dedicate for religious purposes or to dispose of it through testament. The status of ownership and possession of 'Mulk' immovable property was subject to the provisions of the Ottoman Civil Code and not to the Ottoman Land Law. It consisted of plots in cities and villages, houses, buildings, fruit-bearing trees, vineyards, waters, etc., for which the ownership, possession and use belonged to a private party without any public interference or restriction imposed by the state. Apart from the above categories of immovable property, there were also some additional types included in the 'Mulk' land, such as cultivable parcels within residential areas, which were given to conquerors as loot and are known as 'Arazi Usrie' or fragmented land and cultivable parcels, which were left in the possession of the non-Muslim residents and are known as 'Arazi Haratzie' or land upon which a tax known as 'Haratz' was imposed.[40] Subsequently, it is recorded that the 'Mulk' category consisted also of cultivable land, despite the general impression that cultivable land was only part of the 'Arazi Mirie' category property, a category which is analysed below.[41]

2. Category 'Arazi Mirie'

28. This category was the main subject of regulation in the Ottoman Land Law. It consisted of all the cultivable land, which belonged to the State ('State land'). The private party (known as 'mutessarif') would acquire, under a grant from the State, the rights of possession and use of the land, like a tenant under lease,[42] in consideration of 1/10 from the income generated by the land, which is known as 'dekati' and the payment of a lump-sum upon grant (known as 'tapu'). The legal ownership was vested in the State and particularly in the Treasury (the 'Beit-ul Mal'). According to the decision in *Michali Tsinki and others v. The King's Advocate*,[43] the rights-holder of the 'Mirie land' did not enjoy all the powers included in the absolute private ownership concept, but only the powers of use, possession and profit. Thus,

39. Koutas, *supra* n. 32, at 8.
40. Ioannis Pogiatzis, *Land Law* (Coprus de Jure Cyprii, issue 1), 61.
41. *See Sylvestrou et Al. v. Supreme Board of Evkaf* (1959–1960) 24 CLR 153, in Pogiatzis, *ibid.*, 62.
42. *Tsinki et al. v. The King's Advocate*, 9 February 1914, 10 CLR 55, in Pogiatzis, *ibid.*, 64: 'the relationship between the mutessarif and the State is that of a lessee and lessor'.
43. *Tsinki et al. v. The King's Advocate*, 9 February 1914, 10 CLR 55, in Pogiatzis, *ibid.*, 64. According to this case, the 'moutessarif' has no right to drill the land for water without the permission of the owner of the land, that was the State.

despite the fact that he did not have the power of disposal,[44] his right could be inherited by some of his relatives under certain conditions. This right could still get lost, in case he/she had left his land uncultivated for some years.[45] The State would exercise strict controls over this category of immovable property and special permission was necessary for the mutessarif, in order to be able to make any substantial alterations to the property, such as construction, fracturing, planting of trees, etc.

3. Category 'Arazi Mevkoufe'

29. This category of immovable property consisted of the widely known Vakfs,[46] which were, under religious Muslim law, the permanent dedication, by pious Muslims, of any property to religious, charitable, social, educational or any other purpose beneficial to the Muslim Turkish community. This situation was governed by the provisions of a specific law (the Evkaf and Vakfs Law) and there was also an Administrator ('Mütevelli'). The 'Mevkufe immovable property' was split into two categories:[47] (1) 'the real Vakfs', that was a type of a 'Mulk immovable property' (private property), whose ownership was granted for charitable purposes. The real Vakfs were subject to the provisions of specific legislation, namely the Evkaf and Vakfs laws. As regards the real Vakfs, their ownership was supposed to belong to God. (2) 'The non-real Vakfs' was a type of an 'Arazi Mirie immovable property' and subsequently belonged to the State. In this case, since the dedicator did not have the absolute right to property but only the rights of use, possession and profit, the object of the Vakf was restricted only to the enjoyment of the right that the dedicator (moutessarif)[48] was enjoying. On the contrary, if the dedicator was the State, the dedication would refer to the rights of the State over the immovable property. The 'Arazi Mevkufe' category is the only category that was not repealed by Cap. 224.

4. Category 'Arazi Metruke'

30. This category consisted of public plantations, forests, streets, public squares, grazing land, bushes, river beds, seashores, etc. and it was 'res communis' – that is,

44. *See Millington – Ward v. Roubina* (1970) 1 CLR 88: the right of 'moutessarif' is regarded as a right in personam in the sense that it cannot be transferred or granted under a testimony.
45. Koutas, *supra* n. 32 at 9–10. According to Art. 68 of the Code, if the beneficiary of any arable land does not cultivate or take actions to be farmed by another by renting it, but he allows to remain uncultivated for three consecutive years without a reasonable cause, such as for example, fallowing or captivity in the war, the land is returned to Tapu. If the beneficiary who had lost the possession wished to continue the usufruct of the part he had lost, he would have to pay its value (Bedel Misl). If he did not wish to re-acquire his rights, then the possession of the land was given under auction, to another person. *See* in relation *Gavriilidi v. Hadjikyriakou et al.* (1898) 4 CLR 84.
46. *See* in *Sylvestrou et al. v. Supreme Board of Evkaf* (1959–1960) 24 CLR 153.
47. In detail for these categories, *see* Pogiatzis, *supra* n. 37 at 61–71.
48. Koutas, *supra* n. 32 at 11. A basic principle of land law is that you cannot grant a more powerful right than what you have (*nemo dat quod no habet*).

immovable property destined for common use. 'Arazi Metruke immovable property' was split into places which were: (a) used by the public under general terms and without discrimination, such as public streets and squares (communal immovable property) and (b) solely for the use of residents of the beneficiary community or of a complex of villages or communities, e.g., as grazing land or as bush area.[49]

31. The above division corresponds to the current division of communal immovable property, namely immovable property which belongs to the State, but is destined for common use (res communis)[50] and communal immovable property which is subject to the specific provisions of Cap. 224.[51]

32. As regards the legal terminology of communal things in modern land law, it should be noted that common use does not mean common ownership by everyone.

33. Common use therefore refers to the use of immovable things, which belong to the State, but can be enjoyed by everyone. The meaning and the limits of common use depend on the thing, its purpose, time and space. Thus, the meaning of the common use of things does not extend to profit-making purposes.[52] Their use satisfies public interests – anyone can enjoy their use – provided that this enjoyment does not prevent the enjoyment of the others. Exclusive use is not defined.

5. Category 'Arazi Mevat'

34. This last category was defined as isolated and seemingly barren land, unsuitable for cultivation. It was usually rocky or mountainous land, which normally lay at a distance from inhabited areas,[53] was not in the possession of anybody and consisted of the 'Khali land'.[54]

35. It was said of 'Mevat' land that it should have been situated far enough from a village so that the cry of a human voice from the densely inhabited spot cannot be heard. In *Anastasi v. Chatzigiorgi*,[55] this primitive and arbitrary definition was interpreted as a considerable distance. As mentioned above, this category of land belonged to the State (Sultan), but it was also possible for people obtaining State

49. Pogiatzis, *supra* n. 40 at 68; Koutas, *supra* n. 32 at 13.
50. Common use property includes public streets and beaches. *See* s. 3 Cap. 224, where it is defined that the property of the Republic is public streets and beaches that belong to the Republic for public use.
51. For the communal property, *see* ss 3(5) and 19 of Cap. 224.
52. *See* Apostolos Georgiadis, *Real Property Law* 153 (Sakkoulas Publications, 2010).
53. Koutas, *supra* n. 32 at 13.
54. *See Polydorou et al. v. Attorney General of the Republic*, Civil Appeal No. 10657 (2001) 1 CLR.
55. If we turn to the definition of Mevat contained either in the *Mejelle*, or in the *Code de Proprieté Fonciére*, we find that one attribute of these lands is that they must be situated so far from a village that the cry of a human voice cannot be heard. This is no doubt a primitive definition, meaning a considerable distance, and certainly if any person is to claim the full benefit of Art. 1282, or if the State is to purport to grant him such a benefit, the land over which it is to be granted must necessarily be situated, at a considerable distance from any places, where any private person owns either houses or cultivated lands.

permission to cultivate it and in that way it was also possible to convert into 'Arazi Mirie' category or even into 'Mulk', provided that it would have been granted such permission by the Sultan through the approval of the responsible public officer. However, the possibility of converting this land into the 'Arazi Mirie' category, lasted only until 1904.[56]

36. The enactment of the Ottoman Land Law was followed by the establishment of the Land Registry in 1858. In the earlier years of its operation, the Land Registry dealt only with the issuance of deeds stemming from the transfers of 'Tapu Senedi' and 'Hüccet' titles, while at the same time a new type of book was adopted for the registration of those transfers (known as the 'Book with Numbered Pages'[57]). Nevertheless, since the registration of the transfers was not obligatory and as a result transfers were taking place without the issuance of the relevant title, in 1860 a new law came into force, namely the 'General Registration and Valuation Law', which made obligatory the valuation, registration and on-the-spot search of every kind of immovable property. According to this legislation, known as 'Yoklama', the value of the immovable property was appraised through empirical, on-the-spot research, which was nevertheless not accompanied by the drawing up of specific land plans. Similarly, the procedures of registration and issuance of title deed were also simplified. The owner's declaration on honour along with a certificate from the land survey authority seemed enough for the recording into specific registries, known as 'Yoklama Registries'.

B. The Evolution of the Legislative Context: The Commonwealth Influence

37. British rule marked a new era in the history of Cypriot land law. There are two main trends: (1) in principle, the maintenance of the pre-existing registration and recording system and (2) the gradual upgrading and modernization of the procedures and subsequently of the relevant legislation.

38. When, in 1878, Britain took over the governance of Cyprus, the functioning and the working of the Land Registry continued as before. Until 1890, the former procedures, which were adopted during Ottoman rule, continued to be followed. The landmark year was 1890, when the first important reform took place, which promoted the modernization of the registration and recording procedures: most of the former books were replaced by a general 'Register'. The second, very important reform, regarding the registration and titling, took place in 1893. In relation to registrations happening for the first time, which did not concern the transfer of land, a new obligation was introduced, the one of on-the-spot research and drawing up of a specific plan.[58]

---

56. Pogiatzis, *supra* n. 40 at 70.
57. Koutas, *supra* n. 32 at 14.
58. *Ibid.*, 18.

39. Since that time, several laws were enacted.[59] Thus, the milestones in the evolution of the Cypriot land law were the Law 12/1907 and Cap. 224.

40. The improvement of the titling procedures and the registration methodology were the main objectives of Law 12/1907. However, the law came into force later, on 10 February 1919, because of the strong conflict that had arisen before its enactment, which reflected the concern of property owners that new legislation was simply an excuse for the State to increase taxes on land. This legislation introduced a new chapter in the history of the Land Registry, since the provision for the obligatory registration of property rights over land interrelated with the procedure of mapping and land surveying all over Cyprus. In short, the contribution of this legislation can be summarized by the following four crucial points: (1) the provision of the obligatory registration of the immovable property, (2) the mapping and surveying of all the Cypriot land, which was finalized in 1929, (3) the valuation of the Cypriot land and (4) the registration and issuance of title deeds over property.[60]

41. 40. In rationalizing the Cypriot land law, Cap. 224 was of extreme importance and, along with the Wills and Succession Law (Cap. 195), aimed to correct some particularly negative circumstances, which were the outcome of the former problematic legislation and set out procedures. The new legislation attempted to solve two of the main existing problems, namely, the situation of dual ownership, that is the situation of separate ownership over the land and the trees or the buildings existing in it, and the issue of land fragmentation.[61]

42. First, Cap. 224 abolished the five Ottoman categories of immovable property and established four new categories: (1) private property, (2) Vakf property, (3) communal property and (4) property of the Republic. The transition from the old status quo to the new one took place with a number of transitional provisions, which included an explicit correspondence of the former Ottoman categories to each new category of property. According to section 3(2) of Cap. 224, all immovable properties known as Mulk and privately owned as such, at the date of the coming into force of the said Law, would continue to be owned, held and enjoyed as private property.

43. However, the most important reform was provided by section 3(3), where all immovable property known as 'Arazi Mirie' and privately possessed as such, at the date of the coming into force of the Law, would be owned, held and enjoyed as private property. According to this provision, the cultivable agricultural land was no longer property of the State, but of the private party who worked for its exploitation. The only Ottoman category of property which continues to apply in accordance with the provisions of the Cyprus Evkaf Law, subject only to the provisions of sections 36, 37 and 38 of Cap. 224, is the Vakf property.[62]

59. *See* in detail *ibid.*, 19.
60. *Ibid.*, at 23.
61. *Ibid.*, 30.
62. *See* s. 3(4) Cap. 224.

44. The 'Arazi Metruke' immovable property was replaced by the communal property category. In particular, according to section 3(5) all immovable properties, known as 'Arazi Metruke' lawfully held or enjoyed communally by a town, village or quarter, at the date of the coming into force of the Law, would continue to be held or enjoyed as the communal property of such town, village or quarter. Moreover, section 3(6) defines the State Property (Crown Property). According to this provision, all immovable properties known as 'Arazi Mevat' would be owned, held and enjoyed by the Crown as Crown property.

45. Similarly, immovable property other than that specified in subsections (2)–(5) of section 3 and all vacant or unoccupied immovable property, not privately owned or lawfully possessed in the year 1946, that is, at the date of the coming into force of the Law, would be owned, held and enjoyed by the Crown as Crown property as well. It is therefore clearly understood that this section defines as State property not only the land formerly known as 'Khali land', but also all immovable property prima facie not privately owned or lawfully possessed at the date of the coming into force of the Law, in order to avoid cases of immovable property not privately owned or lawfully possessed after the enactment of this law. The concept of the recognition of the State as the lawful rights-holder, in the absence of any other lawful rights-holders is also consistent with the basic principles of feudalism and Ottoman rule as well, when the owner of the land was considered to be, in principle, the representative of the State's authority, who was the King or the Sultan.[63]

46. The second important innovation of the new legislation had to do with the abolishment of the dual ownership concept – that is, the right of separate ownership over plantation, trees, buildings, which were situated upon land belonging to another person.

47. Still, other important innovations were the establishment of a thirty-year prescription period (section 10), the imposition of limits, below which no division of immovable property was possible (section 27), the establishment of the compulsory partition of immovable property to be made among the several parties entitled thereto in the best interests of all persons concerned (section 29), rights of way (section 12), long-term leaseholds, trusts, restrictive covenants and the reservation (section 11(1)(ζ)).

48. As regards the competencies of the Land Registry, semi-judicial powers were allocated to it in many cases, for example in obligatory rights of way (section 11A), separation of immovable property, which is owned by the best interests of all persons concerned (section 29), and the determination of boundary disputes (section 58), etc., all of which are considered to be extremely important.[64]

---

63. In the same line is also s. 47 of the Wills Law, according to which, if, upon the time of death of the inherited, there is no relative up to sixth degree of kinship, then the person is regarded dead without heirs and the intestate part of the fortune becomes property of the Republic.

64. *See* Koutas, *supra* n. 32 at 31.

II. The Concept of Ownership

A. *Unity and Fragmentation*

49. Making references to both continental tradition and common law, the Cypriot land law presents a distinctive approach as regards the unification of the holistic ownership concept.

50. First, and contrary to common law tradition, where ownership is perceived as an aggregate right, which can be divided in smaller and simultaneous estates or interests at the benefit of different persons,[65] ownership over land in Cypriot law is not treated as an aggregate right and always passes as a whole to each consecutive owner.

51. The Constitution of the Republic of Cyprus also follows a unifying approach and protects immovable property, movable property and real rights. More precisely, under Article 23 of the Constitution, the protection of the right to property in Cyprus is guaranteed and defined as a fundamental human right. In this way, the protection of property is formally declared for all the citizens of the Republic of Cyprus. Thus, the protection of property is not absolute, but restricted. According to Article 23(3) of the Constitution, restrictions or limitations, which are absolutely necessary in the interest of public safety or public health or public morals or town and country planning or development and utilization of any property for the promotion of the public benefit or for the protection of the rights of others, may be imposed by law on the exercise of the right to property.

52. Furthermore, Cypriot land law follows the traditional approach of Roman law in relation to the definition and concept of immovable property. Ownership is the direct, absolute and full power over a thing, its interests and uses.[66] As regards the restrictive real rights, the powers, which are vested in the rights-holders in relation to immovable property belonging to another person, are much more limited than the powers of the owner, while at the same time the restrictions stemming from the right of ownership continue to apply.

53. However, in the field of private law, the legal concept of property does not seem to follow a unified approach regarding the regulation of immovable and movable property. In particular, the legal study of Cypriot land law follows the methodology of common law tradition, drawing a distinction between two separate areas of law: (1) the protection of real property, which concerns the protection of immovable property or land property and (2) the protection of personal property,[67] which concerns movable corporeal components, which are not fixtures and other movable

65. Magdalena Habdas, *Property and Trust Law in Poland* 59 (Kluwer Law International 2018).
66. D. Papasteriou, *Land Law, Volume II, Ownership* 8 (Sakkoulas Publications 2008).
67. This distinction, which stems from English law, is historical and due to the different evolution of land law and personal property law. This different evolution is a result of three reasons: (1) the feudal system of possession of land, which was imposed in England right after its occupation by the

incorporeal components, such as securities, shares, intellectual property rights, expertise, clientele or monetary claims. It is subsequently a wide conceptual category, which consists of everything that is not immovable property or real right over immovable property.[68]

54. The distinctive influence of common law tradition over Cypriot land law is manifested by the absence of the concept of the 'thing' (res), which has a unifying dimension in the continental law tradition, since it combines both immovable and movable components. It is also interesting that in the Cypriot legal system, the concept of the thing is defined neither by legislation nor by judge-made rules. The main theoretical distinction into immovable and movable components reflects only partially the above distinction into immovable and movable property. According to the relevant common law tradition, section 1 of Cap. 224 defines immovable property, and whatever does not fall inside that definition, is considered to be personal property,[69] which can consist of both corporeal and incorporeal movable things (chattels). Thus, the category of personal property is much wider that the one of movable things, since it also consists of intangible things.

55. In this context, the regulation of property in the Cypriot legal system is via various specific statutes in the area of private law, which concern immovable and movable components and refer distinctively to immovable and movable/personal property (*see also below* section C. 'Movable and Personal Property'). In general, Cypriot real property law is an interesting mixture of principles and components derived from diverse legal traditions. Nevertheless, this diversity is characterized by a clear dichotomy. The creation and the acquisition of real property rights have, with the major exception of trusts, been mainly inspired by the principles of the continental law tradition, while the protection of real property is formulated on the prototype of English tort law. Indeed, modern Cypriot land law appears to be a peculiar amalgam that has incorporated elements of Roman law, Ottoman law, English law and Greek law.[70]

Normans and conferred to the Crown's ownership (feudal tenure), applying only to immovable property; (2) the possibility of protection of land under claims in rem, under which the re-acquisition of the physical power and possession over land was, in contrast with the claims for the protection of the 'personal property', under which the re-acquisition in rem of the object was not possible up until the middle of nineteenth century; and (3) the several provisions which concerned the succession in relation to the two categories of property. *See*, in detail, Michael Bridge, *Personal Property Law, Calendon Law Series*, 2 (3rd ed., Oxford University Press 2002).

68. This is the category of 'chattels personal', which are historically in common law tradition distinguished from the 'chattels real'. The most typical form of a 'chattel real' is the leasehold, which is hybrid in nature, since it combines both immovable and movable property components.

69. Ugo Mattei, *Basic Principles of Property Law: A Comparative Legal and Economic Introduction* 10 (Greenwood Press 2000).

70. *See* T. Synodinou, *Real Property in Cyprus: In Search of an Identity,* 18 Jahreshefte der Internationalen Juristenvereinigung Osnabrück (IJVO) (2014).

56. With regard to the term of 'ownership' it is hard to find a clear definition of the term in case law.[71] An attempt of definition of term is found in *Christou Orfanides v. the Republic of Cyprus* where it was said that 'conceptually the term ownership denotes proprietorship over an immovable or movable asset and indicates the possibility of that asset being transferred/sold/disposed of'.[72]

*B. Immovable and Real Property (*See Also *Part I)*

57. The Cypriot immovable property law does not contain an official enumeration and classification of real rights. The concept of real rights is not established by law,[73] but is only indirectly and partially recognized via sporadic references to the relevant concept of 'rights in rem' in Cypriot case law.[74] Accordingly, Cap. 224 does not contain any definition or list of real rights.

58. Despite the lack of express recognition and enumeration of real rights in Cypriot immovable property legislation, Cap. 224 contains in disparate sections legal regulation governing specific types of 'property rights' (both estates and interests in respect of land). Taking as a starting point the main conceptual elements of real rights (mainly the absolute effect, the excludability *erga omnes* and the transferability[75]) it could be said that Cap. 224 recognizes a series of rights which could be defined as real rights, even if they are not expressly named as such in the law, with the most powerful and significant of them being the right of 'private ownership'. Except for 'private ownership', the right of possession,[76] easements, usufruct

71. Stéphanie Laulhé Shaelou, Stelia Stylianou & Karolina Anastasiou, 'National Report on the Transfer of Movables', in *England and Wales, Ireland, Scotland, Cyprus*, Vol. II (Wolfgang Faber, Brigitta Lurger eds., Selier, European Law Publishers 2009).
72. *Orfanides v. the Republic of Cyprus* (1994) 4 CLR 1779.
73. *See* on the other hand s. 973 of the Greek Civil Code that defines a real right (or right in rem) as a right securing over a thing a direct power that can be invoked against all persons. For the Greek property law, *see* Y. Karibali-Tsiptsiou, *Property and Trust Law – Greece, International Encyclopaedia of Laws* (Wolters Kluwer, Law & Business 2012).
74. *Flower, etc. v. Hadjiioannou, etc.* (2008) 1B CLR 770; *Markidou v. Killiaris et al. (*1983) 1 CLR 392. ('The rights acquired under a contract for the sale of land are personal and as such, prima facie assignable. A contract for the sale of land does not create an estate in land, that is, rights in rem.')
75. *See* T. Synodinou, *Land Law in Cyprus* 5–6 (Sakkoulas Editions 2011).
76. The right of possession is not defined in Cap. 224. Indeed, Cap. 224 does not establish or even refer to the concept and the term 'possession' except for the case of 'adverse possession'. However, possession of immovable property is what is protected by the two main torts in respect of immovable property by the Cypriot Civil Wrongs Law, i.e., the torts of trespass and private nuisance. This is also confirmed by case law. *See, e.g., Agathocleous Ltd v. Sofocleous* (2000) 1C CLR 1953.

and habitation rights,[77] 'profit à prendre' and the rights created by long-term leasehold and financial leasing[78] and restrictive covenants[79] that have been registered in the Land Registry could also be classified as real rights.

1. The Real Right of Ownership over Land

59. At the core of the legal protection of immovable property traditionally lies the notion of the real right (right in rem), while ownership remains the strongest and fullest real right. The notion of ownership in land law should be distinguished from the notion of property in constitutional law, since the latter is wider and can either refer to corporeal things, which are physically governed, or incorporeal things, such as intellectual creations, patents and trademarks.

60. According to section 2 of Cap. 224, immovable property includes:

(a) land
(b) buildings and other erections, structures or fixtures affixed to any land or to any building or other erection or structure
(c) trees, vines, and any other thing whatsoever planted or growing upon any land and any produce thereof before severance
(d) springs, wells, water and water rights whether held together with, or independently of, any land
(e) privileges, liberties, easements and any other rights and advantages whatsoever appertaining or reputed to appertain to any land or to any building or other erection
(f) an undivided ideal share in any property
(g) land created after sea bedding
(h) Marine area declared as a marina, which is going to be embanked as a land.

61. The above definition presents some similarities, without nevertheless being identical, with the definition of 'land' in section 205(1)(ix) of English Law of Property Act (1925).[80] The category of 'immoveable property', modelled on English law, includes 'incorporeal' components which are also considered as 'realty' and, par consequent, are distinguished from 'personalty' (personal or movable property).

77. It is noteworthy that the usufruct and the habitation rights are not considered as personal easements but as a specific category of rights which are created on the basis of s. 11 of Cap. 224. This was expressly confirmed in the case *Siati v. Siati* (1996) 1B CLR 1349, where it was held that the habitation right in Cyprus is not an easement, since the creation of an easement in Cypriot law requires two tenements, a dominant and a servient.

78. Sections 65A–65IE of Cap. 224 and s. 65ΛA Cap. 224.

79. Section 65IH of Cap. 224.

80. '"Land" includes land of any tenure, and mines and minerals, whether or not held apart from the surface, buildings or parts of buildings (whether the division is horizontal, vertical or made in any other way) and other corporeal hereditaments, also a manor, an advowson, and a rent and other incorporeal hereditaments, and an easement, right, privilege, or benefit in, over, or derived from land.'

According to the definition in Cap. 224, immovable property includes not only tangible, corporeal things, such as land, buildings, trees or waters,[81] but also real rights or proprietary rights over immovable property in general, such as water rights or privileges, easements, benefits in, over, or derived from land or building or other structures such as the right of crossing the lot which belongs to the neighbour (i.e., an example of an easement), the right to restrict the neighbour from constructing a building which would deteriorate your view (i.e., an example of a restrictive covenant) or the right to usufruct from somebody else's land (i.e., an example of a privilege).[82]

2. Limits and Content of Ownership over Land

62. The Roman law rules that the limits of the property of land reach up the sky and deep into the bowels of the earth (*Cuius est solum eius est usque et ad inferos,*[83] known as the *ad coelum* rule) is not applicable in the modern times. In Cypriot land law, the extent of the right to private ownership is defined in section 5 of Cap. 224. According to section 5(1), private ownership of any land extends to the surface and to the substance of the earth beneath the surface and to the space above the surface, reasonably necessary for the enjoyment thereof. Therefore, the owner of the surface is also entitled to dig below the surface and to build above the surface.

63. However, private ownership does not extend to minerals, which belong to the State pursuant to Article 23 of the Constitution. The second subparagraph of section 5(1) introduces an exception as regards the non-extension of private ownership to minerals. The only exception to this rule is the recognition of the right to the substance of the earth beneath the surface without any restriction, on the condition that is an established right before the coming into operation of Cap. 224. Specifically, this exception covers private ownership of any land which lies within the areas specified, for the purposes of this section, on the survey map signed by the Director which was deposited in the Land Registry before the coming into force of this Law, that is 1 September 1946.[84]

64. The notion of minerals includes all materials of economic value forming part of, or derived naturally from, the crust of the earth including mineral oil, pitch, asphalt and natural gas but not minerals whilst in solution or peat, trees, timber and similar kinds of forest produce.

81. Water constitutes immovable property within the definition of that expression in s. 2 of Cap. 224 and its ownership is governed by the provisions of Cap. 224. *See Ashiotis et al. v. M Weiner et al.* (1968) 1 CLR 43.
82. Martin Dixon, *Modern Land Law* 3 (6th ed., Routledge-Cavendish 2009).
83. For its application nowadays with a simultaneous maintenance of its symbolic value, *see* Kevin Gray and Susan Francis Gray, *Elements of Land Law* 14 (Oxford University Press, 2009).
84. *See* Pogiatzis, *supra* n. 37 at Lecture No. 2, 84.

C. Movable and Personal Property (See Also *Part II*)

65. A coherent definition of movable property is absent in Cypriot property law. Movable property is mainly understood in juxtaposition with 'immovable property', which is defined in Cap. 224. Similarly, there is no formal recognition or definition of the concept of a 'thing'. The lack of a developed framework for these concepts could be explained by the influence of the common law methodology in property law, where the focus is not on the 'thing' itself, but rather on some utilities that can be captured from it.[85] While immovable property is thoroughly defined by law, movables are defined by exclusion. 'Objects' that do not fall within the definition of immovable property, are diversely referred to as movable property, goods, fixtures, chattels and 'things' in various pieces of legislation or in case law.

66. For instance, the concept or movable property is sporadically found in specific laws, such as the Wills and Inheritance Law[86] and the Civil Procedure Law (Cap. 6).[87] This inconsistence and unfamiliarity of the Cypriot courts with the term 'movable property', which is also absent from the common law tradition, has been emphasized by the Supreme Court in the case *Hassan Dandelen v. Suleiman Ibrahim.*[88] The Court was called to clarify the meaning of the term 'movable property' as regards a writ of seizure and sale of movable property. The Court first acknowledged that 'movable property' is not a term of English law and that if the legislature had intended the writ to have the same effect as an English writ, it would have used the well-known English law term 'goods and chattels'. The Court further analyzed the meaning of the term from a comparative law perspective. As it was noted, 'Where we find it using a term apparently in some technical sense, but which is not an English technical term, the natural presumption is that the term is one of Turkish law. And upon inquiring whether "movable property" is a Turkish law term and, if so, what it means we find that there is a definition of "menkoul" or "movables" in the Mejellé, in the book concerning sale, Section 128, which in Dr. Grigsby's translation is as follows: "Movable property is everything which can be transferred from place to place, such, as money, merchandise, animals, and things that can be measured and weighed".' As the Court found, this definition is not very clear. In the opinion of the Court, the definition of movable property 'would exclude anything which cannot be moved, without cutting or breaking or severing from the soil, such as buildings and trees or crops not severed from the soil. Moreover, definitions of "movables" are given in the French Civil Code, Book ii., Title 3, Chapter 1, section 520, and in the Egyptian Code, Chapter 1, section 2; in both of these, uncut crops and not collected fruits are clearly excluded. And in the Ottoman Commercial Code, which is founded on the French Code, the terms "movables" and "immovables" are used (for example, in section 241), in the same sense as in the French Code.' For

85. Mattei, *supra* n. 69 at 9.
86. *See* s. 2 of the Cap. 195, where the definition of estate comprises both movable and immovable property.
87. The law refers to the term 'movable property'. It also comprises separate provisions for movable things (s. 16) and immovable things (Part V).
88. *Ahmet HJ Hassan Dandelen v. Suleiman Ibrahim et al.* (V4) (1898) 1 CLR 78.

the Court, the inconsistent use of the terms 'movable property', 'goods' and 'chattels and the rest' seems only to show that the legislation is worded without diligence.[89] In the present case, it was held that 'movable property' shall be understood in the same sense as 'menkoul' in Turkish Law, and that it does not include standing crops.[90] For the definition of 'movable property', the Court adheres to continental law principles and restricts the concept only to movable tangible things (i.e., property that is not attached to land and it can be touched or felt), including money. It is not, however, clear, whether this understanding shall be considered as covering all private law or only the law in question. The application of a fragmented approach on the meaning of 'movable property' has also been confirmed by the Supreme Court's interpretation of the concept of 'movable property' in the Wills and Succession Law (Cap. 195). In relation to the question whether money is also included in the concept of 'movable property' in the context of inheritance upon testament, the Supreme Court held that it depends on the interpretation of the terms of the testament. Therefore, according to the interpretation and spirit of the testament, a monetary sum found in the testator's home safe after his death is not included in the term 'movable property'.[91]

67. On the contrary, personal property, a term familiar in the common law tradition,[92] is a broad term, and refers to any property that is movable, regardless if it is tangible or intangible. It comprises property over movable corporeal components, which are not fixtures and other movable incorporeal components, such as securities, shares, intellectual property rights, expertise, clientele or monetary claims. It is a wide conceptual category, which consists of everything that is not immovable property or real right over immovable property.[93] In *Patiki v. Patiki* the Supreme Court, following English law, clarified that in Cypriot Partnership Law, the partnership share of the deceased in all the assets of the partnership, both movable (personal) and immovable (real) property, shall be considered movable property and denied the argument that the share of the deceased in the movable assets of the partnership is movable property and his share in the immovable assets is immovable property.[94]

68. Another important concept in Cypriot private law is the concept of goods. 'Goods' are defined in the Sales of Goods Law.[95] The definition given is slightly narrower than the concept of personal property, since 'good' means any movable property, except for actionable claims and money. The concept of good includes securities and stocks, unclaimed crops, grass and things that are related to or form

89. *Ibid.*
90. *Ibid.*
91. *Terzis v. Kekkou Petoufas* (2011) 1 CLR 336.
92. *Supra* n. 67.
93. *Supra* n. 68.
94. *D. Patiki v. A. G. Patiki and Co et al.* (V20) (1954) 1 CLR 36.
95. Sales of Goods Law 10(I)/1994. The Cypriot Sales of Goods Law is mainly based on the UK Sales of Goods Act of 1893.

part of the land, which have been agreed to be separated from the land prior to sale or under the contract of sale[96] (*see also* Part II, Chapter 1, §1).

69. Finally, Cypriot law also recognizes the concept of 'chattels', as the latter is understood in English law and the relevant distinction between fixtures and chattels. This was affirmed by Cypriot case law with reference to UK doctrine in *Vereggaria Papakokkinou v. Dimou Paphou,*[97] where it was held that 'Cap. 224 does not specify what a "fixture" is, but it may "*be a building or structure, or structure that is positioned, erected or applied to land or a building so as to constitute part of the land or building. The two key elements answering the question of whether such a structure or building is an appendix (fixture) of the land are: (a) the extent of the attachment and (b) the purpose of the attachment. (See Cheshire's "Modern Law or Property", 12th Edition, p. 138.) According to Woodfall, the appendix refers to objects attached to the earth (see Woodfall "Landlord and Tenant", 27th Edition, p. 695) and acçording to Megarry "includes anything attached to the earth so as to be part of it of the earth" (see Megarry and Wade "The Law of Real Property", p. 643)*".' (*See also* Part II, Chapter 1, §1.)

III. Estate and Patrimony

A. Unity and Fragmentation

70. The concepts of estate and patrimony are not officially established or defined in Cypriot legislation. Cypriot legislation regulates special aspects of estate such as immovable property, goods, intellectual property, movable property, spouses' common property, the estate of a deceased person, etc. Patrimony is generally understood to be a broad concept, which comprises not only ownership rights but also includes obligations and responsibilities that bear an economic value. In this context, patrimony comprises both *erga omnes* property rights and personal rights (in personam), such as obligations arising from contracts and torts. The general patrimony of a person is the sum of their rights and obligations, which, depending on the proportions of the two, can be either active or passive. On the contrary, the notion of ownership is narrower and is established as a real right which is exercised *erga omnes.*

71. The concept of patrimony has been defined by the Supreme Court with reference to Greek case law in the case *Charalambous et al. v. Minister of Finance etc.*[98] It was held that patrimony, an autonomous concept, which is independent of the formal classification of individual property rights in domestic law, includes not

96. Section 2 of the Sales of Goods Law 10(I)/1994. The definition is similar to the definition of "goods" provided in the Sales of goods Act of Ontario: 'Goods means all chattels personal, other than things in action and money, and includes emblements, industrial growing crops, and things attached to or forming part of the land that are agreed to be severed before sale or under the contract of sale.'
97. *Papakokkinou v. Dimou Paphou* (1998) 1 CLR 2398.
98. No. 1480/11 et seq., 11 June 2014. *See also President of the Republic v. House of Representatives of the Republic*, 16 March 2017.

only rights in rem but also all 'property rights', as well as acquired 'financial interests'. In this way, rights in personam are also covered, and in particular, claims arising from legal relations in public or private law, whether recognized by judicial or arbitral decision, or merely arising out of national law, where there is a legitimate expectation, on the basis of the law in force, that they may be enforced in court – that is to say if there is a sufficient legal basis in the domestic law.

72. Section 4 of Cap. 224 refers to the concepts of proprietary right (estate), privileges and interests in land without further definition. The term 'estate' is borrowed from the common law tradition[99] and refers to the legal right to which a holder of land is entitled. Indeed, both the UK Law of Property Act 1925 and the UK Land Registration Act 2002 embrace the theory that land ownership and use are mediated not by the attribution to individuals of any direct ownership of or dominium over the land itself, but by the distribution of intangible jural entitlements (estates) which are interposed between persons and the land.[100] In order for the estate holder to ascertain his rights, it is necessary to decide what type of estate he owns and to know what rights and duties the law attaches to that type of estate.[101]

73. Generally, the concept of estate refers to any proprietary right that a person can enjoy on his/her own land, while the concepts of interests and privileges in land are used in order to define less extensive rights related over land belonging to another person, such as easements, restrictive covenants, life habitation rights and profit à prendre. However, contrary to English law, where there is a closed list of legal estates (mainly the freehold and the leasehold estates) and interests in land,[102] Cypriot law is more evasive, simply mentioning the concepts of estates and interests in land without specifying them. The lack of a precise definition or classification of estates in land is due to the fact that Cypriot property law recognizes the concept of ownership (dominium) of the civil tradition and, therefore, there is only one estate (property) over the land: the real right of ownership. In this context, the provision of section 4 of Cap. 224 is practically pertinent in relation to the category of 'interests' in land.

74. Therefore, contrary to English law, which recognizes that property over land is capable of fragmentation and distribution, Cypriot law recognizes the concept of the legal right of direct ownership of land. The most significant exception to this

99. According to Dixon, the notional entity of the estate was interposed between the tenant and the land, with the consequence that each tenant owned, not land itself, but an estate in land, each estate being graded with reference to its temporal duration. In this context, all proprietary relationships with land fall to be analyzed through the intermediary of an estate. *See* Kevin Gray and Susan Francis Gray, *Elements of Land Law* 57 (5th ed., OUP 2009).

100. Gray & Gray, *supra* n. 99 at 62.

101. E.H. Burn & J. Cartwright, *Maudsley & Burn's Land Law Cases and Materials*, *OUP*, 12 (9th ed. 2009).

102. Sections 1(1) and 1(2) of the Law of Property Act 1925.

unified perception of the concept of property in Cypriot law is the institution of the trust, where a duality of estate ownership is recognized, since equitable ownership is distinguished from legal ownership.

*B. Trust and Fiduciary Mechanisms (*See also *Parts IV and V)*

75. The trust is the main equitable interest which is recognized in Cypriot law. For an analysis of trusts and fiduciary mechanisms, *see* Part I, Chapter 3.

IV. Possession and Title

76. The fundamental distinction between ownership, occupation and possession is not formally established in Cypriot property law. The distinction does not appear in Cap. 224, which is the main source of Cypriot land law. The concept of possession appears more systematically only in the context of the mechanism of adverse possession of immovable property in Cap. 224. These concepts are also sporadically found in Cypriot case law.

77. The establishment of ownership on the basis of Roman law (concept of 'dominium') precludes the understanding of possession as a relationship with a corporeal estate (fee simple, lease or lesser rights in it).[103] This is because, contrary to English law, where there is no absolute ownership of land (in accordance with the doctrine of tenures and estates), Cypriot law recognizes the concept of absolute ownership over land.

78. Possession is defined in case law as the legal situation of occupation of a land which is accompanied by the mental intent of *animus domini*. In this context, possession comprises both an objective element and a mental element (corpus and animus).

79. The concept of possession is distinguished from the concept of simple occupation could be understood as a relationship of fact (physical occupation of a tangible thing or physical presence in a land either personally or through goods, chattels or employees) which is not necessarily accompanied by *animus domini*. *Animus domini* is defined as the will and intent to become the 'owner' of the thing and behave as the owner of the thing. As it was held in Case No. 3011/08, *animus domini* must be exercised in a way that demonstrates the right of ownership over it, in the sense that person who possesses the land, must behave as if he were the owner of the land.[104]

103. Marc Wonaccot, *Possession of Land* 2 (Cambridge University Press 2006).
104. *Constantinou as an Administrator of the estate of Stylianou v. Courides*, No. 3011/08, 13 March 2013.

80. The physical occupation of land is not always 'possession' in the sense that, lacking *animus domini*, it can be justified on other grounds such as the simple allowance or the possessor. In this context, Cypriot tort law recognizes the legal defence of a bare licence, in which there exists the objective fact of a person's local relationship to a real property but lacks the element of physical authority and a mental intent to possess or occupy. Thus, the simple licensee of a property, e.g., the postman who enters the premises to deliver the mail is not considered to be the possessor or the owner of the property. In that case, the owner or the possessor of the property simply allows the licensee the use of the land for certain purposes. As it was held in *Kailis v. Livadiotis,* a bare licence may be revoked at any time and, after revocation, the licensee becomes a trespasser; therefore, he should be allowed a reasonable amount of time to leave and to remove his goods.[105]

A. *Possession*

1. Possession as a Matter of Fact and Possession in Law

81. In Cypriot law, the concept and the nature of possession have been more systematically defined in the mechanism of adverse possession, where possession is defined as the fact of occupying a land with the mental element of *animus domini*, that is when the possessor behaves as the real owner of the land. Since *animus domini* is deduced by the way the possessor behaves (by the possessor's factual behaviour), possession should be seen as question of fact. The absence of the mental element (*animus domini*) turns possession into precarious holding (simple occupation).

82. In *Ikosi v. Karayiannis,*[106] the Supreme Court analyzed the concept of possession with reference to English law and doctrine on torts. As regards the meaning of the expression 'possession', the Court refers to various terms ('possession', 'right of possession', 'legal possession', 'right to possess', 'constructive possession') and notes that these terms generally mean the same thing. Furthermore, the Court draws a distinction between two kinds of possession: (1) possession in fact and (2) possession in law, by recognizing that the first of these does not have the same degree of legal protection as the second. It is quite possible to have de facto possession of a thing without having any bodily contact with it. Possession in fact is prima facie evidence of possession in law but it is not conclusive evidence of it, for possession in law is something more. Possession in law is also known as legal possession. The distinction between possession in fact and possession in law lies in the presence of a certain mental element. Whether this intent exists or not, must generally be a question of fact. As the Court highlights, for possession in law there must be a manifest intent not merely to exclude the world at large from interfering with the thing in

105. *Kailis et al. v. Kostas Michail Levadiotis Ltd et al.*, Civil Appeal No. 133/2012, 28 November 2017.
106. (1971) 1 CLR 189.

question, but to do so on one's own account and in one's own name.[107] This approach was also followed by Cypriot case law. In the case *Agathi Charalambos, as administrator of the estate of Charalambos Neofytou v. Ioannis K. Ioannides*,[108] it was held that possession must be proven through testimony that shows that the non-entitled person is carrying out all the acts that constitute the possession permitted by the nature of the immovable property. There must be possession and considerable use of the entire property at issue, exclusively by the non-entitled person, in a manner and to an extent that precludes the owner from any possession or use of the same property.

2. Possession Versus Property Right

83. Possession, as a matter of fact, is distinguished from the property right, which is a matter of law. Indeed, it is possible for a possessor to exercise, the control in fact over a good, even if ownership is lacking. This is the case of adverse possession where the physical occupation of the thing is done without a legal basis, but over time, can generate rights for the possessor. Legitimate possession is an attribute of the property right, while non-legitimate possession is a possession in fact, based on material control only.

3. Protection of Possession

84. Possession is protected in Cypriot tort law through the torts of trespass and private nuisance. In both cases, the possessor is protected, while the owner (person having the legal title of property) is only exceptionally protected. In general, the owner of the land can only exceptionally bring a claim, for example, when the trespass inflicts damage to the property or when the intervention to the property is of a permanent nature. Specifically, in *Lambrou et al. v. Kefala etc*., it was emphasized that trespassing on immovable property is a tort against the possession of land and that the plaintiff must be the possessor of the land. But, if the intervention is of a permanent nature, then the owner is also entitled to bring a lawsuit.[109] In this context, in *Georghiou v. Andrea*,[110] it was held that the planting of trees was a permanent intervention that gave the landlord who rented the property to others an actionable claim for trespass.

107. Frederick Pollock & Robert Samuel Wright, *Essay on Possession in the Common Law* 17 (Oxford: Claredon Press 1888).
108. *Ikosi v. Karayiannis et al.* (1971) 1 CLR 189.
109. *Lambrou et al. v. Kefala*, Civil Appeal No. 10197 (2000) 1 CLR 1516.
110. *Georghiou v. Andrea* (1998) 1(D) CLR 2311.

B. Title

85. Land law in Cyprus is strongly connected with the operation of the Department of Land and Surveys (the Land Registry). The Department of Land and Surveys is considered to be the oldest governmental department of the public sector in Cyprus.[111] Land registration in Cyprus has a long history. An initial, albeit unsophisticated, system of granting titles started before the enactment of the Ottoman Land Code, i.e., before 1857. However, these deeds of title were not registered. The registration of deeds of title started after the Land Registry was set up in 1858. Formalities are a fundamental element of Cypriot real property law. Various forms of registration of acquisition of ownership have existed in Cyprus since the establishment of the Land Registry. In 1860 it became obligatory to register property rights over land. Two other important legal reforms took place in 1893 and 1907.[112]

86. A fundamental principle of Cypriot land law is that interests or rights over or affecting immovable property are registered and can be traced in the Registries of the Lands and Surveys Department. This was made possible by the General Survey and Registration conducted in the 1920s, which resulted in the adoption of survey plans made to scale for the whole of Cyprus on which each piece of land as it was held then is plotted to scale and numbered.[113]

87. After the division of Cyprus due to the Turkish occupation of the northern part of the island, the Cypriot land registration system suffered a major blow, as the cadastral maps were no longer accessible. Law 55/1975 provided for the possibility of the transfer of immovable property located in the occupied area of the island, after filing the contract of transfer in a special new registry created for this purpose. Law 44/1984 established a procedure for the creation of new cadastral maps for the districts of Kyrenia and Ammochostos, following the notification of title to immovable property by right-holders and subsequent verification by the Land Registry. Thanks to these necessary reforms, the Cypriot registration system managed to endure and to be rebuilt.

88. Registration may be either *ab initio* or by means of transfer. The principal components of land registration records include the Register, the Cadastral Map, the Tax Register and the Certificate of Registration. The Cypriot land registration system aims not only to guarantee legal certainty and security in the acquisition of real rights over land, but also has significant powers in various fields, such as the correction of errors and the establishment of compulsory easements.

---

111. *See* Department of Lands and Surveys of Cyprus, Historical Background, https://portal.dls.moi.gov.cy/en-us/thedepartment/Pages/historical-background.aspx, last visited on 23 December 2019.

112. Koutas, *supra* n. 32 at 18–19.

113. Costas A. Hadjioannou, *Cyprus: Land Law – Immovable Property Law, Cyprus Land Registry, Private Ownership, Restrictions, Acquisitive Prescriptions, Trusts Registration* (6 March 2019), at: http://www.mondaq.com/cyprus/x/787600/agriculture+land+law/Land+Law+Immovable+Property+Law+Cyprus+Land+Registry+Private+Ownership+Restrictions+Acquisitive+Prescriptions+Trusts+Registration.

89. The basic principles that can be generally recognized in cadastral systems are also apparent in the Cypriot land registration system. More precisely: (a) any change in real rights over immovable property, especially by transfer, is not legally enforced until the change or the expected right is registered in the land register, (b) the registered owner of land must give his consent for a change to the entry in the land register, (c) the legal registers are open for public inspection and (d) in land registration, and consequently in the documents submitted for registration, the subject in question (i.e., the person) and object (i.e., the property) must be unambiguously identified.[114]

90. The land registry system in Cyprus is a system of registration of titles of immovable property. This means that the registration does not concern the land, but the title over the land.[115] Title is conferred by law and evidenced by the Land Register. Through the registration, the rights that exist with respect to the specified immovable property are defined. By registering the title, a rebuttable presumption of ownership is established in favour of the title-holder to whom the legal status of 'registered owner' is attributed. The person who wishes to register the title must prove that he/she is entitled to register as its owner.[116] Proof of the right of ownership is, therefore, a necessary prerequisite for the registration of a title over immovable property.

91. Such a right can be acquired either by adverse possession or by derivative acquisition, such as transfer by purchase, inheritance or donation. Since Cypriot land law recognizes the acquisition and transfer of rights and interests on immovable property on the ground of trusts (*see* Chapter 3 below and Part IV, Trust and Fiduciary Mechanisms, Chapter 1),[117] in case of acquisition by purchase the registered purchaser shall prove that he/she is the bona fide purchaser without notice, and thus that he/she took all reasonable care and made enquiry and that having taken that care and made enquiry he received no notice of the trust which affected the property.[118] Therefore, a registered sale does not confer on the purchaser an indefeasible right of ownership.

92. The concept of bona fide purchaser for value without notice has been analyzed by Cypriot courts with reference to the English law.[119] In *Artemis Charalambous Kyprianou v. Christos Mitsi*, it was held that '"notice" is of three varieties: actual, constructive and imputed. It is actual when a purchaser actually knows of

114. For these principles, *see* Jo Hensen, *Basic Principles of the Main Cadastral Systems in the World*, http://www.fig.net/commission7/reports/events/delft_seminar_95/paper2.html.
115. Registration of titles systems are also referred to as 'presumption of correctness systems'. Rights are inscribed in the Registry, which does not consist of a collection of original documentation pertaining to the property, as does the registration of deeds system. *See* Luz M. Martínez Velencoso, Saki Bailey & Andrea Pradi (eds.), *Transfer of Immovables in European Private Law* 10 (Cambridge University Press 2017).
116. *Molla Mustafa HajAhmed v. Abdul Kadir Hassan* (V7) 1 CLR 32, p. 42, at 47.
117. Section 2 of Cap. 224.
118. *Tsiartas et al. v. Alocay Holdings Ltd et al.* (2010) 1 CLR 1523.
119. *See Akil Hussein Arnaout v. Emine Hussein Zinouri*, Civil Appeal No. 4012, 1953.

the existence of the equitable interest. It is constructive when the interest would have come to his knowledge if he had made such enquiries as he ought to have made. Imputed notice covers actual or constructive notice to his agent as such in the transaction in question.' Specifically, as regards constructive notice, 'it is generally taken to include two different things: (1) The notice which is implied when a purchaser omits to investigate the vendor's title properly or to make reasonable inquiries as to deeds or facts which come to his knowledge' and '(2) The notice which is imputed to a purchaser by reason of the fact that his solicitor or other legal agent has actual or implied notice of some fact. This is generally called "imputed notice".' The main question is what a prudent, careful man ought to do when he is purchasing an estate.[120] In *Akil Hussein Arnaout v. Emine Hussein Zinouri*, it was noted that 'without notice' shall mean that the purchaser under the circumstances had made reasonable inquiries in order to find out whether the vendor in addition to being the holder of title deed was also the undisputed owner in physical possession of the land to be sold.[121] Recently, in the case *Ayoub v. Director of the Land Registry*,[122] the District Court of Limassol analyzed the status of the bona fide purchaser for value without notice with reference to the UK case *Independent Trustee Services Limited v. GP Noble Trustees Limited & Others*,[123] by fully following the principles therein. As stated in the latter decision, '(1)The question of notice is to be determined at the time when the legal estate passes (i.e. the date of purchase);[124] (2) as between vendor and purchaser, title passes even if there is a subsequent total failure of consideration and is not re-vested in the vendor;[125] (3) where a bona fide purchaser subsequently transfers the property to a volunteer or even to persons with notice of a prior equitable interest, those transferees nevertheless take free of such interests: see Wilkes v Spooner [1911] 2 KB 473 where (at p. 483) Vaughan-Williams LJ said that: "It cannot seriously be disputed that the proposition which I quoted from Ashburner's Principles of Equity, p. 75, is good law". It is as follows: "A purchaser for valuable consideration without notice can give a good title to a purchaser from him with notice. The only exception is that a trustee who has sold property in breach of trust, or a person who has acquired property by fraud, cannot protect himself by purchasing it from a bona fide purchaser for value without notice. (4) The effect of a transfer of property to a bona fide purchaser is to extinguish any prior equitable interest."'[126,127]

---

120. *Kyprianou as Administrator of the estate of Anna Constanti Koutsouki v. Mitsi et al.* (1975) JSC 1179.
121. *Akil Hussein Arnaout v. Emine Hussein Zinouri*, Civil Appeal No. 4012, 1953.
122. *Ayoub v. Director of the Land Registry*, No. 5165/2012, 20 November 2018.
123. *Independent Trustee Services Limited v. GP Noble Trustees Limited & Others* [2012] EWCA Civ 195.
124. *See Macmillan Inc v. Bishopsgate Investment Trust plc (No. 3)* [1995] 1 WLR 978 at p. 1000.
125. *See Westdeutsche Landesbank Girozentrale v. Islington LBC* [1996] AC 669, which confirmed that a claimant under such a contract did not have a proprietary remedy based on a resulting trust because the relevant time for testing the conscience of the transferee was that of his receipt of the property which predated the failure of consideration.
126. *See Re Diplock* [1948] Ch 465 (at p. 537).
127. *Ayoub v. Director of the Land Registry*, *supra* n. 122.

93. As noted in *Hjikaterini Nicola v. Charalambos Christophi*, the application of a more flexible approach, which is based on morality (equity) and public policy reasons, was justified by the endeavour to avoid harshness arising in certain cases from the fact that well recognized legal rights in immovable property, were not transferable under ordinary legal contract. Specifically, 'if the rights were not registered, or if the property did not happen to be registered, as it was very frequently the case, especially in the earlier days, property rights could not be legally transferred, without prior registration of the property. Absentees, incapacitated persons, or obstinate heirs, often blocked the way. But the flow of human affairs in the ordinary life of the people of Cyprus, went down its course, sometimes over, and sometimes round, these legal impediments. Unregistered property changed hands from father to son, from seller to buyer, or from grantor to grantee, although the legal title to the property remained caught on the legal pegs. And when the good faith upon which such transactions were founded, became too weak or too old to support them, the matter ended in litigation. The Courts called these "private sales" to distinguish them from "official" or registered transfers; and treating them as "illegal", they refused to enforce them. But this often resulted in harshness and unfair consequences, which the Courts endeavored to mitigate by resorting to methods which they called equitable principles.'[128] The situation was problematic, since courts often interpreted the Ottoman Law in a way that precluded not only the transfer of title, but even the creation of contractual obligations, so that no damages might be awarded for a breach of these obligations.[129]

94. In the case *St. George's Car Hire Ltd et al. v. Makedonias Gavrielidou et al.*, the above principles were applied in relation to the recognition of proprietary interests belonging to the purchasers of land vis-à-vis the registered owners of land. The key elements of this case are that the landowners signed an agreement with a land developer knowing from the outset that the developer would sell the apartments to third parties. The land developer then left the project unfinished and the purchasers of the apartments completed the project at their own expense, again with the knowledge of the landowners, who benefited from these actions by the purchasers. The Court held that the law of equity prevents the landlords from claiming their property rights vis-à-vis the purchasers. Even if there is no contractual relationship between the landowners and the purchasers, the law of equity gives substantive property rights to the purchasers and the landowners' property rights shall cede.[130]

95. 94. In the landmark cases *Petsa et al. v. Petsas*[131] and *Pirillou v. Konari*,[132] the Supreme Court dealt with the protection and the obligations of a purchaser of an immovable property which is subject to a constructive trust. It was held that the principles of the law of equity do not allow the purchaser to ignore and discharge the obligations of his predecessor, since the principles of the law of equity can

128. *Nicola v. Christofi et al.* (1965) 1 CLR 324.
129. *The Estate of the Deceased Osman Ahmed Pasha v. Mehmed Osman Pasha*, 19 C.L.R. 226.
130. *St. George's Car Hire Ltd et al. v. Makedonias Gavrielidou et al.* (2006) 1 CLR 47.
131. *Savva Argyrou Petsa et al. v. Papatheocharis Petsas*, Political Appeal No. 8491, 28 June 1996.
132. *Pirillos v. Konnari* (2000) 1B CLR 1153.

extend to also cover third parties whose own conscience is bound and, as a result, they are deemed to substitute the trustee in his/her obligations vis-à-vis the beneficiary of the trust. Third parties are bound by the trust, if they are not purchasers for value and without notice, as in the case, *inter alia*, of the trustee's heirs who acquire the trustee's property. On the one hand, the principle of privity of contract forbids the purchaser, as a third party to the trust, to challenge the validity of the trust, unless the trustee acts under the guidance of the beneficiary. On the other hand, equity protects the beneficiary against the bad faith of the purchaser and, in this case, the trust creates a property interest on the immovable property and the beneficiary of the trust can ask for the property to be registered on his/her name.

96. Registration can only be done by the owner of the land, who is defined as the person entitled to register as the owner of immovable property.[133] The registered owner is considered the owner who is entitled to own immovable property and is registered in the Land Registry. This creates a prima facie evidence of ownership. Anyone who wants to challenge the title, or part thereof, must prove that the registration was made due to an error or fraud and that the claimant holds a better title or the person who registered the title has lost his/her right. The validity of a registration is enhanced by the details that are included, as well as the delineation of the immovable property. The delineation of land is made by comparing the registration with the Government Survey plan and if there is any correlation, then the extent of ownership is the extent of ownership to which the possessor of the land is entitled.[134] Most registrations today are identical to the survey plan in use and the piece of land they refer to is exactly what is shown in the survey plan.

97. As regards the rights and interests that can be registered, apart from ownership, registration can also be effected for long-term leases, trusts, easements, usufruct and habitation rights, restrictive covenants, mortgages and charges.

V. The Legal Effects of Registration

98. The registration of transfer in the Land Registry is a rebuttable presumption of ownership for the rights-holder and of the validity of the registration as well. The certificate of registration is only prima facie evidence of ownership, which can be rebutted if it can be established that the registration was effected in the holder's name in error.[135] Subsequently, in *Theodorou v. Hadjiantoni*, it was mentioned that a 'natural boundary might be of immense help in ascertaining an error in the original registration or in a boundary dispute'.[136] In *Christos Agathocleous Ltd v. Sofocleous*, which was an action regarding the tort of private nuisance, it was held that the certificate of registration is the most orthodox and appropriate way to prove

133. Section 2 of Cap. 224.
134. Section 50 of Cap. 224.
135. *Theodorou v. Hadjiantoni* (1961) CLR 203. This rule was reasserted in *Socratous v. Mezou* (1975) 1 CLR 62; *Savva v. Petrou* (1985) 1 CLR 127.
136. *Loizou, wife of Theofilou v. Christodoulou Polemiti* (1998) 1C CLR 1349; *Theodorou v. HadjiAntoni* (1961) CLR 203.

ownership, without being the only way, since in this case the testimony concerning the status of the plaintiff as the lawful owner of the property in question was enough to prove the validity of the ownership, despite the absence of the relevant certificate.[137]

99. Section 50 of Cap. 224[138] provides that the area of land covered by a registration of title to immovable property is defined as the area of the plot with which the registration can be associated on any Government survey plan or any other plan made to scale by the Director of the Department of Lands and Surveys.[139] The loss of the records of the Land Registry and the loss of the certificates of registration themselves for reasons related to the history of Cyprus mean that it is also possible to have recourse to secondary evidence in order to establish a registered title over a particular plot of land, once the absence of primary evidence has been satisfactorily explained.[140]

100. The legislation does not provide any governmental guarantee of title or any government indemnity. Any person who disputes the facts related to a registration can seek rectification either by application to the Director of the Department of Lands and Surveys[141] or to the Court. Additionally, the general legal regime of tort liability for negligence is theoretically applicable. However, there is no relevant case law.

VI. The Land Registry's Transparency Function

101. The registration of title is intended to act as a mirror, reflecting to potential purchasers and any other interested person the full range of real property rights and burdens applicable over a specific parcel of land. In this context, only the definitive record provided by the register can be taken into account, and there is no need for a retrospective examination of title deeds or other documents outside the scope of the Register.[142] Nevertheless, the Land Registry's transparency function is regulated in order to safeguard the balance with the right of privacy and personal data protection.

102. In general, access to the records of the Land Registry is possible where there is a legitimate reason for it. The question of access to cadastral maps is set out in section 51A of Cap. 224. Under this provision, any interested person can submit

137. *Christos Agathocleous Ltd v. Sofocleous* (2000) 1 CLR 1953.
138. Section 50 defines that 'the area of land covered by a registration of title to immovable property shall be the area of the plot to which the registration can be related on any Government survey plan or any other plan made to scale by the Director: Provided that where the registration cannot be related to any such plan such area shall be the area of the land to which the holder of the title may be entitled by adverse possession, purchase or inheritance.'
139. *Ioannou v. Constantinou et al.* (1999) 1B CLR 749.
140. *Panagi v. Zouvani* (1987) 1 CLR 58.
141. *See* s. 61 of Cap. 224.
142. Gray & Gray, *supra* n. 99 at 190.

an application to the Land Registry, requesting information. The law, however, defines the persons who may submit such an application. In this respect, the term 'interested person' refers to any owner or holder of other real property rights and his/her successors, any person who intends to purchase an immovable property – provided that they produce some documentation proving their capacity as a purchaser, such as a contract of sale – and the mortgagee. The plaintiffs in an action against the owner of immovable property and some categories of professionals, such as land valuers, real estate agents and advocates (lawyers) are also deemed to be interested persons. The law, nonetheless, allows, somewhat arbitrarily, the Director of the Department of Lands and Surveys to enlarge the category of interested persons at his/her discretion. Section 51A(2) of Cap. 224 provides that the term 'interested person' comprises also every person to whom the Director of the Department of Lands and Surveys provides such information on specific grounds.

103. For a long time, the Land Registry would provide information to credit institutions on immovable property belonging to registered owners, even though credit institutions were not classified as 'interested persons' in Cap. 224. Section 51A has been recently amended and now expressly establishes the Land Registry's right to provide information to credit institutions.[143] In respect of the provision of such information to credit institutions, the strategic choice of the legislator has been to introduce a flexible procedure that favours an easy and quick provision of information without an a priori review of the claim. In this context, the law stipulates that the Land registry will provide immediately the information to the credit institution that requests it, without examining the reasons justifying the provision of information which are invoked by the credit institution in its claim. Nonetheless, a necessary prerequisite is that the credit institution should have already obtained a general authorisation by the Department of Lands and Surveys for submitting such claims.

104. At the same time the credit institution is under an obligation to inform the person whom the requested information concerns about the filing of the request with the Land Registry. The person whose real property the information was requested for, has the right to submit a request in writing to the Land Registry asking the Director to proceed to *a posteriori* scrutiny regarding whether the credit institution had reasonable grounds to request the information. The preferential treatment of credit institutions is partially justified, since after the economic crisis, the number of debtors who cannot repay their loans has increased sharply. The respect for personal data protection is also safeguarded by the severe consequences for the credit institutions in case they submit a claim for requesting information without reasonable grounds.[144] On the other hand, the lack of an *a priori* control of the claims and the transfer of the burden to question the legitimacy of the claim to the person, whose property the information is required for ends up, in practice, with an opt-out

143. Christos Ioannou, *Cypriot Land Law* 62 (Nomiki Vivliothiki 2014).
144. The law provides for heavy fines up to EUR 250,000 and for the biennial revocation of the general permission given to the credit institution by the Department of Lands and Surveys.

system of generalized and poorly supervised processing of personal data that is not respectful of the right to personal self-determination.

105. In the case of *Muriel Beaumont v. Papacleovoulou,*[145] the court clearly affirmed that lawyers are considered to be interested persons in the sense of section 51A of Cap. 224. Moreover, the Court thoroughly examined the duties of a lawyer in respect of checking deeds of title in cases where immovable property is purchased by a foreigner. According to the court, in this case the lawyer is bound by a greater obligation to ensure that all the requirements of the law are met, and that his/her client's interests are safeguarded.

106. However, even if lawyers are considered to be 'interested persons', the Department of Lands and Surveys must ensure that information is provided in accordance with the requirements of personal data protection. In this context, in 2009 the Office of the Commissioner for Personal Data Protection issued a decision[146] against the Land Registry for providing information to a lawyer. The Director of the Land Registry argued that the information was disclosed lawfully under section 51A of Cap. 224, since the survey certificate was given to a lawyer, who brought legal proceedings before a court for the settlement of a dispute arising from a divorce. However, the lawyer's application form requesting the provision of information was never found in the Land Registry's records. Consequently, the Commissioner issued a stern warning to the Director of the Land Registry to take appropriate organizational and technical measures to ensure data security and protection. It was also held that the Director was obliged to inform the subject of the personal data on the basis of section 11(1)(3) of Law 138(I)/2001 on personal data protection, for disclosure of the data to a third party.

145. *Beaumont v. Papacleovoulou* (2010) 1A CLR 525.
146. Decision 9/9/2009.

Part I. Immovable Property and Real Property

Chapter 1. General Classification of Property Rights

107. In the Cypriot legal system, the concept of real rights refers more broadly to the concept of 'rights in rem', which originally stems from Roman law, but which appears in civil and common law as well.[147] Indeed, despite the lack of an express definition of real rights in the Cypriot immovable property law Cap. 224, there is still an indirect recognition of these, via sporadic references to the relevant concept of 'rights in rem' in Cypriot case law,[148] which are often distinguished in case law from 'rights in personam'. At the same time, due to the lack in codification, there is also a lack in classification of real rights.

108. The lack of a systemic development of the classification of real rights is partially the outcome of the influence of common law tradition, which does not recognize the concept of ownership as dominium, that is the absolute and exclusive power over the immovable thing,[149] following on from the doctrine of the Crown's ownership over the land.[150]

147. *See* Harold Greville Hanbury & Ronald Harling Maudsley, *Hanbury and Maudsley Modern Equity* 18 (12th ed., Jill E. Martin ed., Stevens, 1985): 'It can also be used to distinguish a right to property from a chose in action. It seems that its proper meaning in the present context is a right enforceable against the world with respect to a particular thing. It seems to be assumed throughout that a legal owner does have rights in rem. Rights, that is, against all the world with respect to property.'
148. *InFlower, etc. v. Hadjiioannou, etc.* (2008) 1B CLR 770, a right in rem is mentioned ('The case law also confirms that a right over land is created only in case where the sale of the immovable property takes place under a written contract, which is registered to the Land Registry, on the basis of the Sale of Land (Specific Performance) Law, Cap. 232, and only then, the buyer acquires a right in rem over the immovable property, which can constitute the subject of specific performance'), while in *Markidou v. Killiaris and Another* (1983) 1 CLR 392 the concept of estate in land is listed in the category of rights in rem: 'The rights acquired under a contract for the sale of land are personal and as such prima facie assignable. A contract for the sale of land does not create an estate in land, that is, rights in rem.'
149. According to Roman law, it is regarded to be one and only concept of ownership over a thing, and thus all the other real rights which constitute restrictions of ownership are in a competitive relationship (*iura in re aliena*). *See* I. Sonti, *Contributions to Theory of Land Law* 54 (A. N. Sakkoulas Publications 1986).
150. The person who used the land based his right directly or indirectly on the King. The characteristics of the feudal system were that no person was regarded to be the owner of the land in the sense of private property as it is defined in Cap. 224. The people, who used to provide services, acquired as

109. Except for the right of ownership or absolute private property, easements, usufruct and habitation rights, 'profit à prendre',[151] the rights created by long-term leasehold that have been registered in the Land Registry pursuant to sections 65A–65IE of Cap. 224[152] and restrictive covenants that have been registered pursuant to section 65IH of Cap. 224, under the term that can be enforced against the successors in title of the defined servient tenement,[153] fall within the category of rights in rem. Unregistered rights (mainly equitable rights) can also be established mainly through the mechanism of trust.[154]

consideration the right to use and possess the land (tenure). *See* E.H. Burn and J. Cartriwight, *Chesire and Burn's Modern Law of Property* 14 et seq. (17th ed., Oxford University Press 2006).

151. As regards the nature of *profit à prendre* as rights in rem and especially the distinction of profit à prendre from the licences, *see* the case *Savvas Manoushios and others of Kalogrea v. The Forest Department* (15 November 1952). *Profit à prendre* are interests or advantages in relation to an alien immovable property, which provide to their right-holder the possibility to profit from the property, e.g., wood, metal, hunting, grass for grazing, etc. They are similar to easement without, nevertheless, being identical, since, as it will be further analyzed, the existence of a dominant and servient tenement is not required as it is with easements. Thus, their common feature is that they do not provide a right of possession, but a right of specific use of the foreign property. For the profit à prendre, *see* Gray & Gray, *supra* n. 99 at 598–601. A profit (short for *profit-à-prendre* in Middle French for 'right of taking'), in the law of real property, is a non-possessory interest in land similar to the better-known easement, which gives the holder the right to take natural resources such as petroleum, minerals, timber, and wild game from the land of another. *See also* https://www.gov.uk/government/publications/profits-a-prendre--2/practice-guide-16-profits-a-prendre.

152. *See* among others *Aggelidis and Filippou Ltd v. Spyros Colocassides Estates Ltd* (1991) 1 CLR 327, 332–333; *Apollonio Private Hospital Ltd v. C & S American Heart Institute Ltd et al.* (2011) 1(A) CLR 379: 'In Cyprus, lease creates a contractual relationship among the parties, unless it is a lease of a land for more than 15 years, which creates a real right, provided that it is registered to Land Registry on the basis of sections 65A-65IE (Part IV) of the Immovable Property (Tenure, Registration and Valuation) Law, Cap. 224.'

153. Dennis Campbell (ed.), *Neocleous's Introduction to Cyprus Law* 879 (2nd ed., Center for International Legal Studies, Yorkhill Law Publishing 2009).

154. Section 4 of Cap. 224.

Chapter 2. Legal Interests

110. A fundamental distinction in English Land law is the distinction between legal and equitable interests. While the transfer of the legal title carries with it, prima facie, the absolute beneficial interest in the asset which is transferred, there are cases where another person is able to establish a basis upon which equity would intervene on (his or) her behalf.[155]

111. The distinction between legal and equitable interests is historically grounded on the fact that legal rights were enforceable only in common law courts, while equitable rights fell within the jurisdiction of the Court of Chancery. Differences between the two categories exist in relation to the focus (form or substance) and the remedies available at law and in equity.[156]

112. Cypriot legislation does not officially distinguish between legal interests and equitable interests in land. In this respect, it could be *a priori* assumed that all interests fall into the category of legal interests. This assumption could be based on section 4 of Cap. 224, which provides for the exclusion of common law and the law of equity, at least to some degree, from Cypriot land law. Section 4 provides that no estate, interest[157] or right in any immovable property shall be created, acquired or transferred except under the provisions of Cap. 224. As a consequence, it is not possible to create, acquire or transfer property rights over immovable property on the grounds of common law and the law of equity. Therefore, section 4 introduces an important departure from section 29(1)(c) of the Cypriot Courts of Justice Law of 1960 (Law 14/60) that provides for the general application of English common law and equity law in Cyprus.[158]

113. Section 4 of Cap. 224 has a long history, since it was promulgated as a reaction to the decision of Judge Halinnan in the case *of Agni Kontou v. Maria Parouti*, which attempted to expand the application of English law to the Cypriot law of real

155. Gray & Gray, *supra* n. 99 at 821.
156. *Ibid.* 72–73.
157. In *Lordos & Anastassiades et al. v. The District Officer of Limassol et al.* (1976) 2 CLR 145, it was held that a building permit cannot be treated as an 'advantage; in the sense such term is used in s. 4 of the Immovable Property (Tenure, Registration and Valuation) Law, Cap. 224. In this context, the argument that a building permit cannot be transferred otherwise than in accordance with the provisions of Cap. 224, with the inevitable result that it does not run with the land, is rejected. Furthermore, the Court held that a building permit is a licence in rem. It is issued, in relation only to the proposed building operations on the land concerned, in accordance with plans submitted for that purpose. Therefore, it does not lapse upon transfer of the ownership of the land on which the building operations are to take place, or have commenced taking place, but it runs with the land.
158. Section 29(1)(β) of Law 14/60 states that the courts of Cyprus, in all civil and criminal proceedings, shall apply the following: the Constitution of Cyprus, the Laws that are still applicable under s. 188 of the Constitution, the Common Law and the principles of Equity, and all laws applicable in Cyprus before 1960.

property.[159] The exclusion of English common law and the law of equity have been constantly affirmed by Cypriot case law.[160] In this context, the Cypriot Supreme Court has affirmed that the influence of English law shall be taken into account only in respect of principles that derive from Roman law and are, as a result, common to Ottoman law and English law, such as in the case of easements. Consequently, courts must be very careful when the parties invoke English case law, even as persuasive precedent, due to the particular features of the Cypriot immovable property law that differentiates it from English land law.[161]

114. The principle, however, is not absolute. Section 4 introduces also certain exceptions, the most important of them being the case of trusts.[162] As will be demonstrated in Chapter 3, equitable (unregistered) interests are also recognized mainly through the institution of the trust, where a duality of estate ownership is established. Specifically, trusts are expressly excluded from the ambit of section 4 of Cap. 224, while Cypriot case law, inspired by English law, has from time to time affirmed the possibility to acquire land though the equitable mechanism of proprietary estoppel, despite the restrictive wording of section 4 of Cap. 224.

---

159. *Kontou v. Parouti*, 19 CLR 172, 6 February 1953: 'The combined effect of the Immovable Property Law and the Courts of Justice Law might well be that, since the law of the Ottoman Land Code has ceased to apply, and as no other provision has been made, the path is clear for the application of common law.'
160. *See Millington – Ward v. Roubina* (1970) 1 CLR 88; *Cyprus Cinema & Theatre Co. Ltd v. Karmiotis* (1967) 1 CLR 42; *Hadjikyriakou v. Fina (Cyprus) Ltd* (1978) 2 J.S.C. 322.
161. *A. Gheorgiou v. K. Gheorgiou Andrea* (1998) 1 D CLR 2311.
162. For the exception established with s. 4 in respect of trusts, *see Miltiadous v. Miltiadous* (1982) 1 CLR 797; *Odysseos v. Pierris Estates et al.* (1982) 1 CLR 557.

Chapter 3. Equitable Interests

115. The regulation of 'land' in the Cypriot legal system is built on a fundamental contradiction. While the meaning of the concept of land itself, as established in the statutory definition of land, bears significant conceptual similarities to the relevant definition in England, the significance of this finding is undermined by a statutory aphorism. Indeed, on the basis of section 4 of Cap. 224,[163] the application of common law and of the law of equity is prohibited as regards the creation and acquisition of property rights in respect of land.[164] In this context, it could be said that all rights and interests in land are *a priori* legal (and not equitable).

116. However, even if the application of the law of equity is expressly excluded by section 4 of Cap. 224 in respect of the acquisition of real property, equity still has a significant role to play through the mechanisms of trusts, specific performance and, despite the restrictive wording of section 4, of proprietary estoppel.

§1. Trusts

117. Trusts that form the principal device of equity for the acquisition of property rights outside a system of registration are expressly excluded from the ambit of section 4 of Cap. 224. Nevertheless, the legal recognition of trusts has been controversial since another provision of Cap. 224, section 65IE regulates only express trusts, and it is now a matter of debate as to whether the special provision of 65IE precludes the recognition of trusts that are not express trusts. Section 65IE states that: '(1) Any trust which relates to immovable property is not considered valid unless it is established βυ document (trust deed) signed by the person entitled thereto or by will. (2) The founding document of the trust (trust deed) or the covenant as appropriate, must be registered to the relevant Register of the Department of Land.' So, the literal interpretation of this provision could permit a reading that in order to be valid, all trusts have to be established by document and have to be registered.

118. The exact meaning of section 65IE was discussed thoroughly in the case of *Christophorou v. Christophorou*,[165] where the Court examined the relationship between sections 4 and 65IE, and especially whether the second has tacitly abolished the first. The Court held that the exclusion of trusts in section 4 is not limited to express trusts, but encompasses trusts generally, including constructive, as well as resulting trusts. This interpretation was found to be consistent with previous case

163. Immovable Property (Tenure, Registration and Valuation) Law, Cap. 224.
164. For an analysis of Cypriot land law, *see* Synodinou, *supra* n. 75.
165. *Christophorou v. Christophorou* (1998) 1 CLR 1551.

law that recognized acquisition of property via constructive or resulting trusts without examining the relationship between sections 4 and 65IE.[166] This finding was also indirectly confirmed in the *Pirillos v. Konari* case, where it was held on the one hand that only express trusts created in compliance with the provisions of section 65IE can be registered, while on the other hand the creation of a constructive trust was recognized.[167] On the basis of the above, it was held that the fact that a trust is not established in the manner provided by section 65IE of Cap. 224, in order to be considered as a valid express trust, does not preclude the creation of a constructive trust, if such a need arises from the circumstances of the case.[168]

119. On the basis of section 65IE of Cap. 224, trusts are divided into 'registered trusts' and 'unregistered trusts'. The entry of the trust in the public registry enables its enforcement *erga omnes*. For unregistered trusts, the impact of the trust affects not only the original trustee but also many categories of persons under the rules of 'bona fide purchaser' or the equitable doctrine of notice.[169] (For an analysis of the concept of trust and relevant case law, *see also below* Part IV, Trust and Fiduciary Mechanisms, Chapter 1.)

§2. Specific Performance

120. Another exception to the general prohibition of the application of the law of equity in Cypriot property law is the case of specific performance. A special piece of legislation, the Sale of Land (Specific Performance) Law (81(I)/2011), permits the acquisition of ownership of land in the case of a contract of sale of land that has not been properly executed by the vendor. This law was one of the first institutions of English law that was transplanted into Cypriot law.[170] In order to obtain specific performance, a series of formalities and deadlines is prescribed by the law. First, the contract of sale must be registered in the Land Registry within a period of six months after its conclusion. Registration of the contract of sale of immovable property under the provisions of the Sale of Land (Specific Performance) Law operates as an encumbrance with respect to such immovable property from the date of its registration at the Land Registry. Therefore, it will create a right in rem and consequently it will impede the transfer of the land to another person by the vendor. Accordingly, the declaration of any subsequent transfer will not be accepted by the Land Registry.[171]

---

166. *Miltiadous v. Miltiadous* (1982) 1 CLR 797; *Pentavkas v. Pentavka* (1991) 1 CLR 547; *Constantinou v. Demosthenous* (1992) 1 CLR 621; *Orphanides v. Orphanides* (1998) 1 CLR 179; *Clerides v. Stavrides* (1998) 1 CLR 521.
167. *Pirillos v. Konnari* (2000) 1B CLR 1153.
168. *Konstantinou Tsillara v. Spyrou Kyriakou*, Nos 13/2016, 1746/2011, 13 October 2016.
169. Gray & Gray, *supra* n. 99 at 80.
170. The first legislation governing specific performance in respect of contracts of sale of land was the Sale of Land (Specific Performance) Law of 1885.
171. *Ayios Andronikos Development Co. Ltd v. The Republic of Cyprus through the Minister of Interior, the Director of Lands and Surveys and the Minister of Finance* (1985) 3D CLR 2362.

121. Law 81(I)/2011, which replaced Cap. 232, has brought about significant improvements. It is now possible to proceed to registration of the property in the name of the purchaser upon specific performance, despite the existence of a prior mortgage. Under previous legislation, in order for the mortgaged property to be transferred to the purchaser, the vendor had to have paid off his mortgaged debt to the creditor. Where the vendor was unable to perform his/her obligations against the creditor, the purchaser could not activate his/her right for specific performance, unless he/she paid off the mortgage debt himself/herself. The new legislation enabled the purchaser, when the object of the sale is mortgaged, to pay the amount due each time, under the Sale Contract, to the mortgage creditor directly and not to the vendor. When the purchaser pays that part of the mortgage debt which corresponds proportionally to the value of the property he/she has purchased, as compared to the total value of the property mortgaged, the Court may issue an order for specific performance, ordering the registration of the property in the name of the purchaser free from the encumbrance.[172]

122. A question that has led to contradictory findings in case law is whether registration of the contract of sale also creates a constructive trust to the benefit of the purchaser. In *Odysseos v. Pierris Estates Ltd*, the Court held that although the contract of sale creates a constructive trust, the contract cannot be enforced, either by the purchaser or by an assignee, in the absence of strict compliance with the provisions of the Sale of Land (Specific Performance) Law, since the existence of a constructive trust cannot, in Cyprus, create an estate in land, unless there is compliance with the provisions of the said Law.[173] On the other hand, in *Wheeler and others v. Messios and Sons Limited and others*,[174] it was held that the encumbrance that arises out of registration of the contract of sale does create a constructive trust, whose beneficiary is the purchaser.

123. Another question that has been posed before the Cypriot courts is that of whether the general provisions of Cap. 149 in respect of the specific performance of contracts can apply simultaneously to the Sale of Land (Specific Performance) Law. In *Iordanou v. Anyftos*, which has been confirmed consistently in later case law, the Court ruled that specific performance in respect of immovable property can be ordered only under the Sale of Land (Specific Performance) Law and that the relevant section 76 of the Contract Law is not applicable to the sale of land.[175]

§3. Proprietary Estoppel

124. Specific reference shall be made at this point to the legal mechanism of proprietary estoppel, since there is an ambiguity as regards its application in Cypriot

172. Department of Land and Surveys, Deposit of Contract of Sale of Immovable Property, The Sale of Land (Specific Performance) Law 81(I)/2011, at: https://portal.dls.moi.gov.cy.
173. *Odysseos v. Pierris Estates Ltd et al.* (1982) 1 CLR 557.
174. *John Richard Wheeler et al. v. A Messios and Sons Limited et al.* (2006) 1 CLR 1239.
175. *Iordanou v. Anyftos* (V24) 1 CLR 97.

land law. Indeed, section 4 of Cap. 224 expressly exempts trusts from its scope. At the same time, Cypriot courts have adopted a nuanced approach to the issue. While the Supreme Court had initially affirmed the application of proprietary estoppel in Cypriot land law,[176] later in the landmark decision *Vereggaria Papakokkinou v. Dimou Paphou*,[177] it reversed earlier case law by denying the possibility to recognize property rights over land on the basis of proprietary estoppel. As it was categorically stated: 'The provisions of [s]ection 4 of Chapter 224 are restrictive as regards the recognition of privileges over immovable property and prohibitive as regards the adoption of rules of equity. Recognition of real rights on the grounds of the equitable mechanism of proprietary estoppel would be in complete contradiction with the provisions of [s]ection 4, which do not allow the application of the rules of common law and of equity in the creation of real property rights in Cyprus. The rights that may be acquired over immovable property cannot be other than those expressly provided in [s]ection 4 of Cap. 224.'

125. However, even later case law has again recognized the possibility to claim property rights on the basis of proprietary estoppel. In *Tsialis v. Hatziandreou*,[178] the appellant had constructed a house above the ground floor on a plot owned by the respondent following a written agreement between both parties permitting the construction. The Supreme Court affirmed that according to the principles of proprietary estoppel, it would be unfair to allow the respondent to withdraw from the agreement, since the latter was based on the written promise of the respondent and had been awaiting the transfer of the property to him. The Court referred to *Stylianou v. Papacleovoulou* decision,[179] which was issued in 1982, where it was stated that 'It is established that a party, making a promise, cannot resile therefrom when it would be inequitable for him to do so notwithstanding the absence of a legally recognised relationship between the promisor and the promisee. And it is inequitable for the promisor to resile from his promise whenever, as a result of such representation, the promisee has modified his position in a way that it would be unjust for the promisor to withdraw from his representations; provided always, that the representations made are clear and unambiguous, such as could lead the promisee to act upon them' and that 'proprietary estoppel forms part of the doctrines of equity and as such is applicable in Cyprus in accordance with s. 29(c) of the Courts of Justice Law, 14/60. The application of proprietary estoppel in Cyprus was also mentioned in the case *Ioannis Antoniou Chrysostomou v. Eleni Christou Antoniou Frangou et al.*[180] Similarly, in the case *Tsangari v. Gavriilidou*,[181] the Supreme Court affirmed the possibility of the recognition of property rights on the basis of trusts by adding that such rights may also be claimed in the case of a proprietary estoppel or estoppel by possession as held in the case *Odysseos v. Pierris Estates and others*, which was decided before *Vereggaria Papakokkinou v. Dimou Paphou*. The application of proprietary estoppel in a case of a dispute between neighbours

176. *See Stylianou v. Papacleovoulou* (1982) 1 CLR 542.
177. *Papakokkinou v. Dimou Paphou* (1998) 1 CLR 2398.
178. *Tsialis v. Hatziiandreou et al.* (2000) 1 (B) CLR 1250.
179. *Stylianou v. Papacleovoulou* (1982) 1 CLR 542.
180. *Chrysostomou v. Fragkou et al.* (2000) 1 CLR 622.
181. *Tsangari v. Gavriilidou et al.* (2003) 1 CLR 472.

over the ownership of a piece of land, was affirmed in *Loizou v. Antoniou*[182] case, where the Supreme Court decided that the appellant was prevented on the grounds of proprietary estoppel from claiming the recovery of the land in question. The Court, by referring to English case law and specifically to the case *Taylor Fashions Ltd v. Liverpool Victoria Trustees Co*,[183] stated that the criterion for the application of estoppel is not whether or not the appellant knew the cadastral status of the property with respect to her rights. What is relevant is only whether, under the circumstances of the specific case, it would be unfair for the land owner to benefit from what was, in essence, a common mistake – that is, a mistake that had been shared by both sides. That is to say, what is crucial is whether or not it would be unfair to invalidate the basis – which was ex post proved to be incorrect – on which the concerned parties had acted.

126. The issue of the appropriate remedy to be ordered by the court in case of a proprietary estoppel has been discussed in a series of cases. In several cases where the application of proprietary estoppel was affirmed, the court ordered the transfer of the disputed property to the person who benefited from the proprietary estoppel.[184] Another question that was examined by the courts has been the possibility of awarding damages instead of an injunction. In *Loizou v. Antoniou* the Supreme Court reversed the finding of the first instance court that, due to the concurrent application of section 4 of Cap. 224 and of the findings of the case *Vereggaria Papakokkinou v. Dimou Paphou*, it was not possible to award damages in the case of proprietary estoppel, but only to issue an injunction to stop the trespass. In this context, damages were awarded[185] and this was further affirmed in the case S*ophocleous Andreas Michalakis and another v. Pavlos Elias Pavlou.*[186] As regards procedural issues, and contrary to promissory estoppel,[187] the non-inclusion of the argument of proprietary estoppel in the relevant pleadings does not deprive the parties of the right to raise the matter at the Hearing of the case, provided that the facts, as evidenced by the testimony, justify the application of proprietary estoppel.[188]

182. *Loizou v. Antoniou* (2007) 1 CLR 1035.
183. *Taylor Fashions Ltd v. Liverpool Victoria Trustees Co* [1981] 1 All ER 897.
184. *Stylianou v. Papacleovoulou* (1982) 1 CLR 542; *Tsialis v. Hatziiandreou et al.* (2000) 1(B) CLR 1250; *Christostomou Bros Company Ltd v. Theodorou Kapnisi*, No. of Claim 1707/07, 9 January 2013.
185. *Loizou v. Antoniou* (2007) 1 CLR 1035.
186. *Michalakis et al. v. Paul* (2012) 1 CLR 2047.
187. *Loizou v. National Bank of Greece (Cyprus) Ltd*, Civil Appeal No. 163/2010, 10 March 2015.
188. *Ioannou v. Bank of Cyprus Funding Ltd* (1999) 1 CLR 1522.

Chapter 4. Limited Interests

127. Apart from the owner's right to absolute private property, it is possible that several other rights could be enforced over immovable property or privileges in favour of other immovable property or third parties, and act as charges by: (a) binding the property without affecting its use, e.g., the mortgage, (b) or by restricting its use in a particular way, as is the case with easements, profit à prendre and restrictive covenants.

128. Easements constitute a very important category of limited real rights over the land of another person. Similarly, limitations to the right to ownership over immovable property, which end up creating restrictive real rights, could also be the result of usufruct and habitation rights and of restrictive terms and restrictive covenants.[189]

129. A special category of restrictions to the right of ownership is the real charges, which bind the land under certain conditions, in order to secure a claim. These charges are created by legislative provisions or by the registration of the mortgage or the filing of the contract according to the provisions of Law 81(I)/2011. Furthermore, a real right is created by the registration of a long-term leasehold according to the provisions of sections 65A–65EA of Cap. 224.

130. According to the above legal mechanisms, the real interests acquired by a third party over foreign immovable property are only limited real rights, since they limit the fullest and most absolute real right, that is the right to absolute private property.

§1. Usufruct and Habitation

131. Another important restriction to the enjoyment of the right of ownership comprise the real rights of usufruct and habitation. In both cases, the real rights are enforced in the interest of a person and not of another immovable property. As a matter of fact, according to Greek land law, the above rights constitute personal easements. However, this is not the case in the Cypriot legal system, which follows the English legal tradition and recognizes only the notion of real (non-personal) easement (a form of predial servitude, which always presupposes a dominant and a servient estate).

132. This was expressly confirmed in the case *Siati v. Siati*,[190] where it was held that a reservation of habitation in Cyprus is not an easement, since the creation of

189. As will be analyzed below, restrictive covenants are hardly distinguished from easements in their function.

190. *Siati v. Siati* (1996) 1B CLR 1349.

an easement in Cypriot law requires two tenements, a dominant and a servient and the protection of rights in favour of the owners and possessors of the latter over the first.[191]

133. The legal basis for the creation of the real rights of habitation and usufruct is section 11 of Cap. 224. Specifically, habitation and usufruct rights shall be acquired according to section 11(1)(a) under a grant or under exchange or under the transfer of immovable property upon section 11(1)(ζ).

134. Any infringement of the habitation and usufruct rights, provided that the possession right belongs to the habitation and usufruct rights-holder respectively, could be prohibited by an injunction, provided that these rights restrict the owner of the property which is charged with usufruct/habitation from taking any actions that would constitute trespass to these rights and to the possession and usufruct powers, which stem from them.[192]

135. Both rights need to be registered according section 11(1)(ζ) of Cap. 224. However, the Supreme Court has adopted a flexible approach on formalities. Specifically, it was held with regard to a usufruct right that was orally agreed but not registered in the Land Registry, that such a right could be recognized as a valid right on the grounds of section 11(1)(γ) of Cap. 224, which provides that such a right can be recognized with a court decision.[193]

I. Usufruct

136. The usufruct right provides to its right-holder the right to use and profit from the value of the foreign immovable property. In other terms, the rights-holder can not only use the immovable property in relation to its nature but also profit from all of its benefits either directly or through a leasehold.[194]

137. However, the usufruct right-holder does not have all the powers stemming from the right of ownership or absolute property. He/she can use and profit from the value of the immovable property, but not dispose of it. Subsequently, he/she does not have the right to divest the usufruct-charged immovable property, or to charge it with other easements, mortgage or other charges over it.

138. The above powers rest with the registered owner of the immovable property, who is, in legal terms, the 'bare owner'. Therefore, in cases where usufruct rights are enforced, the owner of the property enjoys the right of ownership without the powers of use and profit ('bare ownership'), while the usufruct right-holder

191. *Ibid.*
192. In relation to the habitation right, *see ibid.*
193. *Diomidous et al. v. Diomidous et al.*, Political Appeal Nos 329/2011, 343/2011, 12 October 2017.
194. Nikolaos Triantos, *Easements, Transcription, Land Registry* 22 (Nomiki Vivliothiki 2000).

enjoys the full right of use and profit from the value of the property, provided that the usufruct deed of establishment does not reserve some powers regarding the use and profit for the bare owner.[195]

139. Thus, it should be noted that in cases where the usufruct right coexists with the bare ownership right over the same immovable property, the balancing between the enforcement of both real rights is very important, so that neither the use nor the profit power will result in a change in the nature and purpose of the thing or its substantial reduction of its value, and that nor will the enforcement of the bare ownership right hinder the establishment of the usufruct right. This encapsulates the general rule that the usufruct right-holder shall use and profit from the value of the alien thing, while at the same time he/she shall not change the integral substance of the thing (*Ususfructus est jus alienis rebus utendi fruendi salva rei subtantia*).[196]

140. In this context, the usufruct right-holder shall not, for example, change the purpose of use of a residential house into a shopping centre. Nevertheless, he/she could make some minor alterations, such as changing the variety of the seasonal plantation. The usufruct right-holder shall exercise his/her powers with due diligence, so as to prevent damages to the property, except those due to normal use, wear and tear.

141. Cypriot courts have not dealt extensively with the legal mechanism of usufruct. In the case of *Vrahimi v. Kouloumbri,* the Supreme Court briefly mentioned the concept of usufruct, without further elaboration. The usufruct right was not affirmed, since a necessary prerequisite for the lawful creation of a usufruct right is the agreement of all the co-owners of the property to which the usufruct shall apply.[197] A subsequent case which is indicative of the confusion of Cypriot courts in relation to the definition, the content and the extent of the usufruct right is *Savvas Charalambous Savvides v. Eleni Charalambous Savvidis.*[198] This case concerned the issue of the conflict of interests between the holder of the usufruct right and the owner of a property. According to the first instance court, the issue was essentially whether a person (such as the respondent) was entitled to a usufruct right that, in addition to his/her right to receive the 'fructus' of the property, allowed the usufruct rights-holder to prevent the owner or one of the co-owners of the property, who claimed that he operated his own lawful business within the estate, to enter the property for the purpose of running his business. The first instance court sought some guidance on the relevant provisions of the Greek Civil Code for the delimitation of rights of the holder of the usufruct right. However, the decision was overturned by the Supreme Court. More particularly, the Supreme Court, after finding that the legal regime of usufruct is a novel issue which has no specific definition or regulation in Cypriot law, held that the provisions of the Greek Civil Code could not

195. *Ibid.*
196. Dimitrios Theofanopoulos, *System of Roman Law, Real Property Law* 170 (Athens 1900).
197. *Vrahimi v. Kouloumbri* (1992) 1 CLR 836.
198. *Savvas Charalambous Savvides v. Eleni Charalambous Savvidis*, Civil Claim No. 390/2008, 13 June 2012.

form a basis to resolve the present dispute, because the key issue of the dispute was not the finding of a situation of usufruct and the definition of the respective rights of the usufruct holder vis-à-vis the property right of the owner or the land, but the claim of the respondent holder to receive part of the profits of the business which is held by the property owner.

II. Use and Habitation

142. The habitation right does not confer the full power of use of the immovable property, but only the power of exclusive use of the property as a residence, including the power to possess it. The above definition refers also to the relevant distinction in Justinian's legislation of Roman law, where the concept of habitation (*habitatio*) was recognized as a specific category of personal easement and not as a usufruct right.[199] The extent of the subject and object of the habitation right would, in principle, be defined by the habitation establishment deed, upon which the habitation right itself is based.[200]

143. Thus, the habitation power extends also to the common parts of the building, like a corridor, bath or yard, provided that this is necessary for the residential use of the property. Any limitation or restriction of the habitation right regarding this specific part of the property, e.g., only to the house and not to the yard, should be explicitly provided with the concession of the property.[201] Habitation rights can be established for more than one person, and in this case, every single one of them would have the right to use the property as a residence. The notion of exclusivity means that the habitation right-holder (or the right-holders) could use the property as a residence by excluding the registered owner, who is deprived of this possibility. The exact scope of this power under Cypriot law is a matter of interpretation of the deed.

144. The habitation right-holder shall not profit from the value of the property, or have the right to rent it to third parties. A typical case of a habitation or usufruct right being established under a proviso upon the transfer of the immovable property is when a parent transfers immovable property to the child by retaining the right to reside in it for a lifetime (habitation) or to use and profit from it for a lifetime (usufruct).

199. Theofanopoulos, *supra* n, 196, 187; Giannoula Karibali-Tsiptsiou, *The Full Personal Easement of Habitation, Contribution to the Analysis of Easements* 26 (Sakkoulas Publications 1986).
200. Karibali-Tsiptsiou, *supra* n. 199, 30.
201. *Siati v. Siati, supra.*

§2. Building and Planting Rights

145. The Roman law principle of *aedificium solo cedit*, which means that the structure built on a piece of land shares the legal fate of the land, is followed in Cypriot land law. According to this general principle, plants, buildings or any edifice which is annexed permanently to the land belongs to the owner of the land. Indeed, one of the most significant changes brought about by Cap. 224 has been the abolition of 'dual ownership' – that is, of the possibility of separate ownership for the land and buildings or plants on the land. This was achieved mainly through the provisions of sections 22, 23, 24 and 30 of Cap. 224. Before the introduction of those provisions, separate ownership over the land and buildings or plants on the same land was common. This was mainly due to the law of succession at this time, which in relation to 'arazi mirie' property provided that the surviving spouse could not inherit any rights over the 'arazi mirie' land, while she could inherit rights only on buildings and plants (category of 'arazi memlouke').[202]

146. Section 22 of Cap. 224 defines the legal status of plants growing in a wild state on any land and states that such plants shall be deemed to be the property of the owner of the land. Section 22 established a transitory period according to which any grafted wild tree on any land, any tree or vine planted on any land, any spring found, or any watercourse or channel opened or constructed on any land, any building or other erection or structure erected on any land, any fixture affixed to any land or to any building or other erection or structure shall be deemed to be the property of the owner of the land unless another person is registered as the owner thereof or, being entitled to be so registered, applies for registration within two years from the date of the coming into operation of Cap. 224 or within two years from the date on which he became entitled so. If they are grafted, planted, found, opened, constructed, erected or affixed after the date of the coming into operation of Cap. 224, a legal and non-rebuttable presumption of ownership in favour of the land owner is established, since they shall be deemed to be the property of the owner of the land and any dealing affecting such land shall be deemed to include any such wild tree, tree, vine, spring, watercourse, channel, building, erection, structure or fixture, being the property of the owner of the land.

147. Section 23 prohibits the transfer of separate rights and interests in land and in plants or buildings on this land. According to this provision, where any trees, vines or other thing planted or growing upon any land, though belonging to the owner of the land, are separately registered in his/her name, he/she shall not be separately entitled to transfer or mortgage the same, unless he/she transfers or mortgages the land on which they stand; and any transfer or mortgage of any such trees, vines or other thing planted, or growing upon any such land shall be deemed to include the transfer or mortgage of the land belonging to the same owner.

148. Section 24 establishes a pre-emption/option right in case of transfer of separate ownership rights over the land or plants and fixtures/buildings erected on

202. Christos Ioannou, *Cypriot Land Law* 31 (Nomiki Vivliothiki 2014).

the land. When any trees, vines or other thing or any buildings or other erections or structures are planted, grown, or erected, upon any land belonging to a person other than the owner of any such trees, vines, thing, building, erection or structure and either of the mentioned owners has made a declaration before the Land Registry that he/she has agreed to sell his/her interest to a third party, the transfer of the interest shall not be registered unless (a) the owner selling his/her interest satisfies the Director of the Land Registry that the other owner does not wish to purchase such interest at the price at which is being sold or the prospective purchaser advertises the proposed sale thereof or brings it to the knowledge of the other owner and the other owner does not acquire same.

149. Finally, section 30 provides for the readjustment of rights where the owner of trees and of structures is not the same person. Where any tree, vine, building or other erection or structure is owned by a person other than the owner of the land whereon the same is standing, the Director of the Land Registry may, on the application of any person having an interest in the land, tree, the vine, building or other erection or structure, make a readjustment of the interests of the parties therein so as to ensure that in no case shall a tree, vine, building or other erection or structure be owned by a person other than the owner of the land whereon same is standing.

150. Special attention shall be given to agreements commonly known in English law as 'building leases', where a tenant rents land in order to build houses, shops, offices, etc. The ownership of the buildings which are constructed by the tenant on the basis of such an agreement was discussed in the case *Apex Ltd v. Argyridou.*[203] The Court, in relation to the construction of a building by a tenant under the agreement that it would belong to the owner of the plot of land after thirty years, recognizing the fundamental rule of Cap. 224 that any buildings and fixtures erected on land become the property of the landlord, finally concluded that the building to all intents and purposes belonged to the tenant and not to the owner for exploitation, use or occupation purposes and that the owner of the land would be entitled to possess it upon the expiry of the agreement, although he remained the owner of the building against third parties.

§3. Leasehold Interests: Chattels Real (*See Also* Part II)

I. Form and General Content of the Contract of Lease

151. There is no formal definition in Cypriot legislation of the contract of lease. In general, lease is the contract whereby one contracting party (the landlord) assigns the other (the tenant) the absolute use of a property for a certain period of time, while the tenant accepts the obligation to pay the agreed rent. A lease (tenancy) is to be distinguished from a licence for use in several ways. In general, the nature of the relationship created between the parties is independent of the words used, while the Court should not only review the relevant deed but also consider the transaction

203. *Apex Ltd v. Argyridou* (1989) 1 CLR 265.

as a whole. The granting of an exclusive right of possession is of crucial importance, while monthly payments are not deemed enough in order for a tenancy contract to be affirmed.[204]

152. As a general principle of Cypriot contract law (Chapter 149), formality is not a prerequisite for the conclusion of the contracts, which can, therefore, be validly concluded either in writing, orally or following a certain behaviour of the parties. As an exception to this rule, section 77(1) of the Contracts Law (Cap. 149) provides that a contract relating to the rental of immovable property, for a period of more than one year, is not valid and enforceable unless it is written and signed at the bottom of the contract by any party to the contract who should also have legal capacity), who have signed as well. According to case law, where the tenant takes possession of the property and pays for the rent on the basis of an invalid contract of lease, the tenancy becomes a tenancy automatically renewed on an annual or monthly basis (periodic tenancy), depending on whether the rent is payable annually or per month.[205] Periodic tenancies are based on invalid tenancy agreements due to the non-compliance with section 77 of Cap. 149 or by oral agreement where the rent is paid periodically and the period of validity of the tenancy is not clearly defined.

153. Regarding the content of the contract, there are no mandatory minimum requirements of what needs to be stated in a lease contract. Some essential elements that a contract should include are: (a) the object of the tenancy agreement (defined as the 'leasehold'), (b) the fee owed by the tenant to the landlord for use of the dwelling ('rent'), (c) an agreement to hand over the exclusive use of the dwelling and (d) duration: according to Cypriot law,[206] a tenancy agreement in which the duration is not defined by the parties, does not constitute a valid contract, and is therefore null and void. Moreover, the tenancy agreement must also include the start date of the tenancy.[207]

II. Special Protection of Tenants by the Rent Control Law

154. Cypriot tenancy law is characterized by the existence of a special rent control law known as the Rent Control Law (Law 23/1983). The law imposes serious

---

204. *Aggelidis and Filippou Ltd v. Spyros Colocassides Estates Ltd* (1991) 1 CLR 327; *Michailidou v. Municipality of Nicosia* (1997) 1(A) CLR 18; *Karesiou v. Karapita et al.* (2002) 1(A) CLR 338. *See* T. Konistis, *TENLAW: Tenancy Law and Housing Policy in Multi-level Europe: Tenant's Rights Brochure for CYPRUS*, National Report for Cyprus, Team Leader: Elena Bargelli, National Supervisor: Tatiani Eleni Synodinou, https://www.uni-bremen.de/fileadmin/user_upload/fachbereiche/fb6/fb6/Forschung/ZERP/TENLAW/Reports/CyprusReport_09052014.pdf, last visited on 20 December 2019.

205. *Georghiades & Others v. Lambis* (1976) 8 J.S.C. 1332; *Petrolina Ltd v. Vassiliades* (1975) 1 CLR 289.

206. *Alpan Furnishings Limited v. Savva Dimadi* (1989) CLR 170.

207. Konistis, *supra* n. 204.

restrictions and limitations on tenancy agreements. The Rent Control Law protects statutory tenants against eviction, controls the adjustment of rents and regulates relations between landlords and tenants.

155. The Rent Control Law has a long history and has been amended many times. The first legislation was voted before Cypriot independence and was known as Cap. 86 – Rent (Control) Law. The Cap. 86 was partially replaced by the Rent Control (Work Dwellings) Law of 1961, which was further modified by Law 39/61. The latter provided for fixed rent of work dwellings as well as restricting evictions from them. The Cap. 86 was amended by Law 8/68, which replaced the Rent Councils with the District Courts. After the Turkish invasion, the Law on Immovable Residential Dwellings (Provisional Provisions) of 1975 was enacted. This law was repealed by the Rent Control Law of 1975 (Law 36/1975). Law 36/1975 repealed all previous legislation, including Cap. 86. Finally, Law 36/1975 was repealed by the Rent Control Law of 1983 (Law 23/1983), which is still in force today, though it has also been subject to various amendments. The political philosophy behind the enactment of the Rent Control Law of 1983 is connected with the tragic event of the Turkish invasion of Cyprus. Thus, the special protection of tenants was obviously a matter of urgency at the time, since almost 1/3 of the Cypriot population had to flee their homes.[208] The law applies both to tenancies for residential as well as for commercial leases. As regards commercial leases, special provisions regulate a previous tenant's right to claim compensation for the goodwill of the commercial dwelling.[209]

156. The above legislative initiatives were identical to the English legislation in force at the time, and more specifically the Increase of Rent and Mortgage Interest (Restrictions) Act 1920, Landlord and Tenant Act 1927, Rent and Mortgage Restrictions (Amendment) Act 1933, Furnished Houses (Rent Control) Act 1946, Landlord and Tenant (Rent Control) Act 1949 and 1954, as well as the Rent Acts of 1957, 1965 and 1977. Therefore, English case law is very instructive for the interpretation of Cypriot Law. However, the landlord-tenant relationship shows a greater complexity in England, where although the vast majority of tenancies is controlled, they do not easily become statutory. In contrast, in Cyprus, almost all tenancies inevitably become statutory, unless the dwelling in question is of recent build.[210] The Rent Control Law of 1983 is applicable to tenancies of properties (buildings under or for rent for a dwelling or shop) situated within the boundaries of the 'controlled/ rent restriction area' which were completed before 31 December 1999. The 'controlled/rent restriction area' is prescribed as such by a decree of the Council of Ministers. More specifically, the legislation that is in force today applies to all large city centres, to buildings completed before 31 December 1999[211] do not fall within this protective regime.

208. *Ibid.*
209. Section 13 of Rent Control Law 23/1983.
210. Konistis, *supra* n. 204.
211. Amending Law 20(I)/2001.

157. In *Constantinou v. Attorney General of the Republic*,[212] it was held that the law is also applicable when the owner of the property is the State. Following this decision, the Rent Control Law of 1983 was modified in order to expressly provide the above ruling.[213]

158. According to section 2 of the Rent Control Law of 1983, a statutory tenant means a tenant who at the expiration or termination of the first tenancy continues to be in the possession of the premises. Tenancy means any lease, demise, letting or holding of premises whether in writing or otherwise, by virtue whereof the relationship of landlord and tenant is created, but does not include rental of land used for agricultural purposes or rental of petrol stations or rental of motor vehicle parking, or rental of furnished dwellings or apartments which is shorter than six months or hotel rentals or rental of tourist accommodations. The extent of the exclusion of the rental of petrol stations was examined by the Supreme Court in the case *Lukoil Cyprus Ltd v. Charalambos Fellas et al.*[214] The Court clarified that while section 2 of the Rent Control Law of 1983 states that the term 'tenancy' does not include the rental of petrol stations, it nevertheless also provides that the right of possession and the determination of the rent or consideration from the sublease or the licence of use between a service station and the petroleum company is governed and regulated by the provisions of the said Law. 'First tenancy' is defined as the first rental of the property by the respective tenant and its duration is determined by the document of the tenancy agreement or the oral agreement or, where there is a lack thereof, by the method of payment of the rent. In *Christou Nicos Developments Ltd. v. Panagiotis Tofini*, the Supreme Court examined whether 'first tenancy' also covers an invalid contract of lease due to the non-compliance with the provision of section 77(1) of the Contracts Law (Cap. 149) and held that it did.[215] It was further decided that a monthly lease does not expire at the end of each month, but continues until its termination with the appropriate termination notice.[216]

159. Therefore, tenancy contracts are divided into those belonging to the free market ('contractual tenancies') and those falling within the application of the Rent Control Law of 1983 ('statutory tenancies'). A tenancy will be regulated either by Cap. 149 or the Rent Control Law. So, no statutory tenancy can arise while the contractual tenancy still exists. In relation to the termination of a 'contractual tenancy', if the contract has a clear term, termination occurs when this term expires. If it is not clear, or if a tenancy document is invalid pursuant to the provisions of section 77(1) of Cap. 149, a periodic contractual tenancy is born, which terminates with a notice of termination or at the expiration period provided for in the invalid tenancy document. A 'contractual tenancy' is also terminated if the landlord exercises his/her right to enter the lease and take possession of it ('forfeiture').[217] As regards the

212. *Constantinou v. Attorney General of the Republic* (1997) 1 CLR 741.
213. Section 2A (added by the Law 150(I)/2002).
214. *Lukoil Cyprus Ltd v. Charalambos Fellas et al.* (2012) 1 CLR 364.
215. *Christou Nicos Developments Ltd. v. Panagiotis Tofini* (1998) 1 CLR 1990.
216. *See also Michael v. Yianni* (1998) 1(D) CLR 2052.
217. Lefkia Kammitsi, President of Rent Control Court, Lecture on Rent Control, Limassol, 19 April 2007.

form of the notice of termination, no specific form is required (it can be in oral or in writing), but the notice shall be clear and shall define the termination of the existing tenancy at a specific time.[218]

160. If a specific tenancy does not fulfil the conditions of Rent Control Law of 1983, then any dispute arising from the tenancy contract is dealt with by the District Court. As regards the jurisdiction of the Rent Control Courts and the District Courts, in *Papagheorghiou v. Karayiannis*,[219] the Supreme Court held that 'There is no question of the District Court and the Rent Control Court having concurrent jurisdiction on the same dispute. If the dispute refers to any matter which either – (a) arises during the application of the Rent Control Law of 1983, or (b) concerns any incidental or supplementary matter, the Rent Control Court has exclusive jurisdiction to determine such dispute under section 4(1) of the Law. In all other cases the jurisdiction rests with the District Court. No difficulty arises in cases which fall under category (a) above. The main theme of the Rent Control Law is: i. The restriction of the power of the Court to make eviction orders to the cases exhaustively enumerated in section 11(1) of the Law, ii. The regulation under section 8 of the Law on the rent payable in respect of premises to which the Law applies, iii. The granting of compensation to the tenant in certain cases under the provisions of sections 12, 13 and 15 of the Law, iv. The granting of a new tenancy to the tenant under the provisions of section 14 of the Law.'

161. Section 27(1) of the Rent Control Law of 1983 provides that existing contractual terms between landlord and tenant are applicable if the tenancy becomes statutory. This was applied in *Rodosthenes Christina v. Georginas Orati Fourouklas*, where it was held that the express term in the original invalid lease agreement between the parties, according to which the landlord was obliged to ensure to the tenant peaceful possession and use without interference, continued to apply.[220] More specifically, if a tenant is unlawfully or unjustly deprived of the physical possession of the lease by an act of or with the knowledge and consent of the landlord, then, despite the absence of physical possession, the tenant may nevertheless be entitled to apply to the Court for an order of possession.

162. Section 11 of the Rent Control Law of 1983 provides the cases in which eviction of the tenant can be lawfully made. These are, *inter alia*, the cases where the rent due is in arrears, where the tenant is guilty of nuisance or persistent annoyance to persons in the same or neighbouring premises, when the condition of the property has deteriorated owing to acts of waste or the neglect or default of the tenant, when the tenant subleases the property contrary to an express prohibition of sublease, where the premises are reasonably required by the landlord for occupation as a residence or as business premises for himself or another member of his family, where the premises are required by the landlord for the substantial alteration or

218. *Glykys v. Ioannides* (V24) 1 CLR 220; *Michael Charikleia v. Vavel Boutique Ltd* (2007) 1 CLR 241.
219. *Papagheorghiou v. Karayiannis* (1988) 1 CLR, 571.
220. *Rodosthenes Christina v. Orati Fourouklas* (2010) 1 CLR 1154.

reconstruction or demolition. The last condition was subject to significant changes in 1983, where the legislator departed from the provisions of the previous legislation and designed this ground in such a way so as to tighten the prerequisites for recovery of possession for the purpose of alterations to a building. The criteria for application of this condition have been analyzed in the case law. In *Lamarco Ltd. v. Heraclis G. Kranos*,[221] it was held that the alterations must be substantial and radical. Specifically, 'they must be made for the purpose of the development of the building and must result to radical and total change of it. The interpretation of this paragraph should not be approached with a dictionary. The teleological or purposive interpretation coupled with the ordinary and pragmatic meaning of the words should be employed.' In this context, it was noted that 'changes to be qualified as substantial and radical must be extensive and fundamental in character. They must be made for purposes of development. If the general structural character of the building remains unchanged, they fall short of satisfying this requirement. Not only the changes contemplated must be themselves substantial and radical, but must also entail sequentially thereto the radical and total transformation of the building effected for purposes of developments.' Overall, 'no exhaustive definition can be given. It is a question of degree depending on the facts and circumstances of each case, having regard to the totality of the work proposed to be done'.[222]

163. Significant provisions are also sections 12 and 13 of the Rent Control Law of 1983, which provide for the compensation of the tenant in case of eviction. Specifically, when by the reason of carrying on by the tenant in the premises of a trade or business a goodwill is attached thereto and by reason of the eviction the tenant will suffer a loss, the court may require the landlord to pay the tenant additional compensation.

III. Timeshare Contract in Cyprus

164. The legal status of timesharing contracts has been harmonized in the EU[223] and was implemented in Cyprus by Law 34(I)/2011 in respect of certain aspects of timeshare, long-term holiday product, resale and exchange contracts. A timeshare contract is defined as a specific kind of lease for the duration of more than one year under which a consumer, for consideration, acquires the right to use one or more overnight accommodation for more than one period of occupation.

165. As this specific kind of lease was traditionally seen as deceptive (the consumer was led to believe he did acquire some property right on the land), the legislator added some protective provisions: imperative pre-contractual information, a right of withdrawal and the principle of no advance payment.

---

221. *Lamarco Ltd. v. Heraclis G. Kranos* (1987) 1 CLR 336.
222. *Poyatzis v. Pilavakis* (1988) 1 CLR 411.
223. Directive 2008/122/EC of the European Parliament and of the Council of 14 January 2009 on the protection of consumers in respect of certain aspects of timeshare, long-term holiday product, resale and exchange contracts.

IV. Protection of the Tenant in Case of Transfer of the Leasehold

166. Provided that the Rent Control Law of 1983 does not apply, in case of transfer of the property to a third party during the tenancy contract, the question of the protection of the tenant arises. The Supreme Court dealt with the issue in the case *Pantelis Charalampidis v. Georgiou Andrea Konstantinou.*[224] It was held that anyone purchasing a dwelling, aware that a tenancy contract has been signed on said dwelling, is in a position of a constructive trustee vis-à-vis the tenant (possessor) and commits to respecting the obligations of his predecessor.

167. Transfer of the leasehold following death causes some legal difficulty. Traditionally, lease contracts, apart from the long-term leases, which are registered in the Land Registry under the provisions of Cap. 224 (*see below* at §4), are considered to be contracts in personam. As regards the continuation of the contract in case of the death of one of the parties, a lease contract is a personal contract which is terminated by the death of one contracting party.[225] However, the same principle may apply here, and the successor may be entitled to continue the lease through the principle of constructive trust. In the case of a registered lease, Cap. 224 states in section 65(A) that the term 'lessor' also encompasses administrators and successors.

§4. Emphyteusis Through the Registration of a Long-Term Lease and of a Financial Leasing

168. A limited-term ownership right arising from long-term lease registration was introduced into Cypriot law after the amendment of Cap. 224 by Law 2/1978.

169. In principle, the contract of lease acts in personam is regulated by contract law and does not, in principle, have any in rem effect.[226] However, it is possible for the lessee to acquire a real property right over the leased real property if certain conditions are met. In the case *Attorney General of the Republic v. Thanos Hotels Suppliers Ltd,* the legal mechanism of a long-term lease of an immovable property lease, that was previously unknown in Cypriot law, was introduced, in order to enable a tenant to acquire a limited-term immovable property right. The right acquired by the lessee is related to the land and constitutes a form of ownership which is subject to transfer.[227]

224. *Charalampidis v. Konstantinou*, Civil Appeal No. 85733 (1996) CLR.
225. *Rolandis et al. v. The Republic of Cyprus* (1991) 4C CLR 1750.
226. *The Attorney General v. The Water Board of Nicosia* (1961) CLR 1.
227. *Attorney General of the Republic v. Thanos Hotels Suppliers Ltd* (2003) 1A CLR 558. *See also Cyprus Tourism Organization v. Charilaou* (1998) 1 CLR 607 (where it was held that the contract of lease of state property which, was registered in the Land Registry – on the basis of the provisions of the law on State Property (Lease Registration) of 1967 (Law 49/67), which was at this time in force – creates a right in rem). It should be noted that Law 49/67 has now been abolished.

170. If the lease has been registered under Cap. 224, a real right is created for the benefit of the lessee. This right is not considered as a property right for taxation purposes.[228] A lease can also be registered in relation to real estate belonging to the State in accordance with the provisions of section 18 of Cap. 224.[229] The real right of the lessee can be transferred, mortgaged and inherited.[230] In the case of transfer of the leased property, through succession or otherwise, the lessee's successor in title shall acquire the right in rem for the period of the original lease of the property which has not expired and may be registered independently of the duration of this period. The real right acquired through the registration of the lease may be transferred under the terms and conditions of Cap. 224, but may not be subject to any assignment.[231] In the case *Attorney General of the Republic v. Thanos Hotels Suppliers Ltd*, regarding an agreement between a lessee and a third party for the sale of the registered leasehold right, it was held that Cypriot law does not provide for the assignment of the leasehold within the meaning of the term 'assignment' as defined in law. All that it provides is the transfer of a right in rem under the conditions laid down therein. Assignment, within the legal meaning of the term, results in the disposal of a right in personam and not of a right in rem.

171. If the lease is not registered, no real right is created. The lease contract remains personal, is terminated with the death of the parties and does not give rise to a right on the lease that can be inherited.[232]

172. The registration of a long-term lease is possible only for long-term leases exceeding fifteen years. If, at the date of the application for registration of the lease, the lease period which has not yet expired together with all the renewal periods which are clearly provided for in the contract of lease does not exceed fifteen years, then the lease shall not be registered.[233] The real right acquired by the registration of the lease may be subleased, if sublease is not prohibited by the lease. In this case, if the duration of the sublease is longer than fifteen years, then the sublease must also be registered in order for the lessee to acquire a real right.[234]

173. Necessary prerequisites for registering the lease are the validity of the contract of lease, an express provision in the lease contract that the lease shall be registered pursuant to section 65B of Cap. 224, the exact definition in the lease contract of the beginning and the end date of the lease, as well as the proof of registration of ownership over the real property that is leased in the lessor's name.[235]

228. *Administrative Court, Domoplex Ltd. v. The Republic of Cyprus*, Joined Cases Nos 889/2014 & 890/2014, 3 April 2019.
229. *See Cyprus Tourism Organization v. Charilaou* (1998) 1 CLR 607.
230. Section 65Γ Cap. 224.
231. Section 65E Cap. 224.
232. *Rolandis et al. v. The Republic of Cyprus* (1991) 4C CLR 1750.
233. Section 65B(4)(ι) Cap. 224.
234. Section 65Δ Cap. 224.
235. Section 65B(4) Cap. 224.

174. The original lease contract may be amended by a subsequent contract between the lessor and the lessee and the amending contract may replace the previous one in the registration. However, if substantial terms of the lease contract are amended by the subsequent contract, such as those relating to the term of the lease, or the rent, then the subsequent contract shall not be regarded as an amendment to the original, but as a new contract.[236]

175. For the duration of the real right created by the registration of the lease, the lessor shall be liable for the taxes and charges payable by the owner of the immovable property, but he is entitled to request reimbursement from the lessee of any tax or fee paid.[237] Furthermore, the owner of immovable property in respect of which a real right of long-term lease has been acquired through the registration of the lease shall not be entitled to grant a right of easement on such property without the written consent of the lessee.[238]

176. At the same time, the lessee shall have the same powers as the lessor in taking any judicial, administrative or other measures to protect and improve or take profit of the immovable property that has been leased provided that the improvement and enjoyment of the property fall within the framework provided or reasonably implied by the lease contract.[239]

177. The cancellation of the lease or the sublease may be effected by the Land Registry upon provision of satisfactory proof of termination of the lease and in the event of the termination of the lease before its expiry on the condition that the lessor or the lessee has given his written consent.[240] Under the Immovable Property Acquisition (Aliens) Law (Cap. 109), third-country nationals and Cyprus companies controlled by them shall require permission from the Council of Ministers before entering into a lease of immovable property for a period exceeding thirty-three years.

178. The Cap. 224 also provides for the registration of a financial leasing whose duration is longer than ten years.[241] 'Financial leasing' means a special contract of lease which constitutes a way of financing, without being a loan agreement and which is set out in writing, in accordance with the provisions of Part V in the case of immovable property, pursuant to which the lessee receives exclusive possession of some of the property from the lessor in exchange for the payment of an agreed lease, and which contract expressly provides the lessee with the right to purchase the property throughout the term of the contract or its renewal.[242] The registration of financial leasings is similar to the model of the long-term lease. Upon registration the lessor is granted an in rem right that is subject to the terms of the financial

236. Section 65ΣΤ(4) Cap. 224.
237. Section 65Θ Cap. 224.
238. Section 65H Cap. 224.
239. Section 65Λ Cap. 224.
240. Section 65I Cap. 224.
241. Section 65ΛA Cap. 224.
242. Section 2 of the Law on Financial Leasing of 2016 (Law 72(I)/2016).

leasing agreement and can be transferred and inherited.[243] In case of transfer, forced sale or inheritance of the right, this right is transferred for the period of the lease which has not expired.[244]

§5. Use and Habitation/Occupation

179. Use and habitation/occupation rights are established pursuant to section 11 of Cap. 224. For these rights, *see* §1.

§6. Easements and Profits

I. Introduction

180. As regards limited real rights over immovable property, easement occupies a central position, along with the relatively similar in function concepts of restrictive covenants and profit à prendre, which are not, however, identical for historical reasons.[245]

181. Easements can provide important advantages, such as better utilization of the immovable property or increasing the profits from the exploitation of the cultivation of land.

182. In an attempt to define this right, it can be said that easement is the absolute and dominant real right over an alien immovable property (known as the servient, praedium serviens or servient tenement), which provides limited power in favour of another immovable property (which is called the dominant, praedium dominans, or dominant tenement) or in favour of another person.

183. Upon the establishment of an easement, some of the powers of the owner of the servient tenement split away and fall under the easement right-holder. Therefore, the owner of the servient tenement shall accept the enforcement of the easement and the restrictions stemming from this enforcement.[246]

184. The above definition is relevant to the theoretical distinction of easements in the civil law tradition into real and personal, and corresponds only partially to the legal construction of easements in the common law tradition, where the establishment of an easement requires the existence of two properties, the dominant and the servient.

243. Section 65ΛΒ Cap. 224.
244. Section 65ΛΔ Cap. 224.
245. Papasteriou, *supra* n. 66 at 1.
246. Triantos, *supra* n. 194 at 49.

185. Real easement is the real right which is established in the exclusive favour of another immovable property. In other terms, in case of a real easement, there are always two properties, the dominant and the servient. The subject of the easement right is the dominant property, who is indirectly the beneficiary. Therefore, easement is not extinguished after the death of the right-holder. The real easement is a charge over the immovable property only, but not over the movable things lying on it.

186. On the contrary, the personal (gross) easement is a charge over a specific immovable property in favour of a specific person.[247]

187. Cypriot case law, evidently influenced by the legal theory and judge-made rules of common law tradition,[248] recognizes only the concept of real (non-personal) easement. In this context, habitation and usufruct rights in Cypriot legal system are not recognized as personal easements and thus, they constitute a specific category of real rights, which are established pursuant of section 11(1)(f) of Cap. 224.

188. Every easement is a restriction of the right of ownership. The benefit of the easement right-holder no longer belongs to the owner of the thing, nor does it continue to lie under his/her dominance, but presents quantitative or qualitative changes.[249]

189. At this point, the specific concept of the profit benefits of the natural sources of an alien immovable property should be noted, namely the 'profit à prendre' rights, which are not regarded as easements *stricto sensu*, since Cypriot law recognizes only the concept of real easements, given that their establishment does not always require the co-existence of a dominant and a servient property.[250] In other terms, 'profit à prendre' rights could exist 'in gross[251]', that is possibly taking the form of personal easements.[252] Thus, they constitute restrictions and charges over alien immovable property, which provide to the rights-holder the right to use the property in such a way without depriving the owner of the property from the right to possession, while it is possible for these rights be transferred during life or after death, in this way being similar to easements.

190. Furthermore, easement is similar to restrictive covenants, which also refer to two immovable properties, restrict the use of the alien immovable property in a

247. Christian H. Kälin, *International Real Estate Handbook: Acquisition, Ownership and Sale of Real Estate, Residence, Tax and Inheritance Law* 276 (John Wiley & Sons 2005); Velencoso, Bailey & Pradi (eds.), *supra* n. 115 at 303; Russ VerSteeg, *The Essentials of Greek and Roman Law* 159 (Carolina Academic Press 2010).
248. *See Hawkins v. Rutter* [1892] 1 QB 668, D.
249. Papasteriou, *supra* n. 66 at 5.
250. Dixon, *supra* n. 82 at 363.
251. Chris Bevan, *Land Law* 393 (Oxford University Press 2018).
252. That would be, more specifically, a personal easement of usufruct. *See* Theofanopoulos, *supra* n. 196, 186.

specific way and act in rem, provided that they have been registered with the Land Registry. Restrictive covenants act as 'negative' easements in the sense that they prohibit the burdened property owner from doing something. Certain differences between them, however, exist, such as the fact that a restrictive covenant requires a promise, while an easement may be acquired by a long-term user (prescription). Thus, despite the similarities with easements, restrictive covenants will be examined in a separate section of this monograph, since they are specifically regulated in Cap. 224.

II. General Principles Regarding Easements

191. There are some general principles regarding easements, which are broadly similar in both the civil law and common law tradition.[253]

192. The first basic principle is that the easement should be beneficial for the right-holder (*servitus utilis esse debet*). In other words, the easement shall generate a direct or indirect benefit to the right-holder, that is to the dominant immovable property, provided that this is the case of a real easement.[254]

193. A benefit could be an improvement or a convenience in the use of the dominant immovable property, for example by offering a view or passage or, possibly, a benefit to the commercial business that is being carried on to the servient property.[255] Thus, the benefit is not necessarily exclusive to one sole dominant immovable property, but may serve more properties.[256]

194. The second principle is that no one can establish an easement over his/her immovable property (*nemini res sua servit*). This is the 'principle of segregation' between the servient and the dominant immovable property.[257] The important effect of this principle is that, where the owner of the servient and the dominant immovable property is the same person, there will be a subsequent absorption of the easement.[258]

195. The third principle refers to the fact that an easement cannot be established if it confers a positive obligation on the owner of the servient immovable property, that is to act in a certain, positive way (*servitus in faciendo consistere nequit*). The person burdened with the easement shall omit to do some acts or put up with some actions of the easement right-holder.[259]

253. For these principles, *see* Theofanopoulos, *supra* n. 196, 163–164.
254. *See* Dixon, *supra* n. 82 at 320.
255. It is possible for example to be the right of placing a sign in the neighbouring plot for the hotel located in the servient tenement: *Moody v. Steggles* (1879) 12 Ch D 261.
256. *Re Ellenborough Park* (1956) Ch 131 (easement of enjoyment of a park, which belongs to the possessors of more residences).
257. *See Roe v. Siddons* (1888) 22 QBD 224.
258. Dixon, *supra* n. 82 at 319.
259. Papasteriou, *supra* n. 66 at 8.

196. An easement, as a real right, should restrict the right of ownership. For example, the owner of the servient property is restricted from building a high wall or the owner of the dominant property should be able to pass through the servient property.

197. Finally, the fourth principle provides that the real easement refers always to a certain immovable property, either dominant or servient. An easement cannot be regarded independently from an immovable property (in gross).[260] Specifically, an easement should necessarily be relevant to a specific dominant tenement and act in favour of it and charge on a specific property. The above rule, which is critical for determining the creation of an easement in common law tradition, was established in *Ackroyd v. Smith.*[261] When the Court was asked to determine whether the right of way which was allowed by the former owner of the land, was an easement or just permission, it ruled that it was permission, since it was a right of way for the general benefit of anyone without discrimination – owners, users and visitors – and not a right attached to the specific land. As long as this component is missing, it constitutes a contractual and not a real right.

198. In this context, a real easement is distinguished from a profit à prendre,[262] given that a profit à prendre, as already mentioned above, does not require the existence of a dominant and a servient tenement and therefore, it could be in gross. The relevant benefits refer to the possibility of the right-holder(s) to enter the alien immovable property (servient tenement) in order to profit from it in a certain way, for example by bushing, grazing, fishing, etc.,[263] while, nowadays, their practical significance is limited.

199. In *Tsiamanta v. Tsiamanta*, the Court, deciding the issue of the right of way, defined clearly the particularity of the Cypriot legal approach in relation to easements and the historical influences on the current provision. According to the decision, the Cypriot law on easements, as regulated by Cap. 224, constitutes a codification of the pre-existing rules and not of the common law. Thus, taking into account the fact that both Ottoman and English laws were influenced by Roman law, it is true that some principles regarding easements may be identical. In this context, it was accepted that an easement can only be established in favour of a specific immovable property, while it cannot result in a substantial possession of the alien land in a way that restricts its lawful owner.[264]

260. *Rangeley v. Midland Ry. Co.* [1868] 3 Ch App 306. *See* Dixon, *supra* n. 82 at 318–319.
261. *Ackroyd v. Smith* (1850) 10 CB 164.
262. In Cap. 224, there is a reference to the concept of profit in the definition of the immovable property in s. 2 (ε), in s. 4 (1) and in s. 11. According to these rules, profits are regarded as immovable property, while at the same time they can be created only on the basis of Cap. 224, as is the case with all the other real rights.
263. *See* M.F. Papandréou-Deterville, *Le droit anglais de biens* 294 (L.G.D.J. 2004).
264. *Tsiamanta v. Tsiamanta* (1990) 1 CLR 97526. The case concerned the claim of the registered owner of the servient tenement against her sister, the right-holder of a right of way, for trespass due to the drilling and use of a pit for drainage, the construction and the use of a stairway and the installation

III. Creation of Easement

200. It could be easily assumed that the concept of the easement is defined in line with the party autonomy doctrine, which governs English and Cypriot private laws. Thus, it is very important to remember that easements are real rights and are enforced in rem in a way that binds third parties, the successors in title of the servient and the dominant tenement. In this regard, the need to ensure the legal stability and certainty in the field of the immovable property transactions could not allow the matter to be settled in accordance with the full freedom of the parties concerned.

201. The scepticism with which English law regards the unlimited recognition of new types of easements is explicitly manifested in *Keppel v. Bailey*,[265] which is considered to be the milestone of the numerus clausus principle, not only in relation to easements but also in relation to real rights in general in the common law tradition.[266] Thus, despite the negative trend in recognizing new types of easements, the concept of the numerus clausus principle in relation to easements has taken a flexible form and the case law has recognized several deviations. Besides, it is possible for rights or interests upon which easements cannot be enforced, to be recognized by the related concept of restrictive covenants.[267]

202. The legal scepticism extends also to the ways that easements and other real rights regarding immovable property can be created. In Cypriot land law, the ways that easements can be created are provided in section 11 of Cap. 224, not in detail, but along with other forms of creating other real rights or interests, such as the restrictive terms and the habitation and usufruct reservations. It is explicitly defined that no right, liberty or interest shall be created in any other way except under the ways provided. Again, it can be argued that this is an implicit reassertion of the principle of exclusion of the law of equity from Cypriot land law, as this is, as mentioned before, explicitly provided by section 4 of Cap. 224.

203. In this respect, it can be said that there are two main ways of establishing an easement, namely, through the acquisition of easement by transfer/grant and through the acquisition of easement by the continuous and uninterrupted use for

---

and use of a washing brush in such a way that it constituted trespass on the strip used for the passage. In fact, the claimant was challenging the extent of the right of way. The District Court accepted the existence of an easement as regards the passage of drainage of the respondent from the servient tenement due to acquisitive prescription. The appellant, who was the owner of the servient tenement, based her argument on case law *Copeland v. Greenhalf* [1952] 1 All ER 809, according to which there is no valid easement when the certain use confers the deprivation of use and profit to property from the owner of the servient tenement. In this case, the rule from *Copeland v. Greenhalf* [1952] 1 All ER 809 was reasserted in Cypriot law, but its application in this case was rejected because it was ruled that the use of the stairs, the washing brush and the pit did not confer an exclusive possession of the strip of the passage from the respondent-owner of easement.

265. *Keppel v. Bailey* (1834) 2 My & K 517(1822-34), All ER Rep. 10.

266. Thus, the application of this principle relates also to the fact that new restrictions may be created by the restrictive covenants. *See* Papandréou -Deterville, *supra* n. 263 at 294.

267. Gray & Gray, *supra* n. 99 at 617.

more than thirty years, which is similar but not identical to the concept of the 'acquisitive prescription', as will be further analyzed below.

204. In English law, the main legal basis for the establishment of an easement is by transfer.[268] In addition, it was accepted that the transfer is inferred as evidence of an easement even in the case of a long and continuous use of a land, since the long and continuous use of a land is considered to stem from a transfer under law, contract or testament.[269]

205. Section 11 of Cap. 224 provides that an easement can be acquired via a grant from the owner thereof duly recorded in the books of the Land Registry. Therefore, it seems that the registration of the grant in the Land Registry is necessary for the establishment of an easement. The acquisition of an easement by transfer/grant presupposes that the easement is sufficiently specific, so as to be possible for it to become the object of the transfer[270] and that the assignor has the right to transfer (rule of *nemo dat quod non habet*). In practice, the transfer is conducted by filling in a special application form in the Land Registry, where information about the servient and the dominant tenement is given, along with a full description of the transferred right.

206. Apart from grant, an easement can be acquired under a written proviso upon the transfer of the immovable property, pursuant to section 11(1)(ζ). This is the case when the transferor/predecessor-in-title reserves the easement right upon the immovable property which transfers to the acquirer. In this context, the predecessor-in-title could, for example, retain the right of way over the transferred immovable property (servient tenement) in favour of his/her own neighbouring immovable property (dominant tenement).[271]

207. Another important way of acquiring an easement, which usually refers to a right of way, is through the uninterrupted and undisputed use of the alien immovable property for a full period of more than thirty years. This is the case of acquisitive prescription, which is similar but not identical to the original acquisition of immovable property under the concept of adverse possession.[272]

208. The main condition for the easement to be acquired in such a way is the possession to be enforced as a right, *nec vi, nec clam, nec precario*, namely without

268. In the case *Re Ellenborough Park* ((1956) Ch 131–140), Danckwerts defined the substantial elements of easements in common law, among which is that the right acquired under easement may be the subject of a grant: '(1)There must be a dominant and a servient tenement; (2) an easement must accommodate the dominant tenement, that is, be connected with its enjoyment and for its benefit; (3) the dominant and servient owners must be different persons; and (4) the right must be capable of forming the subject-matter of a grant.'
269. Papandréou-Deterville, *supra* n. 263 at 299;. Dixon, *supra* n. 82 at 353.
270. *See* Aldred's Case (1610) 9 Co Rep 57b.
271. For the proviso of easement, *see* Gray & Gray, *supra* n. 99 at 679.
272. For the distinction of s. 11 of Cap. 224 from the adverse possession of s. 10, as regards the concept of use, *see Thrasyvoulou v. Thrasyvoulou* (1984) 1 CLR 411; *Hadjidemosthenous v. Georghiou* (1969) 1 CLR 187.

force, without secrecy, without permission.[273] The requirement 'without force' means that the use must not be contentious. The second condition means the use ought to have been 'open', in the sense that an ordinary owner of land, diligent in the protection of his interests, would have, or must be taken to have, had a reasonable opportunity of becoming aware of the use. The third condition means that the use must not have been permitted by the owner or made with the owner's consent since if permission is asked or consent given then the servient owner would be acknowledging that no right exists and this would go against prescription.

209. The explicit and positive act of permission, given by the owner of the servient tenement, in relation to the enforcement of the easement, excludes the acquisition of the easement via acquisitive prescription, since the condition of *nec precario* is not satisfied ('without permission'). Nevertheless, in deciding the existence of an easement, a decisive affirmative factor is the knowledge and the passive tolerance of the owner of the servient tenement, since the prescription depends on the approval from the owner of the servient tenement of the easement as a right. In other words, the fact that the easement is being enforced without force and without secrecy, and subsequently without the opposition of the owner of the servient tenement, is evidence of passive approval of the easement as a right.[274] However, in many cases, the distinction between the tolerance of the easement from the owner of the servient tenement and the consent can be extremely difficult. In addition, it is even possible that the use may have started with the consent of the owner of the servient tenement for a certain period of time, but continued after the expiration of the period without consent. In this case, the calculation of the prescription period will start from the time the consent expired.[275]

210. An interesting example in English case law of the recognition of an easement via prescription due to the long use of the property without secrecy and without the opposition of the owner of the servient tenement is the case *Dalton v. Angus*. According to the facts of the case, a building, which was first used as a house and then was converted into a factory, was built in the extreme limits of the neighbouring soil, on which another building had been built. Subsequently, the conversion put significant lateral pressure on the soil under the adjoining house. When the owner of the adjoining building pulled it down, he brought down the factory as well. According to the House of Lords, despite the rule that an easement shall be exercised without secrecy (*nec clam*), a right to lateral support from the adjoining land had been acquired by the owner of the factory, without the owner of the servient tenement having to know about the increase in the lateral pressure due to the conversion of the building into a factory.[276]

273. *Thrasyvoulou v. Thrasyvoulou, ibid.*; *Valana v. Elia* (1983) 1 CLR 730; *Christophorou v. Vouria* (1994) 1 CLR 624; *Kyprianou v. Pillacouri* (2000) 1C CLR 1873.
274. Gray & Gray, *supra* n. 99 at 673. *See also Voskou v. Hadjipetrou, supra.*
275. Dixon, *supra* n. 82 at 357.
276. *Dalton v. Henry Angus & Co* [1881] UKHL 1.

211. In contrast to the acquisition of immovable property via adverse possession, the provision of section 11 for the acquisitive prescription of an easement, that has been exercised by the same person who invokes it, or by those from whom receives his claim, has been discussed as it consists also of the exercise by people not particularly close to the person who invokes the easement. More specifically regarding the right of way, in *Christodoulos (Alias Tooulis) v. Michael Hadjipetrou*, the Court ruled that according to the former Ottoman legislation and the English law in relation to the computation of the thirty-year period, it was right to add the years during which the current owner of the dominant tenement exercised the right of passage, to the years that one or more predecessors of the dominant tenement exercised the right, even if one of the predecessors was a stranger and even if the current owner bought the land from him and did not inherit it, the meaning of Cap. 224 remained the same.[277]

212. The plaintiff must prove that he/she had been using the same passage for thirty years.[278] This is the reassertion of the principle that the easement should be specific. The easement should concern the use of the specific part of the servient tenement for at least thirty years. In *Ponou v. Ibrahim*, it was ruled that the claimant of the right should prove that he/she was using the specific part of the servient tenement, and in this context the use of an alternative passage over the land of the servient tenement depending on whether it was cultivable or not, would exclude the establishment of the easement.[279]

IV. Compulsory Acquisition of the Right of Way

213. The specific case of the compulsory acquisition of the right of way is provided by section 11A of Cap. 224. This provision can be enforced in cases where the immovable property is deprived of the necessary passage to a road, that is when the property is landlocked.

214. Thus, the right of way is not only limited to passing through the neighbouring immovable property but also concerns the possibility of diverting water, sewage or any other liquid through channels, tubes or other appropriate means. The compulsory grant of the right of way is justified by the need for full use and utilization of the landlocked property.[280]

215. The concept of the compulsory acquisition of the right of way was introduced in Cyprus in 1967. Until then, there was no law imposing on any landlord the obligation to grant a right of way to a neighbouring property for the reason that the latter had no access or satisfactory access to a road.[281] The above provision is

277. *Voskou v. Hadjipetrou* (1964) CLR 21.
278. *Hadjidemosthenous v. Georghiou* (1969) 1 CLR 187.
279. *Ponou v. Ibrahim* (1970) 1 CLR 78. *See* also *Kyprianou v. Pillacouri, supra*.
280. K. Kountourisis, *Compulsory Grant of Way of Right* 28 (P.N. Sakkoulas Bros Publications 1986).
281. I. Pogiatzis, *supra* n. 40, §2, 241 (Nicosia 1988).

related to the provisions of sections 1012–1017 of the Greek Civil Code, but, although in Greek law the direction of the passage, the extent of the right to use it and the compensation to be paid are determined by the Court, in Cypriot law, these are determined by the Director of the Land Registry, who in this case exercises quasi-judicial power.[282] In this context, it is necessary to have sufficient justification for the decision by the Director of the Land Registry, similar to a judgment handed down by a court of justice.[283] The determination of the position of the way is at the discretion of the Director, and the Director's powers, which are set out in section 11A of Cap. 224, are in the sphere of private law.[284] The necessary condition for the application of section 11A is the existence of a landlocked immovable property – that is, either there is no way to access the immovable property or any access is considered to be inadequate for the suitable use, development or utilization of the property.

216. Except for where the passage has been abolished or has become inadequate due to the unprompted decision of the owner of the landlocked immovable property, the reasons why the property became landlocked are not investigated.[285] The immovable property may have been landlocked from the beginning or may have

282. *Georghiou v. Hadjifessa* (1970) 1 CLR 58. As it is noted in this case, 'the Land Registry Clerk, who is acting on behalf of the Director, in the capacity of an arbitrator in a quasi-judicial capacity under the law, finds himself in a very difficult position in trying to comply with the provisions of rule 6 (2). He finds himself between Schylla and Charybdis. If he makes a full comparison of the various possible routes, then there may be a complaint that he made that comparison and he reached his conclusion without giving notice to the interested persons as regards the alternative routes and that he, consequently, failed to comply with rule 6 (2), and his decision is vitiated.

If, on the other hand, he fails to make any comparison at all, or to give any consideration to the alternative routes suggested by the owner of the servient tenement, then he may be faced with the complaint that, without considering the matter at all, he came to the conclusion that there was no other suitable property or properties for the creation of access over them, as envisaged in the opening words of rule 6 (2). We must say that the Director finds himself in an unenviable situation.' For an analysis, *see* T. Synodinou, 'The Land Registry in Cyprus: Between Formalism and Realism', in *Grundbuchfunktionen im europäischen Rechtsvergleich (Functions of land registers in European Comparative Law Perspective)*, Das Grundbuch im Europa des 21, Jahrhunderts (A. Wudarski ed., Duncker & Humblot 2016).

283. *Charalambous v. Aristo Developers Ltd* (2009) 1 CLR 834. As regards the statement on the reasons of the decision, the Regulations of 1956 provides as following: '6.-(1) The Director shall, when so requested by a person aggrieved by any order, notice or decision of the Director made or given under the provisions of the Law, who signifies his intention to appeal against such order, notice or decision, furnish such person with a statement of his reasons therefor, which statement shall be filed with the Registrar together with the summons (Form 2). (2) Where an office copy of the summons (Form 2) is served on the Director under the provisions of Rule 5, he shall, within fourteen days after the date of such service, file with the Registrar a statement of his reasons for the order, notice or decision appealed against, unless he shall have previously supplied such statement to the person aggrieved under the provisions of paragraph (1) of this rule: Provided that the Director may, within the aforesaid period of fourteen days, apply to the Court ex parte for an extension of time, and shall forthwith give notice of any extension allowed by the Court to all parties to the proceedings.(3) On filing his statement of reasons with the Registrar, the Director shall leave, for each party to the proceedings, a copy thereof for service plus a duplicate of such copy for the affidavit of service.'

284. *Peyiotis a.a. v. Polemides* (1982) CLR 442; *Kafieros et al. v. Theocharous et al.* (1978) 1 CLR 619; *Kramvias et al. v. Theodosiou* (2000) 1A CLR 267.

285. Pogiatzis, *supra* n. 40 at 243.

become landlocked due to real or legal facts, for example land alterations and other natural causes, which led to complete or almost complete deprivation of a passage to a road or to inadequate access to it or to the abolishment of the public road by the State.[286] The immovable property shall be considered landlocked, even if its owner used a dirt road for many years to pass through his/her property, which crosses many neighbouring properties, provided that he had not acquired a registered right of way, despite the multiannual use, and the passage granted under section 11A by the Director was shorter and had the advantage of not traversing more properties.[287]

217. The Immovable Property (Granting Way) Rules of 1967 define in detail the procedure of granting a right of way by the Director. The procedure differs depending on whether there are immovable properties other than the servient tenement, upon which the right of way could be established or not. If, in the opinion of the Director, there are no other properties that are suitable to provide a passage, he/she proceeds to determine the direction of the passage and the amount of the compensation.

218. On the other hand, if the Director believes that there are probably other properties, which are suitable for providing a passage to the landlocked property, he/she suspends the delivery of the judgment, in order to choose among the more suitable properties, after their owners have been notified.

219. The Director's discretion in choosing the most suitable immovable property shall be exercised in such a way as to minimize the damage, the nuisance or the inconvenience caused by the acquisition of the passage,[288] while the essential elements taken into account in making the decision are the surface, morphology, need for constructing walls, eradication of trees, the use or the intended use by the servient tenement of the part of the land granted or the need of avoiding a passage with multiple corners.[289]

220. The extent of the right should reflect the profit-making utility of the landlocked immovable property, and along with the necessity of granting way, should be objectively evaluated based on the type, the needs and the position of the landlocked property and the servient tenement and not based on the subjective opinion of the owner of the landlocked immovable property.[290] All the registered owners of the immovable property should participate in the procedure so that the decision that the Director issues is legitimate.[291] Despite the fact that the Director's decision is taken under an administrative procedure, it does not constitute an administrative act,

---

286. Kountourisis, *supra* n. 280 at 32.
287. *Koumis v. Kountourou* (1992) 1B CLR 1312.
288. *Kafieros et al. v. Theocharous et al.* (1978) 1 CLR 619.
289. Pogiatzis, *supra* n. 40 at 253.
290. Kountourisis, *supra* n. 280 at 34; Argyris Stavrakis, *Granting a Way of Right under Sections 1012-1017 of Civil Code, Law & Economy* 13 (P.N. Sakkoulas 2009).
291. *Hadjisavva and Others v. Loizou* (1982) 1 CLR 218. For the necessity of adding the new owner as a defendant in the action for the establishment of easement of way in case the owner has changed, *see Hadjitheodosiou v. Ioannou* (1996) 1B CLR 764.

but is considered to be a decision in the field of private law. In this context, the decision can be appealed before the District Court pursuant to the procedure in section 80 of Cap. 224.

221. The District Court has the competency not only to annul the decision but also to replace it, provided that all the necessary evidence has been furnished. If the Court does not have all the information which would have enabled it to substitute the Director's decision with its own, the Court may, depending on the circumstances, order a new on-the-spot examination.[292]

222. According to current case law, the Court's jurisdiction is not limited only to reviewing the legality of the decision, but extends also to its accuracy and to the regulation of parties' rights in justice.[293] The order of the District Court can be appealed before the Supreme Court of Cyprus within fourteen days from the day that the judgment is handed down.

V. Enforcement of Easements

223. The enforcement of easements is also considered to be an important issue. Where the enforcement leads to an abuse, there would be a violation of the right of property (private nuisance or trespass).

224. An easement, either acquired in one way or another or under section 11A via compulsory acquisition, is a real encumbrance binding both the registered owner of the property and its subsequent owner.[294] The easement right-holder should exercise the right with restraint[295] and within reasonable limits, which are dictated by the type and the content of easement. Otherwise, the use could be considered excessive ('excessive user').

225. In *Michael Panayi v. Georghios Nicola Lefteri*, the Court ruled that the passage of a flock of sheep of the owner of the dominant tenement for seventeen continuous years by the servient tenement, without the opposition of the owner of the latter, does not constitute an alteration in the nature of an easement, whose exercise had started forty years ago for agricultural purposes, without this meaning, however, that there was a right of way in general for other reasons.[296]

226. In relation to excessive exercise of the way of right, the case law has been concerned by the distinguish between the trespass to immovable property and nuisance. According to *Zinonas Chrysanthou v. Chrissoula Pagkratiou*, the Court, after

---

292. *Patsalides v. Damaskinou et al.* (2004) 1B CLR 1248.
293. *Kafieros v. Theocharous* (1978) 1 CLR 619; *Peyiotis v. Polemides* (1982) 1 CLR 442; *Athanasi et al. v. Hadjimama et al.* (1990) 1 CLR 208; *Koumis v. Kountourou* (1992) 1 CLR 1312; *Patsalides v. Damaskinou, ibid.*
294. *Andreou v. Chrysostomou* (2006) 1B CLR 820.
295. Theofanopoulos, *supra* n. 196, 193.
296. *Michael Panayi of Vassili v. Georghios Nicola Lefteri of Vassili* (1958) (V23) 1 CLR 204.

highlighting that the concept of immovable property is defined differently in Cap. 224 than in Cap. 148, in which easements are excluded from the definition, proceeded by relating the practical importance of the distinction of the definition in these two chapters and ruled that the examination of the excessive use, namely whether it is a trespass or a nuisance, is a theoretical and academic matter and in both cases the restitution is the same.[297]

227. Finally, the right of way cannot deprive the owner of the servient land of the possession of the land or deprive any third party of the possession of land where the third party, on the grounds of a recognized and lawful right, exercises such possession, on the condition that in any case the exercise of the right of way for the benefit of the dominant property is not impeded.[298] In this context, the construction of works, for the benefit of the dominant land, following the grant of a right of way, constitutes trespass. In the light of this finding, the compensation paid by the dominant property to the servient property is paid only for the acquisition of the right of way and not for the acquisition of the immovable property on which the right is exercised. The construction of works is permissible only to the extent that the right of way could be exercised comfortably and safely. On the contrary, the construction of an entrance on the part of the immovable property which is covered by the right of way was held to be inadmissible.[299]

VI. Legal Effect of Easement

228. According to section 12 of Cap. 224, where an easement or other advantage has been acquired pursuant to section 11 in respect of any immovable property, it shall be deemed to be attached to such property and to be included in any dealing made with such property. In fact, this is a legislative reassertion of the basic common law principle, that easement is an attachment to the immovable property and constitutes a 'part' of it, in the sense that there can be no easement that does not belong to a particular immovable property. As it was held in *Kanara v. Protopapa*, 'The right of way is not the subject of separate ownership of land. The right of way is an easement which extends the ownership right of the dominant real estate and limits the right of ownership of the servient property.'[300]

229. In relation to the acquisition and transfer of an easement, sections 11 and 12 of Cap. 224 are exclusively applicable, while the application of the Immovable Property (Transfer and Mortgage) Law (Law 9/1965), along with the common law and the law of equity are prohibited. The ways of creating an easement provided by section 11 (law, grant, continuous, long use, registration) are reflected grosso modo in the ways of establishing an easement in English common law (legal easements), which, nevertheless, recognizes the application of the law of equity in recognizing

297. *Chrysanthou v. Pagkratiou* (1998) 1B CLR 675.
298. *Tsiamanta v. Tsiamanta* (1990) 1 CLR 97526.
299. *Odysseos v. Papadouri*, No. 217/12, 10 September 2018.
300. *Kanara v. Protopapa* (1999) 1 CLR 801, 806.

an easement right, as is also the case for other property rights over immovable property (equitable easements). Cypriot law, by prohibiting the application of the law of equity in the creation of an easement, safeguards the security in the transactions, since, in that way, the potential buyer of the servient tenement is more easily informed of the existence of the restriction stemming from the easement.

VII. Abolishment of Easement

230. The abolishment of easement can take place either voluntarily or compulsorily. The voluntary abolishment takes place via abandonment by notice in writing to the District Lands Office. When the easement right has not been exercised for the full period of thirty years without interruption, it shall be deemed to have lapsed.[301] The way of right shall be compulsorily nullified by the order of the Director of the Land Registry, when it is no longer necessary due to the construction of a public road or other way or due to another reason.

231. In this case, the owner either of the servient or the dominant tenement makes a claim for the abolishment of the right of way to the Director, who examines the case, decides, announces the decision and proceeds with the abolishment of the right after thirty days of the announcement.[302] This is an exclusive competence of the Land Registry which precludes the hearing of the claim for abolishment by a District Court. However, the District Court was found competent to judge on the question of an error as regards the boundaries of the neighbouring properties since the case fell within the ambit of 'deceit'/error of contract in the sense of Cap. 149 (Contracts Law).[303] In examining the case, the argument that the way of right had been abandoned for more than thirty years cannot affect the Director's decision.[304]

§7. Licences

232. In general, licences are permissions granted to a specific person (licensee) to use the licensor's land for an agreed purpose, which, without permission, would constitute an act of trespass.

233. The concept of licence in relation to immovable property has been analyzed by the Supreme Court in the case of *Apollonio Private Hospital Ltd v. C & S American Heart Institute Ltd & Others*,[305] where the Court defined the concept of licence and distinguished it from the concept of tenancy. As regards the definition of 'licence' and the categories of licences, the Court fully adopted the relevant definitions of UK law. It was held that the traditional concept of licence refers precisely

301. Section 12(2) of Cap. 224.
302. Section 12(3) of Cap. 224.
303. *Ioannou et al. v. Shiakalli* (2013) 1 CLR 1877.
304. *Christodoulou v. Chrysostomou* (2006) 1B CLR 820.
305. *Apollonio Private Hospital Ltd v. C & S American Heart Institute Ltd et al.* (2011) 1(A) CLR 379.

to permission or tolerance to legitimize what would otherwise be considered as an illegal interference with the land. The Court, by referring to UK case law[306] and doctrine, stated that the permission may emerge through a multitude of different situations and that the main categories of licence are: bare or gratuitous licence, the licence coupled with a grant (or licence), the contractual licence and 'licence by estoppel', which is considered as a new right *in alieno solo*. The 'licence by estoppel' is not considered as an alternative or a substitute for tenancy, but as an independent right.[307]

234. Bare or gratuitous licences relate to cases where the landowner simply allows the access to his property without any contractual or proprietary rights being granted and can be revoked at any time. The main difference between bare or gratuitous licences and contractual licences is that the contractual licence includes a consideration from the licensee for the benefit of the licensee. A 'licence coupled with a grant (or an interest)' enables the granting of a licence while granting a limited land right, such as, for example, permission to enter the land for the purpose of purchasing timber. The permission to enter the land under these circumstances cannot be revoked.[308] This category of licence comprises the permission to enter a property which is accompanied by an interest in land, such as when conferring to the licensee the right to go on another person's land for the sole purpose of removing something from the land. In this case, the licence comprises the rights granted under profit à prendre to access an interest, coupled with the right to enter the land in order to exploit the interest.

235. Then, the Court examined the significance of the distinction between 'tenancy' and "licence' in Cypriot law. As the Court affirmed, the distinction between the concepts of 'tenancy' and 'licence' is more important in English than in Cypriot law in the sense that in the UK leases create 'estates in land', whereas a licence merely provides temporary rights, at the will of the owner, so that the licensee can enter the land or the premises for a purpose that would otherwise be unlawful. In Cyprus, the lease merely creates a contractual obligation between the parties unless it is a lease of land for more than fifteen years, which creates a real right if it is registered in the Land Registry pursuant to Articles 65A–65IE of Cap. 224.[309] Renting in Cyprus under the relevant legislation can, of course, bring about beyond contractual obligations and statutory protection due to its conversion into institutional renting.

306. *Winter Garden Theatre (London) Ltd v. Millennium Productions Ltd* [1946] 1 All ER 678, 680.
307. Cedric D. Bell, *Land: The Law of Real Property* 13 (3rd ed., Old Bailey Press, 2003); *Pascoe v. Turner* [1979] 2 All ER 945.
308. *Apollonio Private Hospital Ltd v. C & S American Heart Institute Ltd et al.* (2011) 1(A) CLR 379.
309. *Aggelidis and Filippou Ltd v. Spyros Colocassides Estates Ltd* (1991) 1 CLR 327.

§8. Restrictive Covenants

236. Restrictions to the right of property, which can lead to the creation of a real right and a real charge over an alien property, can be introduced with restrictive terms and covenants. In Cypriot land law, which is constructed around the concept of registration with the Land Registry, restrictive terms and covenants acquire real power only when they are registered with the Land Registry.

237. These restrictions can be defined as a restriction and encumbrance, imposed over the immovable property, which restrict the owner from carrying out a certain act or use and development of the land, which would normally fall under his/her property right. Thus, their detachment from the concept of contract or easement makes it possible to argue that they could be characterized as sui generis real rights.[310]

238. These restrictions are, for example, an agreement restricting the construction of a building that has more than a certain number of floors, the condition or the agreement under which the reconstruction should be made at a particular distance from a neighbouring property, the agreement that the immovable property will not be used for commercial purposes, but is destined only for residential use, the agreement that the particular physiognomy of the building will not be altered, the restriction on the exercise of a particular commercial activity, such as that the property should not be transformed or used for the construction of a factory, a brothel, or for the operation of a landfill, livestock, slaughterhouse, competing enterprise, etc.

239. The distinction between restrictive term and restrictive covenant is difficult and mostly concerns the way of establishing these restrictions rather than their functioning. Equally difficult is the distinction of these two concepts from the concept of easements, especially in the case of the restrictive covenants.

240. In particular, the distinction between the real easement and the restrictive covenant is mostly historical, and it is probable that in both concepts, the outcome would be the same. Typical cases, where the above concepts are applied, are when defining the use of the land between two neighbouring properties or when restrictions over the use of residential complexes are imposed or over lots resulting from land fragmentation.

241. It is possible that the restrictions over the use of the specific immovable property may be agreed in the context of the principle of private autonomy of the parties and the freedom to contract, just as it is possible that positive obligations may be agreed in relation to the property. These agreements have been particularly

310. G.L. Newsom, *Preston & Newscom's Restrictive Covenants Affecting Freehold Land, Property and Conveyancing Library* 9 (8th ed., Sweet & Maxwell 1991).

popular since the nineteenth century, when the lack of complete residential development plans made the private autonomy in this field extremely important.[311] Despite the fact that the enforcement of the agreed terms of the parties was always possible, the doctrine of privity deprived these private legal instruments of a part of their meaning. The law of equity would solve the difficulty of enforcing these terms against third parties and especially between the rights-holders of the contractual parties who came to this agreement. Recognizing in rem powers in the restrictions to property, in fact new real rights, was a slight deviation from the principle introduced in *Keppel v. Bailey* that the private autonomy cannot recognize new real rights.[312] Thus, over the years, this possibility has been delineated by the introduction of strict criteria. In principle, the in rem (*erga omnes*) power is recognized only for restrictive terms and covenants and not for contracts which impose a positive obligation.[313] Furthermore, like in the case of easements, the restriction should be relevant to a specific dominant tenement, which would benefit from the restriction.[314]

242. In Cypriot law, the restrictions on the use and development of the immovable property can be inferred, with reservations, upon the transfer of the property based on section 11(1)(f) and upon the concluding of a restrictive covenant based on section 65 IF of Cap. 224. The latter provision, which creates a restriction through a restrictive covenant, is similar to an easement, because it always concerns a specific immovable property that benefits (dominant tenement).

243. Indeed, according to *Sotiriadi v. Vasiliou*,[315] the provision of section 11(1)(f) is not limited to the registration of restrictive covenants which are similar to easements, namely, to a dominant and a servient tenement, but extends also to the acquisition of rights of any kind over immovable property belonging to another person.

244. In principle, the Supreme Court of Cyprus has held that the registration of a restrictive covenant based on section 11(1)(f) is not necessarily similar to an easement. In addition, the Supreme Court disagreed with the District's Court decision that held that the validity of the restrictive covenant was dependent on the sale contracts which concerned the immovable property.[316]

311. Ben McFarlane, Nicholas Hopkins & Sarah Nield, *Land Law, Text, Cases and Materials* 918 (Oxford University Press 2009).
312. *Keppel v. Bailey* (1834) 2 My &K 517.
313. *Haywood v. Brunswick Permanent Benefit Building Society* (1881) 8 QBD 403.
314. Gray & Gray, *supra* n. 99 at 265.
315. *Sotiriadis v. Vasiliou et al.* (1992) 1B CLR 1210.
316. According to the Supreme Court of Cyprus 'the proviso of section 11 (1) (f) of Cap. 224 does not depend on the registration of the foreseen restrictions on the existence of a contractual obligation but on the consent of the parties to the restriction at the declaration of transfer of land. In this case the restriction was included under a common consent in the transfer and subsequently it was registered to the Land Registry as a real charge, that is a charge which co-exists with the possession and ownership of land. Restrictions that are registered based on section 11 (1) (f) of Cap. 224, draw their existence from this registration to the land registry records and not from the contractual or

245. As regards the functioning and the purpose of the proviso, upon which the restrictive covenant is created in relation to the use and development of the property, the Court underlines that 'the immovable property without commenting on any existing rights of a third party. As it is inferred by the wording of the proviso, its purpose is not the establishment of rights over the property of a third party, but the regulation of the use and development of the immovable property, which inevitably responds to the city planning and developing of the environment authority where it is located. The restrictions which are provided under the proviso, are similar to "Restrictive Covenants", as they are known in English Common Law tradition. In English law, the restrictive covenants are contractual and mostly present in sale contracts or leases. Their application is based on the rules of equity and a right to bring an action upon them is recognized for both the first owner and his/her successors. At the same time the restrictions are charged on both the purchaser and his/her successors. Once again, they have parallels in the real charges, which in Cyprus are regulated with the provisions of paragraph (f)* in this way, the restrictions are released from any contractual context' – the proviso of paragraph (f) provides explicitly for the creation of a restriction in the use or development of.

246. The Court, by objectively interpreting the restriction, according to which the residential character of the area along with its value are maintained and promoted, ruled that the appellant, who was the granter of the land and participated in the establishment of the restriction, was eligible to enforce it, provided that he/she continued to possess immovable property in the area and had a direct interest in the residential and environmental development of the area. So, it was possible for the Court to grant him/her as restitution an injunction prohibiting the use of the property for commercial purposes in contravention of the restriction. Thus, at the same time, the Court dismissed the claim for damages, because the appellant failed to prove that he/she had suffered any damage, since it had not been proved that the value of his/her property in the area had suffered any reduction.

247. The above decision is interesting, since it defines the legal nature of the burden of proof created by the proviso of section 11. The real charge that is created does not necessarily grant a real right for the benefit of a specific property, but binds the property in general terms. However, this does not mean that anyone is eligible to bring a claim concerning the enforcement of the covenant since in this case, the legitimate interest necessarily presupposes the connection of the burden with the protection or the benefit of another property, even if the latter is not explicitly defined as the dominant tenement. We could possibly acknowledge an indirect influence of the rule that the plaintiff should still be the owner of the land, which benefits from the burden, in order for the burden to be transferred to the successors of the counterpart and the original owner of the burdened land, when the Court accepts that the appellant is eligible, because he still possess property in the area and has an interest in its residential development.[317]

---

other obligations of the parties who precede the transfer. The consent of the respondents in establishing a real charge is evidenced by the document of transfer.'

317. For this rule, *see* Dixon, *supra* n. 82 at 384, with reference to *Formby v. Barker* 1903, 2 Ch. 539.

248. The above legal mechanisms are listed in the category of real restrictions, since their registration with the Land Registry guarantees the obligation of the future owners of the burdened property to respect them. In this respect and mostly in relation to third parties' commitment, these restrictions establish in rem rights for the benefit of third parties and specifically for the benefit of one or more dominant tenements, similarly to easements. However, if the concept of the real right is interpreted more widely than the real power and a property interest is attributed to it over an alien immovable property, then the nature of the right in rem is to obtain only the restrictions which benefit a specific property and not the general restrictions that serve to improve or maintain indefinitely the character of a specific area, which may be established with a reservation under section 11(1)(g). Thus, even in this case, it is possible to argue, under a wide interpretation of the relevant terms, that the proximity of one property to the burdened property could make it a dominant tenement, even if this case it is not specifically defined as such.

249. Except for the provision of section 11(1)(g) of Cap. 224, a restrictive covenant could be established under a contract independently from the transfer of the immovable property. In this case, the restriction, which charges the immovable property and not the owner, has parallels with the concept of real easement. The restrictive contract binds every new owner of the burdened property, provided that the contract has been registered with the Land Registry.[318] The registration of the restrictive contract takes place through an application of one of the owners of the property concerned to the Land Registry. The contract shall be duly signed by both the owners, and if one of them is not the registered owner, the registration is not accepted by the Land Registry.[319] The legal effect of the registration of the restrictive contract is that by the submission of the contract, an encumbrance (lien) is created, which binds all the successors of the 'burdened property'. The restrictive covenant may be removed or modified by a court order.[320]

---

318. Section 65IH of Cap. 224.
319. Section 65IZG (3) of Cap. 224.
320. Section 65IΘ of Cap. 224.

Chapter 5. Security Interests (*See also* Parts II, IV and V)

250. Immovable property can be encumbered by a mortgage and a charge. These security interests can cover both land and everything attached to the land (fixtures). The Transfer and Mortgage of Immovable Property Law (Law 9/1965) governs the registration of a mortgage and charges over immovable property, while the Companies Law, Cap. 113 governs the procedure for the registration of charges created over the assets of a company. A mortgage or a charge does not constitute an estate in land but rather a contractual right for the benefit of the mortgagee and a charge on the land.[321] Neither a mortgage nor a charge over land are possessory, in the sense that possession does not pass to the creditor. For further analysis of security interests, *see* Parts II, IV and V.

321. Kyriakos Georgiades and Katerina Brandysova, 'Cyprus', in *International Secured Transactions* Chapter 11, https://www.neocleous.com, last visited on 23 December 2019.

Chapter 6. Joint Ownership

§1. Joint Ownership of Immovable Property

I. In General

251. Joint ownership of immovable property is not extensively regulated in Cypriot land law. In general, it may come about in various ways, such as through the purchase of property, through the transfer of property upon donation or through transfer of property upon death.

252. According to section 21 of Cap. 224, 'Where any immovable property is held in undivided shares, all the co-owners shall be entitled, in proportion to their respective shares, to (a) any building or other erection or structure erected upon, or affixed to, the property (b) any tree or vine planted or any well sunk therein (c) any permanent improvement effected therein, whether erected, affixed, planted, sunk or effected by a co-owner or by any other person.'

253. Cap. 224 lacks specific rules for the management of indivisible co-ownership. In this context, no provision exists regarding the liability of a co-owner towards the cost of repairs of a jointly owned property.[322] This absence has been addressed by case law on the basis of the relevant common law rules. In *Ismini Kyriacou Hjiloizi and others v. Irini Iona*,[323] the Court acknowledged that there is no legislative provision in Cypriot law regulating this issue and found that where a co-owner does not consent to the costs of maintaining the common property, he/she is not required to contribute to the repair costs. A co-owner could be reimbursed for the amount he paid for the part of co-owners who did not pay, only if the conditions of unjust enrichment under section 70 of Chapter 149[324] were fulfilled. However, section 70 of the Contract Law (Cap. 149) properly interpreted,

322. As it is stated in *Kyriacou HjiLoizi et al. v. Iona* (1963) 2 CLR 11: 'Until the 1 September 1946, when the relevant provisions of the Mejellé were abolished by the Immovable Property (Tenure, Registration and Valuation) Law, 1945 (now Cap. 224), this matter would have been governed by the provisions in Chapter V of the Mejellé (Articles 1308 to 1328). Under section 1313, when there was a need for repair of a property owned in common which was not "capable of partition, like a mill or a bath," and one of the owners wished to repair it, if his co-owner objected, he could only proceed to do so with the Judge's permission; and if he had done the repairs without obtaining the Judge's permission, then he could not compel his co-owner to contribute to the cost of repairs. Section 1311 provided that if someone, without asking the permission of his co-owner or the Judge, repaired, on his own accord, property held in common, he became a "giver", that is to say, he could not recover from his co-owner any part of the expense from him, whether the property held in common was capable of division or not. And, under section 1323, in case of a private river held in common, those who wished to cleanse the river had cleansed it with the permission of the Judge, and, until the person who objected to such cleansing had paid his share of the cost, he was prohibited from taking benefit from the river.'

323. *Kyriacou HjiLoizi et al. v. Iona, supra.*

324. Section 70 of Contract Law, Cap. 149 provides as follows: 'Where a person lawfully does anything for another person, or delivers anything to him, not intending to do so gratuitously, and such other person enjoys the benefit thereof, the latter is bound to compensate the former in respect of, or to restore, the thing so done or delivered.'

excludes this possibility, since one of the conditions that must be met is that the person for whom the act is done must enjoy the benefit of it. In this case, it would not be reasonable to hold that a person enjoys the benefit of the repairs if, as in this case, he had no option but to enjoy such benefit. Unless the defendant has an option to enjoy or reject the benefit, it cannot legitimately be said that he enjoys the benefit.[325]

II. Co-ownership Applied to Apartment Buildings

254. Apart from the concept of co-ownership, which is established when the immovable property belongs to two or more owners of undivided shares, a particular form of co-ownership is also created in relation to the common parts of buildings, where in parallel with the absolute property right that the owner of a story of a building or an apartment on a story enjoys, he/she also acquires a property right to the common parts of the building which are intended for common use.

255. In Cypriot land law, the concept of common ownership was recognized for the first time under section 6 of Law 26/1946. According to Ottoman Law (Mejelle section 1315), the owner of the upper floor had no right of ownership of the plot, but enjoyed only the right of support to the lower floor and the right to rebuild on the plot in case of a disaster. In other words, the plot on which the building was built, belonged only to the owner of the ground floor. This legal status continues to apply for all the buildings that were registered before 1 September 1946, that is before the date when Cap. 224 came into force.[326]

256. In particular, the concept of common ownership was first provided by section 6 of Cap. 224, which was later abolished and replaced by the more complete and detailed provision of sections 38A-38 ΑΓ of Cap. 224. These sections provide for the possibility of registering as separate private property an apartment, an office or another independent unit,[327] which is combined with the common ownership in the common parts of the building or possibly with limited common ownership, as will be further analyzed below.

257. The law provides the definitions of 'Commonly owned building' and of 'unit'. 'Commonly owned building' means a building consisting of at least five units, even if it belongs mainly to one owner, and will be registered as such according to section 38 ΑΑ of the law. 'Unit' means a floor or part of a floor, room, office, flat, or shop or any other part or space of a commonly owned building, which may be properly and conveniently occupied and enjoyed as a full, separate and self-contained unit for any purpose.

325. *Kyriacou HjiLoizi et al. v. Iona, supra* n. 322.
326. *See Millington – Ward v. Roubina* (1970) 1 CLR 88.
327. According to s. 38 A, a story is a floor or part of a floor, such as an apartment, office, shop, room, storage, etc., which can be easily possessed and used as a full and independent unit.

258. The establishment of an absolute private ownership right over a part of a building requires from the unit to be the object of a separate usufruct and possession right. The common parts of the building are the site on which the building is standing, the foundations thereof, the main walls supporting the whole building, its roof, the elevator, the main staircase leading to the various stories, the main corridors thereof and any other part of the ground or building which is of common use to the owners of the various stories, which are jointly enjoyed. The common parts are commonly owned, possessed and used by all the owners of the separate units in undivided parts.

259. Each one of the undivided shares is proportional to the relationship between the cubic area of the apartment and the total cubic area of the building. The separate registration of an undivided share over the communal parts, without the concurrent registration of the individual apartment or shop in title of the same person, is impossible.

260. Until recently, the share of a common ownership was not regulated by law. The owners were informed neither about their corresponding percentage nor about their rights to the administration of the building. Since 1993 the share (a) for the existing buildings, namely the ones that obtained a building licence before 1993, and the division of the shares was not agreed by the owners, is defined by the Director of the Land Registry on the basis of the comparison between the prices of the apartments with the prices on 1 January 1980 and (b) for the new buildings which obtained or obtain a building licence after 1993 is defined by the owner of the immovable property, so that every purchaser can know a priori the purchasable share to common parts. In particular, section 38Θ provides that the share to the common parts of the building is defined by the owner of the immovable property upon which the building is built on the basis of the proportion between the value of one apartment (unit) with the total value of all the apartments (units). Thus, the Director reserves the right to define a different value if he/she is of the opinion that there is an inconsistency between the value defined by the owner and the real value of the unit.

261. The importance of the owner's share over the common parts of the building is significant not only for the accurate regulation of the obligations of the owners of the units regarding the expenses of the common parts of the building, but also for the cases of destruction of the common building or sale on the basis of a unanimous decision of the owners of the units or compulsory expropriation, where the owners' interests would be analogous to their shares to the communal ownership.[328]

262. Under section 38B(a) the way of establishing common ownership of a building is defined. Common ownership is obligatorily established under law where the building consists of more than five units, even if all of them belong to one and

328. Section 38IZ of Cap. 224.

only owner. If the building consists of two to four units, the registration of the building as communal could take place if the 50% of the owners or two owners of units ask for it.

263. The owner of a separate and self-contained tenement of a communal building enjoys every right deriving from the concept of the absolute private ownership as regards the tenement, which, nevertheless, shall be exercised with respect to the ownership of the other tenements and to the common ownership. The longstanding tenant, who has registered his/her right on the basis of Cap. 224, can also be regarded as the owner of the tenement, unless otherwise defined. The equalization of the rights and obligations of the longstanding tenant with the owner of the tenement in relation to a commonly owned building is justified by the fact that the registration of a long-term leasehold grants to the tenant a real right of ownership, limited in time, as will be further analyzed below.

264. The owner of the unit may make any alterations to the unit provided that they do not prejudice the rights of the owner of any other unit and they do not unduly interfere with the enjoyment by the owner of such other unit, they do not affect the main walls of the communal building, its structure, the external walls and they do not alter the appearance of the building.[329]

265. As already mentioned, the common ownership of a common building belongs, is possessed and is jointly used by the owner of every tenement and belongs to the stories in a certain proportion.[330] Thus, the co-ownership which is created by the concept of common ownership constitutes a special form of ownership, to which the provisions of Cap. 224 in relation to undivided ownership do not apply.[331] In this context, a separate transfer of the share in the common ownership cannot be effected. The milestone of the legal regime of the common ownership is the common use concept over the commonly owned parts, while the exercise of the ownership right takes, for the most part, the form of a right to participate in the common parts with a proportional contribution to the maintenance and restoration costs without the power to exclude the owners of the other stories.

266. An exception to the above rule is the grant of an exclusive use right of a certain part of the common ownership to one unit in the building This part, which is called ‘limited common ownership’, would be specifically provided in the registration of the story, for example, it could define that the owner of a particular ground floor apartment will have exclusive use of the garden located right in front of his apartment. The restrictive common property is regarded as a follower of the unit, which is intended to serve, provided that the owner of the unit cannot dispose it independently from it. As it is defined in section 38B(3)(b) of Cap. 224, every disposition or exchange in relation to unit consists of the share to common ownership which corresponds to the unit and to the probable restrictive common ownership,

329. Section 38Δ of Cap. 224.
330. Section 38 ΣΤ.
331. Section 38Z of Cap. 224.

which was granted for an exclusive use of the unit. The disposition of a common ownership share and of a limited common ownership independently from the unit is void.

267. A 'limited common ownership' can also be established after the registration of the common building (except if it is forbidden by the Regulations) upon the agreement of the 75% of the owners of the stories. However, this is never possible for the main stairway, the structure of the building, the elevators or the corridors, which are the parts or the areas which are destined to serve all the owners. Furthermore, if one of the owners denies his consent to the establishment of a restrictive common ownership, this denial will be reviewed by the Land Registry to assess whether there has been an abusive exercise of his right of ownership. In this context, the Director of the Land Registry has the power to register only a part of the building as a limited common ownership, if he/she considers that the refusal of the owner obviously exceeds the limits imposed by the principle of good faith or by the economic or social purpose of his/her right.

268. The review criteria of the refusal of a unit owner are identical to the ones provided in section 281 of Greek Civil Code regarding the abuse of the right.[332] This obvious influence of Greek law is further evidence of the various influences on the Cypriot land law.

269. As it is defined in section 38A of Cap. 224, a building is regarded as a permanent construction and consists also of the land upon which it has been built. Consequently, the right of the owner of a unit in a commonly owned building concerns jointly the building and the land upon which it has been built. In other terms, the co-ownership share over the communal building is at the same time a co-ownership share over the lot.

270. The obligations of the owners of the units extend also to the maintenance and insurance of the commonly owned building. The participation in the maintenance, repair and administration costs of the commonly owned building is proportional to the area of each unit.[333] If any owner fails to comply, the Administration Committee deposits the relevant amount and can bring a claim to obtain the owed amount.[334] At the same time, the Administrative Committee is obliged to take out insurance for the commonly owned building against fire, thunder and earthquakes.[335]

271. In the concept of commonly owned building, the Regulation, which is an agreement of the co-owners for the regulation of the legal relationships resulting

332. For the abuse of a real right in Greek law, *see* Petros Alikakos, *Abuse of Real Rights, Caselaw Evolutions Regarding the Abuse during the Possession and Exercise of a Real Right* (Sakkoulas editions 2007).
333. Section 38IA.
334. Section 38IA(2).
335. Section 38IB.

from the compulsory co-ownership, is critical. The Regulation constitutes a multilateral agreement in which participants are both the original and any subsequent co-owners.[336] The Regulation concerns the control, the functioning, the administration and the management of the communal building, the legal relationships between the owners of the stories and their rights and obligations regarding the communal building and the communal property.[337]

272. The administration of the commonly owned building is carried out by the Administration Committee. Its establishment is compulsory.[338] Its composition, appointment, responsibilities and duties are defined by the Regulations and Cap. 224.

273. As soon as the commonly building is registered with the Land Registry, the Director can appoint a temporary Administration Committee, which will exercise its powers until the appointment of the first Administration Committee pursuant to the Regulations, provided that the owners of the stories who applied for registration have asked for it.[339] A temporary Administration Committee may also be established if the original Administration Committee has ceased to operate.[340]

274. The primary responsibility of the Administration Committee is to observe the compliance with the Regulation of the joint-ownership building and the control, administration, management and functioning of the common ownership. Nevertheless, particularly important decisions for the commonly owned building, such as deciding whether it should be demolished or sold,[341] are generally taken by unanimous vote of all the owners of the stories.

275. The Administration Committee can bring a claim and respond to a claim for every issue that is relevant to the commonly owned building. In this context, the members of the committee are considered to constitute a composed body with legal status and legal capacity. As mentioned by the Supreme Court in *Christina Talianou v. Administration Committee of Belmar Complex (2002)*, the people who are members of the statutory Administration Committees do not appear in their personal capacity nor are they being sued or sue in their personal capacity.

276. For the purposes of Cap. 224, the people participating in the Administration Committee constitute a lawfully composed body, which can easily be named the Administration Committee with the addition of another distinctive name or attribute for identification purposes or distinction from other similar Administration Committees.

336. Papasteriou, *supra* n. 66 at 627.
337. Section 38ΙΘ.
338. Section 38ΚΒ Cap. 224.
339. Section 38ΚΓ of Cap. 224.
340. Section 38ΚΔ of Cap. 224.
341. Section 38ΙΣΤ of Cap. 224.

III. Partition of Immovable Property Held in Undivided Shares

277. Cap. 224 contains specific provisions about the separation of joint ownership which is held in undivided shares. The separation can be achieved through an agreement of the owners or at the request of one of the joint owners which is addressed to the Director of the Land Registry (compulsory partition).

278. According to section 29 of Cap. 224, 'Where immovable property is held in undivided shares, it shall be lawful for the Director, on the application of any co-owner, to cause a partition of the property to be made amongst the several parties entitled thereto and to register the holdings into which the property is divided in the names of the persons to whom the same are respectively allotted. In making a partition under the provisions of this section the Director shall, as far as possible, apportion the property in accordance with the wishes of the several co-owners, and if the co-owners, though otherwise agreeing with the partition, do not agree as to the holding or holdings to be allotted to each one of them, the question shall be finally determined by the drawing of lots by the Director. Where by reason of the nature of the property to be partitioned or of the number of the parties interested therein or for any other reason, it appears to the Director that it is not practicable to allot holdings of a value corresponding to the respective shares of the co-owners, the Director may order that those co-owners who take holdings of greater value than their due shall pay to those who take holdings of less value than their due or take no holding at all, such compensation as the Director may determine having regard to their respective shares and the values which he allocates to the holdings.' This process does not resolve disputes between co-owners, nor does it expropriate property for the benefit of other co-owners.[342] Under section 29, the Director does not have any discretion.

279. The Director's judgment is limited to whether the property in question can be divided into smaller parcels corresponding to the undivided shares and, where appropriate, to determining financial compensation. The Director shall have no discretion to assign less than the lots provided for in section 27 nor shall he be allowed to not proceed to partition as long as the estate can be divided.[343] The partition cannot be claimed through the mechanism of proprietary estoppel since the partition between co-owners is made only if the conditions of section 27 of Cap. 224 are met.[344]

342. *Achilleos et al. v. Pittaras et al.* (2012) 1 CLR 1590.
343. *Papagheorghiou v. Patsalidi* (2001) 1 CLR 1365.
344. *Mina v. Chimonidou et al.* (1999) 1 A CLR 405.

Chapter 7. Neighbourhood and Urban Problems

§1. The tort of Trespass to Land

I. Various Aspects of the Tort

280. According to section 43 of Cap. 148 (the Tort Law): '(1) Trespass to immovable property consists of any unlawful entry upon, or any unlawful damage to or interference with, any such property by any person. (2) Where the acts complained of are permitted by local custom, such custom if established shall be a defense but in any action brought in respect of any trespass to immovable property the onus of showing that the act of which complaint is made was not unlawful shall be upon the defendant.' The tort therefore corresponds to the traditional common law tort. As explicitly stated in section 43, three different applications of the tort are recognized: the wrongful entry, the unlawful damage and the unlawful interference to the immovable property.

281. Wrongful entry is entry with the consent of the possessor. Even if the defendant has the consent of the plaintiff, the interdiction of access to part of the property could lead, if violated, to the characterization of the tort. In the same way, an abuse of entry or remaining after explicit withdrawal of the consent are covered by this situation. In some circumstances, the consent can be implicit: the silence and lack of reaction of the owner is therefore read as an implicit licence (bare licence), which can be, however, revoked at the discretion of the owner. This has been held in the decision *Aggelidis kai Filippou Ltd v. Spyros Colocassides Estates Ltd* [345] To remain on the land after revocation of the consent does not always lead to trespass. Specifically, if the defendant had a lease contract with the plaintiff, he/she will be protected by the Leasing Law 23/1983 even after the termination of the contract, as long as he/she continues to pay the rent.

282. The trespass to land by interference created certain legal overlaps with the tort of private nuisance. Throwing anything on the land constitutes trespass to land by interference. The third variant concerns a very specific case: the direct act of damaging the land.

283. The list of the three variants of the tort, as stated in section 43, is not exhaustive, as highlighted by the case *Zinonas v. Pagkratiou.*[346] The plaintiff sued his neighbour after he constructed a wall on the road towards his property, violating the easement the plaintiff had on the road. By issuing an injunction and granting damages on the basis of section 43, the Court accepted that a fourth application of the tort exists: the unlawful interference with an easement.

345. *Aggelidis and Filippou Ltd v. Spyros Colocassides Estates Ltd* (1991) 1 CLR 327.
346. *Zinonas v. Pagkratiou* (1998) 1 CLR 675.

II. Characteristics of the Tort

284. The tort is actionable per se, unless, of course, the trespass of land concerns damage to the immovable property. In each situation, the tort traditionally requires that the intention to trespass be proven, even though in the UK, negligent trespass to land is accepted.[347] Section 43 does not provide a precise definition of immovable property or who can sue for trespass to land. The tort is related to the protection of the land but, it intends to protect first of all the interest of the holder (possessor).[348] In the case *Archimandritis Sevastianos Stavrou v. Iera Moni Metamorfoseos*, which related to the invasion of a church by some monks,[349] the decision of the first instance judges to allow damages for trespass to land was overturned by the Supreme Court, as it had not been proven who was the licensee of the church, independently of who was the owner.

285. Immovable property must be understood within the context of the classic adage *cuius est solum, eius est usque ad coelum et ad infernos* (whoever owns the land owns it all the way to the heavens and to hell). That means that immovable property is defined as the surface, subsoil, airspace and anything permanently attached to the land.

§2. The Tort of Private Nuisance

I. Definition and Distinction from Similar Torts

286. The Cypriot tort of private nuisance is very similar to its common law origin. In section 46 of Cap. 148, it is stated that 'a private nuisance consists of any person so conducting himself of his business or so using any immovable property of which he is the owner or occupier as habitually to interfere with the reasonable use and enjoyment, having regard to the situation and nature thereof, of the immovable property of any other person: provided that no plaintiff shall recover compensation in respect of any private nuisance unless he shall have suffered damage thereby: provided also that the provisions of this section shall not apply to any interference with daylight.'

287. The tort of private nuisance must be distinguished from various other related torts. It has little in common with the tort of public nuisance, which is defined in section 45 of Cap. 148 as the 'unlawful act or omission to discharge a

347. *League Against Cruel Sports v. Scott* [1985] 2 All ER 489.
348. As it was held in *Adamou v. Christophi* (1974) 1 CLR 100, 'Trespass, therefore, is actionable at the suit of the person in possession of land, in spite of the fact that he is neither the owner nor does he derive title from the owner. Once, therefore, the plaintiff was in occupation or physical control of the land in question and because he has planted those trees, he is holding the land as a de facto possessor and it is too late for the defendant – who never had any title to the land – or indeed she never genuinely believed the land to be hers, to allege that the plaintiff had no right of action against her because the Government is the owner of that land.'
349. *Archimandritis Sevastianos Stavrou v. Iera Moni Metamorfoseos*, No. 110/2011, 7 February 2014.

legal duty where such act or omission endangers the life, safety, health, property or comfort of the public or obstructs the public in the exercise of some common right'. Furthermore, unlike the situation under UK law, in Cyprus interference with daylight is forbidden, but is not governed by the tort of private nuisance. A specific tort entitled 'interference with daylight' is provided in section 50 of Cap. 148, with strict prerequisites (the owner has to prove that he/she lost the enjoyment of a reasonable amount of daylight due to interference from his/her neighbours, after having enjoyed it for more than twenty-five years, and considering the nature and the situation of the immovable property). This tort has been discussed notably in the case *Akama Theofanou and another v. Niki Ioannou Tsiakoli*,[350] where it was held that the deprivation of daylight in the plaintiff's kitchen due to the construction of a property by the neighbours did not constitute an unlawful interference with daylight as the kitchen was illuminated by other sources of daylight (other windows).

II. Prerequisites

288. Some elements are needed to determine the tort of private nuisance: a habitual interference, a damage that is defined even by the mere deprivation of the normal enjoyment of ownership and an activity that exceeds the level of endurance of the area (objective criterion of a person's comfort). This last condition is the essence of protection as it leads to the use of a balance of interests between the two neighbours. In this context the subjective sensitivity of one owner is generally indifferent to estimation of the level of endurance. In other words, the tort protects the land, not the person. The estimation of level of endurance depends on the nature of the land. For instance, in a commercial area, more traffic is expected; in an industrial area, more smells are tolerated, etc. It has to be understood that the specific nature of an area does not negate the elements of the tort of private nuisance. It is still possible for the owner to sue and ask for damages or an injunction for any land. However, the judge will take into account the nature of the land when assessing the level of endurance. Furthermore, malicious intent of the tortfeasor is not required, but evidence of it plays a decisive role in the estimation of the balance of interests. The prerequisite of habitual interference states that either a repetition or a continuation of the nuisance is needed in order to sue for private nuisance. Therefore, an occasional party does not count as nuisance.

289. The tort is one of the most important tools, along with negligence, in the arsenal of extra-contractual liability in Cypriot law. Some landmark cases can be cited. In the case *Martha Geroudi v. The Electricity Authority of Cyprus*,[351] the plaintiff was demanding compensation from the State as the operation of the neighbouring electric station caused vibrations, odours and noise in her home. The action was dismissed as the Electricity Authority of Cyprus was simply performing a statutory duty. In the case *Chrystothemis Palantzi v. Nicolas Agrotis*,[352] it was found that

350. *Akama Theofanou et al. v. Ioannou Tsiakoli* (1967) 1 CLR 206.
351. *Geroudi v. The Electricity Authority of Cyprus* (1960) Civil Appeal No. 4309.
352. *Palantzi v. Agrotis* (1968) 1 CLR 448.

the noise coming from a printing plant was not a nuisance because it did not exceed the noise level one would expect to hear next to such a factory.

290. The calculation of damages was dealt with in case *Christos Agathocleous Ltd v. Fotini Sofocleous*,[353] where the incessant movements and manoeuvers of the vehicles of a goods distribution company, located in a quiet area, constituted private nuisance. The owners could not rent out the property anymore because of the noise. Specifically, it was held that 'in the matter of nuisance, as a matter of principle, general damages may be claimed, such as for negligence. However, there is a right to compensation not only based on the damage caused to the property but also with a view to reducing or eliminating its rental value of the land.' However, the assessment of compensation is objective: it did not take into account the rental value based on contractual arrangement before the nuisance, but rather the general rental value of the area for this kind of property.

III. The Legitimate Interest to Sue for Nuisance

291. The tort of private nuisance in common law is a tort against the land. A UK landmark case on this issue is the case *Hunter v. Canary Wharf Ltd* [1997] UKHL 14. Several hundred claimants alleged that the defendant, in constructing a skyscraper nearby, had caused nuisance to them by impairing their television signal. Independent of the first legal issue as regards to whether or not a TV signal constitutes part of a normal enjoyment of a land, the case offers a very important solution to the thorny issue of who is eligible to sue for private nuisance. The ruling establishes that only householders with an interest in a property could sue for private nuisance.

292. However, the legal concept of interest to a property may have a different meaning in the UK than in Cyprus, which has been heavily influenced by Greek and Ottoman law in the field of land law. It is worth mentioning the case *Christos Agathocleous Ltd v. Fotini Sofocleous* (already mentioned above), where the plaintiff did not provide any evidence of ownership of the property. However, the court remarked that the behaviour of the plaintiff (as occupier of the property but also having rented the property to third parties) corresponded to the behaviour of the land owner. Therefore, it accepted that the plaintiff was eligible to file the action.

IV. Special Defence for Private Nuisance

293. In addition, to the general defences available, such as an act of God or the public interest, the law of private nuisance created a specific defence. Section 47 of Cap. 148 states that 'it shall be a defense to any action brought in respect of any

353. *Agathocleous Ltd v. Sofocleous* (2000) 1C CLR 1953.

private nuisance that the act complained of was done under the terms of any covenant or contract binding upon the plaintiff which insures for the benefit of the defendant'.

294. Perhaps it is more important to highlight what is not a proper defence for private nuisance. Indeed, section 48 explains that 'it shall not be a defense to any action brought in respect of a private nuisance that the nuisance existed before the plaintiff's occupation or ownership of the immovable property affected thereby'. This issue, known in common law as 'coming to the nuisance', is therefore absolutely solved in Cypriot law: the question of who was first in the land does not play any role in the assessment of the level of nuisance. Indeed, the ownership of the land does not mean that the owner possesses an interest in the nature of the area. If by the passing of time and/or administrative decisions, the nature of the area gradually changes, the first owner is not eligible to claim merely on the basis of having been there before the change.

§3. Resolution of Boundary Disputes by the Land Registry

I. The Competence of the Land Registry in Boundary Disputes and Corrections of Errors

295. In the event of a boundary dispute, the remedies offered are either by decision of the Director of the Land Registry under section 58 of Cap. 224 or by amicable settlement, without changing the registered border, or by amicable settlement which brings about a change in the registered border – that is, by border adjustment.[354] When the dispute is settled amicably and the position of the border is accepted by the concerned parties, then the plan must be revised.[355]

296. Generally, the Land Registry has enhanced powers that give it a quasi-judicial or law-making role in various fields, such as granting easements and changing the terms of easements, powers to accept and reject claims for the registration of the transfer of land, the sale of jointly owned immovable property in cases where it cannot be subdivided,[356] and the demarcation of boundaries between neighbouring properties. It is section 58 in particular of Cap. 224, which grants the Director of the Land Registry powers to settle boundary disputes. Before the enactment of Cap. 224, all cases of boundary disputes were brought before of the Courts, which as a result were burdened with a heavy workload. In addition, the parties bore high costs, which sometimes exceeded the value of the disputed piece of land.[357] The provision of section 58 does not limit the jurisdiction of the courts but, on the contrary, grants technical jurisdiction to the Land Registry within its administrative

354. Andreas P. Ioannidis, *The Land and Survey Department: Jurisprudence and Land Registry Procedures, 2nd Volume,* 288 (Dorographics Ltd 1998).
355. *Ibid.*, 283.
356. Sections 27 and 28 of Cap. 224.
357. Koutas, *supra* n. 32 at §2, 87.

jurisdiction. It should, therefore, not be considered a barrier to the right of access to the courts, since access to the courts is safeguarded under section 80 of Cap. 224.[358]

297. Case law has held that section 58 gives a broad discretion to the Director for the resolution of the dispute.[359] Furthermore, the Director has a duty[360] to determine the outcome of the dispute effectively, and the Director is in the first instance bound to settle the dispute and determine the boundaries, as best he/she can, in the light of the material and the records held by the Land Registry. Subsequently, the Director of the Land Registry is obliged to resolve the dispute on the basis of the available data.[361] On-the-spot examination is one of the elements considered in resolving the dispute, but on-site examination cannot, without sufficient justification, override what is stated in the cadastral map, which most of the time is an authentic guide to boundary disputes, except re the cadastral map is wrong.[362] The law does not envisage any circumstances under which the Director might conceivably be excused from giving a definitive answer to a boundary dispute.[363] However, the decision issued by the Director of the Land Registry is subject to appeal before a Court, under the relevant provision of section 80 of Cap. 224. The question of the time limits within which a person can claim the resolution of a boundary dispute on the grounds of section 58 was examined by the Supreme Court in *Director of the Land Registry v. Caracotou*. In this case, nine years after the boundary dispute was resolved, one of the parties applied for a repositioning of the boundaries to the Director of the Land Registry, who proceeded to redefine the boundaries by stating that his intention was to correct and replace the cadastral map on which the resolution of the dispute had been based. Both at first instance and on appeal, it was held that the actions taken by the Director constituted an abuse of power and had no legal effect, because the time restrictions of section 80 had not been respected.[364]

298. Another important competence of the Land Registry is the power to correct errors. Section 61 of Cap. 224 establishes the procedure for the correction of errors and for the annulment of a registration in the event of an error or omission. Under the relevant provision, the Director may correct any error or omission in the Land Register or in any book or plan or certificate of registration, and the corrected plan, certificate or book shall then have the effect that it would have had if it had not been processed wrongly. The correction aims to restore the authenticity of cadastral maps, books and records. The procedure starts with a notification issued to the person concerned, and the Land Registry's decision is subject to appeal, on the basis of section 80 of Cap. 224.

299. The increased powers of the Land Registry have given rise to confusion, and have occasionally been misused. In this context, it has been clearly affirmed in

358. *Avgousti et al. v. Spyridou*, Political Appeal No. 114/2012, 24 April 2018.
359. *Georgiou v. Argyrides* (2012) 1 CLR 185.
360. *Komodromou v. Olgas Christaki Kokou* (2013) 1 CLR 1442.
361. *Pitsillides et al. v. Nasif* (1982) 1 CLR 426; *Marcou v. Paschali* (2001) 1 CLR 829.
362. *Anastasiou v. Kyprianou et al.* (2002) 1 CLR 1695.
363. *Pitsillides and another v. Nassif* (1982) 1 CLR 426.
364. *Director of the Land Registry v. Caracotou* (2005) 1 CLR 99.

case law that the competence of the Director of Land Registry to make a correction under section 61 does not extend to solving disputes concerning the ownership of property, which are tried by the competent civil court.[365] Case law has also clarified the nature of the errors and omissions that the Director has the authority to correct under section 61. This procedure can be used when the error or omission can be deduced by means of interdepartmental research, on the basis of evidence held in the Land Registry. In cases where it is necessary to seek out and interview witnesses, the case does not fall within the competence of the Director but is subject to judicial scrutiny.[366] In this context, it has been held that the resolution of a boundary dispute through correction that results in a change of ownership status requires relevant evidence and, therefore, lies outside the competence of the Director of the Land Registry, under section 61.[367] Similarly, it was held that the Land Registry is not competent to decide upon issues concerning false representation and fraud, because these are complex legal concepts which can be evaluated only by a court.[368]

II. Judicial Review of the Land Registry's Decisions

300. The decisions of the Director of the Land Registry are considered definitive, and the Director cannot change a previous decision of his own accord.[369] The only way to reverse such a decision is for any person who is aggrieved by the decision to bring an appeal on the grounds of section 80 of Cap. 224.

301. Section 80 of Cap. 224 specifically provides that any person who has a complaint against a decision, notice or order of the Director of the Land Registry may, within thirty days from the date of notification to him of the Director's act, submit an appeal to the Court.

302. In *Mobil Oil Cyprus v. Stavroula Ellina*,[370] it was held that the right of appeal against a decision made by the Director shall be decided on a case-by-case basis and that any person aggrieved by that decision has *locus standi* to submit an appeal against a decision of the Director of the Land Registry. In the case of *Pegioti v. Polemiti*,[371] Judge Stilianides explained that the term 'aggrieved person' is not

365. *Hassidoff v. Santi et al.* (1970) 1 CLR 220; *Director of the Department of Land and Surveys v. Michalaki Georgiou Stavrou*, Civil Appeal No. 156/2010, 24 March 2015; *Socratous v. Mezou* (1975) 1 CLR 62, *Themistokleous v. Christodoulou* (2010) 1 CLR 1177.
366. *Hassidoff v. Santi et al.* (1970) 1 CLR 220; *Hani v. Director of Land Registry et al.* (1999) 1(C) CLR 1760.
367. *Nikolaou et al. v. Director of Land Registry* (2003) 1 CLR 1676.
368. *Hadjisavva Fella et al. v. Hadjisavva et al.* (2002) 1C CLR 2075.
369. *Solomontos v. Papaneocli* (1992) 1B CLR 906.
370. *Mobil Oil Cyprus v. Ellina* (1990) 1 CLR 837.
371. *Pegioti v. Polemiti* (1982) 1 CLR 442.

synonymous with the term 'dissatisfied person', but that the term implies the element of legal complaint. It was further held that the term should be interpreted broadly and assigned to a person having a legitimate interest within the context of administrative law.

303. The Court has broad competence regarding when hearing an appeal. The Court can reverse the decision and can refer the case to the Land Registry for review or substitute the Director's judgment with its own. It can also decide on the merits of the case without, however, being required to do so.[372]

372. *Kafieros et al. v. Theocharous et al.* (1978) 1 CLR 619.

Chapter 8. Agrarian Problems

304. Cap. 224 does not distinguish immovable property on the basis of its use (arable or for building, housing, etc.). The definition of agricultural land is provided in the Law on the Consolidation and Redistribution of Agricultural Property of 1969 (Law 24/1969). According to this definition, agricultural land is any land that is being cultivated or used for agricultural purposes. For the notions of 'immovable property' and 'owner', the law refers to the corresponding definition in section 2 of Cap. 224. Law 24/1969 provides a broad definition of 'agriculture', which includes horticulture, fruit-growing, seed production, dairy farming, animal breeding (including every kind of animal kept for producing food, fleece wool, leather or fur or using the same for cultivation), the use of land for pasture, basket-making, or as a meadow, orchard or nursery-garden, or the use of land as forest where such use is ancillary to the cultivation of land for agricultural purposes. 'Agricultural', with its grammatical variations, shall be construed accordingly.[373]

305. The main problems solved through the implementation of land consolidation measures are the elimination of the small, fragmented and dispersed land plots, the lack of farm roads, the mixed land tenures (i.e., land held in undivided form and dual or multiple ownerships) and irregularly shaped plots of land.[374] In order to solve these problems, the Land Consolidation Department shall have the power to buy, sell, exchange, mortgage and generally dispose of immovable property and to acquire either by compulsory acquisition or otherwise any holdings for the purposes of any consolidation and reallocation measure. For the buying or disposal of immovable property, the approval of the Minister of Interior is also necessary. The consolidation and reallocation of agricultural holdings can be done either voluntarily, by agreement among the owners, or compulsorily, by resolution of the majority or by an order made by the Council of Ministers.[375]

306. As regards a consolidation and reallocation agreement, this must be properly submitted to the Director of the Land Registry. Where the land consolidation and reallocation agreement covers a property charged with the payment of money or against which any right of way, privilege, liberty, easement or other right or benefit registered or recorded in the books of the District Lands Office exists, the Director shall not approve such agreement unless the consent in writing is submitted to him of the beneficiary of such charge or of the owner of the property in whose favour such right of way, privilege, power, easement or other advantage is enjoyed, as the case may be.[376]

307. Where compulsory consolidation and reallocation is decided by the majority of the owners, a provisional committee, which is elected by the owners, shall

373. Section 2 of the Law 24/1969.

374. *See* the website of the Land Consolidation Department, http://www.moa.gov.cy/moa/lcd/lcd.nsf/dmlmission_en/dmlmission_en?OpenDocument, last visited on 23 Dec. 2019.

375. Section 4 of the Law 24/1969.

376. Section 5(2) of the Law 24/1969.

define the area to be consolidated and reallocated and obtain from the District Lands Office a list containing the names of the owners of the affected area, the total holding of each owner and the recorded details for each holding and its aggregate registered or recorded value as at the date of the request. It shall then make the list of owners together with a land plan, in which the affected area is shown. Any concerned person may, within twenty-one days from the date of the publication of the list, lodge an objection with the Director of the Land Registry, stating the reasons why any property shown in the list as belonging to an owner should not be considered as owned by such owner and also to show the reasons why his name should be included therein. Upon such objection being made, the Director of the Land Registry shall as soon as possible investigate the same and give notice of his decision thereon to the objector and to all other concerned persons and shall, if it is amended, republish the list of owners together with a land plan, on which the affected area is shown. The Director of the Land Registry shall prepare the list of owners in accordance with the existing ownership status for all the affected lands, after verifying, on the spot, the current actual owners of each plot and how it was acquired. Any concerned person aggrieved by such decision may appeal to the Court.

308. After the publication of the list as amended by the Director of the Land Registry, the District Officer shall convene the first meeting of the entitled owners who shall decide in this meeting for or against any land consolidation and reallocation measure being applied to their properties. Where a statement in favour of the measures is signed by the majority of the entitled owners, and where those who have so signed own properties which in the aggregate account for more than half of the total registered value of the affected area, it shall be deemed that a land consolidation and reallocation decision has been adopted. A Land Consolidation and Reallocation Committee shall be responsible for organizing and administering the consolidation and the reallocation and shall take any action necessary for the proper carrying out of land consolidation and reallocation measures in the affected area. The Committee shall also proceed to draw up a plan of new roads, watercourses, channels and other works, having regard to existing and possible future needs for access, irrigation, drainage and soil conservation works carried out or to be carried out under the legislation in force for the time being and the overall development of the area.[377] The Law 24/1969 provides some safeguards for pre-existing rights over the lands which are affected by the consolidation and reallocation measures. With regard to leases, any provision for the modification, transfer or cancellation of an existing lease of property within the affected area shall be published together with the consolidation and reallocation plan, and whenever it is decided for compensation to be paid as a result of the submission of objections or appeals, it shall be paid at once by the Committee and shall be recoverable from any person who benefits from the modification, transfer or cancellation of an existing lease, provided that if the Committee finds itself unable to decide whether any benefit accrues to any particular person from the new arrangements regarding leases, the whole amount of the compensation or the balance thereof shall be payable towards the expenses of consolidation and reallocation measures. For encumbrances over the affected lands, the

377. Section 20 of the Law 24/1969.

law provides that any encumbrances shall be ascertained and examined by the Committee who shall advise the owners on means open to them through which they can free the said property therefrom. At the time of the preparation of the land consolidation and reallocation plan, the Committee shall have the power to provide therein for the transfer of encumbrances on to holdings or for amending them or even cancelling them, provided that in such a case compensation shall be payable. Any right of way, privilege, liberty, easement or any other right or advantage enjoyed in connection with roads, channels and watercourses which has been abolished shall be cancelled together with the roads, channels and watercourses.

309. In *Mousiavessiis v. the Republic of Cyprus*, the applicant argued that Law 24/1969 infringed his/her property right under Article 23 of the Constitution, as the consolidation of land is a burdensome measure that results in the deprivation of property, without following the necessary procedure of compulsory acquisition provided in Law 158(I)/99. The Supreme Court, however, did not examine the substance of this argument, since it was found that the applicant's argument was vague and did not provide any evidence on how extensively the property of the applicant will be affected.[378]

310. Finally, the Council of Ministers has the power to decide the consolidation and reallocation if this is necessary for the construction of a dam or other expensive irrigation or other land improvement works to be carried out by the Government. Such a consolidation and reallocation order shall be published in the Official Gazette of the Republic. The procedure to be followed for land consolidation and reallocation following an order of the Council of Ministers shall be the same as that provided by this law in the case of land consolidation and reallocation following a resolution of the owners.[379]

378. *Mousiavessiis v. Republic of Cyprus*, No. 1473/2009, 17 July 2013.
379. Section 39 of the Law 24/1969.

Chapter 9. The Legal Framework of State Guardianship

311. In order to better understand the interaction between private and public law in the field of Cypriot real property law, it is necessary to refer briefly to a striking particularity of the Cypriot legal system: the law of necessity. The hostilities between the two communities posed a number of extremely difficult challenges for the Cypriot legal system. Since the State was structured under the Cypriot Constitution to function on the basis of the cooperation and participation of both communities in its administration, a serious danger of paralysis arose. The answer to this deadlock was provided by the Supreme Court in the famous *Mustapha Ibrahim*[380] decision. Here, the law of necessity was recognized as a fundamental legal axiom that could permit the State to function. Under the law of necessity, in the event of an unavoidable emergency that poses an objective threat to the existence of the State, administrative acts may be undertaken which would have been deemed illegal under normal circumstances.[381]

312. On the basis of the law of necessity, a special law governing the administration and protection of the property of Turkish Cypriots situated in non-occupied zones was promulgated. Law 131/1991 establishes a regime of State guardianship for properties belonging to Turkish Cypriots that are situated in the non-occupied part of Cyprus.

313. The Ministry of the Interior is designated as the Guardian of these properties. In exercising its powers, the Guardian enjoys all of the rights and duties that the Turkish Cypriot owners should have had. Therefore, the Guardian is entitled to manage the property, to collect monies owed to the beneficiary, to raise or defend actions in court relating to such property, and generally, to exercise any rights and to perform all obligations arising from contracts that were concluded between the Turkish Cypriot owners and other persons before the enactment of the Law. As it is expressly stated in the preamble of the law, its primary purpose is for the Guardian to oversee the preservation of these properties. However, the law also serves secondary and other purposes, such as improving the situation of Greek Cypriot refugees who lost their properties in the Turkish occupied zones. Indeed, the Guardian often rents these properties to such refugees.

314. As regards the status of rights, the Guardian certainly has wide-ranging powers, but does not have the right to alienate the property, other than in exceptional cases where this is deemed beneficial for the Turkish Cypriot owner.[382] The guardianship regime is temporary in nature. The law expressly provides that such

380. *The Attorney General of the Republic v. Mustapha Ibrahim* (1964) CLR 195.
381. *See* Constantinos Kombos, *Le Droit de la necessité à Chypre*, in: *Rosseto J. & Joséphides K., La singularité de Chypre dans l'Union Européenne, Diversité des droits et des statuts*, 373 (Mare & Martin 2012).
382. Section 6 of Law 139/1991.

guardianship will come to an end when the 'abnormal situation' created by the Turkish invasion ends.[383] Throughout the period from the entry into force of the Law in 1991 until the end of the situation of 'necessity' and the issuance of a notification to this effect by the Council of Ministers, the Guardian is deprived of the power to grant to the owner the property which is considered as 'Turkish Cypriot property' under guardianship.[384] All monies collected by the Guardian, for example income from leasing the properties, are kept in a special account and will be paid over to the owner of the property once the regime ceases to exist.

315. The conformity of this law with the Cypriot Constitution, and more precisely with Article 23 of the Constitution governing the protection of property, has been examined by the Cypriot Supreme Court. The Supreme Court has consistently found the law to be in compliance with the Constitution on the grounds of the law of necessity,[385] which allows limitation of the exercise of fundamental rights, such as ownership. In this context, it was held that depriving the owner of the right to exercise ownership is justified it is temporary and imposed by the need of maintaining the social order.[386] Furthermore, the guardianship of abandoned Turkish Cypriot properties by the Republic is part of public policy, and therefore any agreement between individuals attempting to circumvent or even neutralize the provisions of Law 139/1991 will not be enforceable.[387] The status of State guardianship was also found by the Cypriot Courts to be compatible with the European Convention on Human Rights.[388] As it was held, the aim of the law is to protect the properties which have been abandoned and to correspond also to the needs of the refugees which had to leave their properties in the occupied part of Cyprus.[389]

316. In general, the Guardian has all the rights and obligations that the Turkish Cypriot owner would have.[390] At the same time, the recognition in law of the Turkish Cypriot owner as the sole and true owner of the real property has been consistently confirmed by the courts. Nonetheless, the owner of the property cannot have the possession of the land[391] and cannot dispose of it without the permission of the

383. Section 2 of Law 139/1991.

384. *Fezile Ahmet v. Republic of Cyprus*, No. 1482/2010, 24 September 2012.

385. *Solomonides Ltd et al. v. Attorney General et al.* (2003) 1(B) CLR 1275; *Mehmet Shakir et al. v. Republic of Cyprus et al.* (2013) 3 CLR 54.

386. *Ahmet Mulla Suleyman v. The Republic of Cyprus*, No. 99/2005, 21 May 2007.

387. *Alexandrou v. Eleftheriou*, No. 2043/2011, 22 June 2015. *See also Nadjiye Mushawar et al. v. Republic of Cyprus*, No. 405/2011, 18 July 2013, where, as regards the transfer of the property by the Turkish Cypriot owner to a company established in Cyprus, it was held that the transfer of Turkish Cypriot property on the condition of safeguarding the possession of the property by the refugees is not possible, since there was no proof that the Cypriot company was controlled by Turkish Cypriots.

388. *Oguz Onkaya et al. v. Attorney General et al.*, No. 1314/13, 27 March 2014.

389. *Natia Christodoulou v. Minister of the Interior*, as the Guardian of Turkish Cypriot Property through the Attorney General of the Republic, No. 331/2014, 29 July 2016.

390. *The Lost Resort Ltd v. Municipality of Paphos*, No. 1283/2016, 13 January 2017.

391. The rights of possession and management of the property are subject to strictly necessary restrictions in accordance with Art. 23.3. of the Constitution. *See Ahmet Mulla Suleyman v. The Republic of Cyprus, supra* n. 386.

Guardian. Any such transaction shall be deemed to be unlawful and contrary to public policy if the Guardian's prior consent is not obtained.[392] Therefore, it is possible to transfer the property to the children of the owners with the consent and permission of the Guardian.[393] Since the Guardian is not considered to be the owner of the property, the Guardian is not competent under Law 139/1991 to give consent for the compulsory acquisition of immovable property by the State and the only person who can challenge the legality of the expropriation is the Turkish Cypriot owner.[394]

317. A question that has led to contradictory decisions of the Supreme Court in the past was that of whether the guardianship regime could still apply if the Turkish Cypriot owner moves to the non-occupied zone for permanent residence. More specifically, section 2 of Law 139/1991 provides that all properties belonging to Turkish Cypriots who do not have their residence in the non-occupied zones are subject to guardianship. This provision was interpreted as enabling the law to apply to properties belonging to Turkish Cypriots who did not have their permanent residence in the non-occupied areas on 1 July 1991, the date on which the law entered into force. While in the case of *Arif Moustafa v. Ministry of Interior*[395] the distinction drawn among Turkish Cypriots between those who had their permanent residence in the non-occupied zone at that date and those who did not was held to be unjustifiable and arbitrary, in its later case law the Supreme Court took the opposite view.[396] Accordingly, even if a Turkish Cypriot subsequently moved to non-occupied Cyprus, this would not justify the full restitution of his right of ownership, because once a property has come under the guardianship regime, it should remain under this regime for as long as the 'abnormal situation' continues.

318. The guardianship also applies to Vakf property,[397] despite their reinforced protection in Article 23(10) of the Constitution.[398] Vakf property includes both movable and immovable Muslim religious property as well as objects and subjects of

392. *Perihan Mustafa Korkut or Eyiam v. Apostolou Georgiou* (2008) 1B CLR 905.
393. *Fezile Ahmet v. Republic of Cyprus*, *supra* n. 384.
394. *Kiazim Halit et al. v. the Republic of Cyprus*, No. 18/2005, 29 November 2006. As regards the consent of the Guardian of Turkish Cypriot Property to the expropriation and acceptance of the amount of the compensation, the Guardian's consent does not deprive the Turkish Cypriot owners of the expropriated property from the legal interest they have to object to the expropriation. Nonetheless, after the amendment of Law 139/1991 with the Law 9(I)/2010 the owner can have recourse to court only on the grounds of s. 6 of Law 139/1991 (the owner shall bring an action before the District Court with a claim against the Republic and the Guardian for the alleged infringement and claim for the infringement the remedies provided for in this section) *See Shahap v. Republic of Cyprus*, No. 205/03, 4 May 2018.
395. *Arif Moustafa v. Ministry of the Interior*, No. 125/2004, 24 September 2004.
396. *Ali Ibrahim Houssein Basma v. The Republic of Cyprus*, No. 1353/2008, 3 September 2009; *Perihan Mustafa Korkut or Eyiam v. Apostolou Georgiou* (2008) 1B CLR 905; *Stavrou Georgiou v. Minister of Interior*, No. 5/2014, 9 January 2015.
397. *Solomonides Ltd et al. v. Attorney General et al.*, *supra* n. 385; *Ms Mishas Investments Ltd v. Minister of Interior*, No. 938/2012, 04 April 2014.
398. According to this provision, '10. Notwithstanding anything contained in this Article, no deprivation, restriction or limitation of any right provided in paragraph 1 of this Article in respect of any Vakf movable or immovable property, including the objects and subjects of the Vakfs and the properties belonging to the Mosques or to any other Moslem religious institutions, or any right thereon

the Vakufis and properties belonging to the mosques or any other Muslim religious institution.[399]

319. Nevertheless, the legal situation underwent a significant change in 2010. The law was amended, and it is now possible for a Turkish Cypriot to apply to the Ministry of the Interior for his property to be removed from the regime of compulsory guardianship. The Guardian can do this by means of a reasoned decision only in exceptional circumstances, one of which is a situation whereby the Turkish Cypriot moves to non-occupied Cyprus for permanent residence.[400] If the Guardian refuses to agree to the restitution of the property to the Turkish Cypriot, the latter can bring an action before the competent District Court.[401] However, even if restitution is ordered by the Court, it may have significant adverse consequences for the original owner, since the law provides that the owner might be obliged to compensate either the Guardian or the person who occupied the property with the Guardian's permission, for the cost of repairs and other expenses incurred with a view to the upkeep or improvement of the property.[402]

320. As regards the judicial protection of the property, the Guardian is the competent person to bring an action for trespass and not the owner. Specifically, for a Turkish Cypriot owner to apply to the Court for any claim in relation to his property covered by the provisions of Law 139/91, it is a prerequisite that he/she shall first refer to the Guardian and only if his/her claim is dismissed can the owner bring an action before the District Court.[403]

321. The compliance of the remedies of the amended law with the European Convention on Human Rights was examined by the European Court of Human Rights in the case *Kazali and Others v. Cyprus*,[404] where it was held that 'the new provisions in Law 139/1991 are formulated in broad terms and by express reference to the guarantees of the Convention as interpreted by this Court. They allow the applicants to make a claim to the Custodian alleging a violation of their Convention rights and, in the absence of a favourable response, to lodge a case in the District Court. The remedies available include an order for restoration of the property and an order for payment of compensation to cover pecuniary and non-pecuniary damage as well as costs and expenses.' In this context it was also held that 'Law 139/1991 as amended provides an accessible and effective framework of redress in

---

or interest therein shall be made except with the approval of the Turkish Communal Chamber and subject to the Laws and Principles of Vakfs and the provisions of paragraphs 3, 4, 7 and 8 of this Article shall be subject to the provisions of this paragraph: Provided that restrictions or limitations for the purposes of town and country planning under the provisions of paragraph 3 of this Article are exempted from the provisions of this paragraph.'

399. Costas Paraskevas, *Cypriot Constitutional Law* 397 (Nomiki Vivliothiki 2015).
400. Section 3(b) of Law 139/1991.
401. Section 6A of Law 139/1991.
402. Section 6A(6) of Law 139/1991.
403. *Oguz Onkaya v. Attorney General*, No. 1314/13, 27 March 2014.
404. ECHR, *Ali Kamil Karamanoglu and others v. Cyprus*, No. 49247, 6 March 2012.

respect of complaints about interference with the property owned by Turkish Cypriots.' This finding was also confirmed in *Mehmet Yilmaz v. Republic of Cyprus*.[405]

405. ECHR, *Mehmet Yilmaz v. Republic of Cyprus*, No. 4722/05, 28 August 2012.

Part II. Movable Property and Personal Property/Chattels

Chapter 1. General Classification

§1. Tangible Movable Property: 'Fixtures/Chattels' and 'Goods'

322. As already mentioned, there is no general statutory definition of tangible movable property in the Cypriot legislation, while the concept of movable property is subject to various definitions depending on the legislation.

323. Due to the influence of English law and doctrine, the common law principles on fixtures and chattels are also applicable in Cyprus. More specifically, although the concept of fixtures and chattels is not expressly established in Cap. 224, an indirect reference to these concepts results from the definition of immovable property in section 2. According to this definition, the concept of immovable property also comprises buildings and other erections, structures or fixtures affixed to any land or to any building or other erection or structure and trees, vines, and any other thing whatsoever planted or growing upon any land and any produce thereof before severance.

324. The law of fixtures is founded on the maxim *quicquid plantatur solo cedit.* That is, whatever is attached to the land becomes a part thereof. Chattels that are so affixed to the land as to become a part of it, lose its character as chattel and pass with the ownership of the land. Buildings and structures that are firmly attached to the earth are 'fixtures', while attachments that are not firmly connected to the earth are 'chattels'. To determine if a land-related object is a 'fixture', emphasis shall be given to whether its actual connection to the earth is continuous and stable and also to the objective purpose of its connection to the earth.[406] This was further affirmed in Cypriot case law with reference to UK doctrine in *Vereggaria Papakokkinou v. Dimou Paphou,*[407] where it was held that 'Cap. 224 does not specify what is a "fixture", but may be said to be a building or structure, or structure that is positioned, erected or applied to land or a building so as to constitute part of the land or building. The two key elements answering the question of whether such a structure or

406. Gray & Gray, *supra* n. 99 at 33 et seq. *See D'Eyncourt v. Gregory* (1866) LR 3 Eq 382; *Leigh v. Taylor* [1902] AC 157; *Elitestone Ltd v. Morris and Another* [1997] 1 WLR 687.
407. *Papakokkinou v. Dimou Paphou* (1998) 1 CLR 2398.

building is an appendix (fixture) of the land are: (a) the extent of the attachment and (b) the purpose of the attachment. (See Cheshire's "Modern Law or Property", 12th Edition, p. 138). According to Woodfall the appendix refers to objects attached to the earth (see Woodfall "Landlord and Tenant", 27th Edition, p. 695) and according to Megarry "includes anything attached to the earth so as to be part of it of the earth (see Megarry and Wade *The Law of Real Property*, p. 643)".'

325. Furthermore, the legislation related to the sale of goods, which was prior to 1994 part of the general Contract Law (Cap. 149) gives a definition of 'goods'. According to section 2(1) of Law 10(I)/1994 on the sale of goods, '"goods" means every kind of movable property other than actionable claims and money and includes stocks and shares, growing crops, grass, and things attached to or forming part of the land which are agreed to be severed before sale or under the contract of sale.' The distinction in Cyprus between immovable and movable property follows the UK's dichotomy between real property and personal property. It has been ruled for instance that a ship is a kind of movable property.[408]

326. However, this reference to the notion of goods in the sale of goods legislation cannot be extended to all legal issues related to movable property. Characteristically, the legislator has added another definition of 'goods' in the part of the Contract Law (Cap. 149) related to bailments. According to section 106 of Cap. 149, 'goods' means 'every kind of movable property and includes bills of exchange, promissory notes, bonds whether in customary forms or no other that those secured by mortgage of immovable property, share certificates or share warrants for shares in a company'. It is explained however that this definition is to be used only as regards bailment contracts.

§2. Intangible Movable Property and Choses in Action

327. There is no evidence in the definition of section 2 that intangible movable property is not included in the definition of goods. However, in the English case *St Albans City and District Council v. International Computers Ltd*,[409] the court declined to apply the category of goods to a software. Also, in the US case *Moore*[410] it has been ruled that mere information (in this case the DNA of a patient used by a doctor in order to obtain a patent) is not protected as a good. The court found that Moore had no property rights to his discarded cells or to any profits made from them.

328. Intangible movable property is therefore governed by intellectual property law. For original content, the Copyright and Related Rights Law of 1976 (Law 59/1976) will apply. As regards industrial property law, patents are governed by the Patents Law of 1998 (Law 16(I)/98). Trademarks are governed by the Trade Marks

---

408. *Panayiotis v. 'SHIP MARIA'* (1983) 1 CLR 497.
409. *St Albans City and District Council v. International Computers Ltd* [1996] 4 All ER 481.
410. *Moore v. Regents of the University of California* 51 Cal. 3d 120; 271 Cal. Rptr. 146; 793 P.2d 479.

Law (Cap. 268). Designs are governed by the Designs Law of 2002 (Law 4(I)/ 2002). In all cases, the European Union's intervention in this field has been substantial, resulting in the harmonization of the existing legislation on industrial property and, to a large extent, the harmonization of copyright laws too.

329. Copyright law provides to the author (defined as the creator of the original content) economic and moral rights. The economic rights, as harmonized by the EU legislation, are the right of reproduction, the right of communication to the public, the resale right, the right to distribution and the rental right. The moral rights are imposed by the Berne Convention for the Protection for Literary and Artistic Works law, which Cyprus ratified in 1960, and are twofold: (1) the right of paternity and (2) the right to protect the integrity of the intellectual work. In Cyprus, following the common law tradition, transfer of all the economic rights (assignment of property) is allowed. Contracts related to the assignment of rights are to be in writing. Furthermore, copyright law recognizes neighbouring rights, that are economic rights given to intermediaries to the creation (film or music producers, broadcasting organizations, artists/interpreters, database producers).[411]

330. Inventions are protected by patents upon registration at the Registrar of Patents' office. It has to be proven that the invention is new, involves an inventive step and is susceptible of industrial application. Cyprus is a member of the Patent Cooperation Treaty (The International Patent System) and of the European Patent Convention since 1998.

331. Both trademarks and designs receive a double, hybrid protection. A registration procedure exists, where the office examines the distinctive character of the trademark and whether similar or identical prior marks exist, or the novelty and the individual character of the design. As regards designs, this dichotomy is inscribed in the legislation, as harmonized at EU level. As regards trademarks, unregistered trademarks will still receive a protection under the tort law Cap. 148 section 35. The section prescribes in Cypriot law the common law tort of 'passing-off'.[412] Section 35 states that 'Any person who by imitating the name, description, sign, label or otherwise causes or attempts to cause any goods to be mistaken for the goods of another person, so as to be likely to lead an ordinary purchaser to believe that he is purchasing the goods of such other person, shall commit a civil wrong against such other person: Provided that no person shall commit a civil wrong by reason only that he uses his own name in connection with the sale of any goods.' Two substantial prerequisites are therefore to be found: that the plaintiff has created, by use in the Cypriot market, an intangible asset, closely related to his/her name, brand or product, and that a risk of confusion exists in the mind of the average consumer due to the imitation of this intangible asset by the defendant.

411. For an analysis of Cypriot copyright law, *see* T.E. Synodinou, *Copyright news from Cyprus*, 261 Revue Internationale du droit d'auteur (2019).

412. *Jonitexo Ltd. v. Adidas* (1984) 1 CLR 263.

§3. FUNDS (CAPITAL; INVESTMENT FUND)

332. Cyprus legislation on sale of goods differs from the UK as it includes stocks and shares in the definition of the goods, following the example of the corresponding Indian legislation.[413] This particularity has been adopted by the jurisprudence, that applies the sale of goods disposition to the transfer of stock and shares.[414] The main significance of the insertion of stocks and shares in the sale of goods framework lies in the application of section 56 of the Law 10(I)/1994 related to the calculation of the damages allowed to the seller. Independently of the value of the shares, the seller is entitled to demand the price fixed by the contract, as held in the case *Christofi v. Kleanthous.*[415]

333. It has to be noted that while the English version of the legislation refers to stocks, which can be construed in a strict manner (as the Indian Courts have done[416]) in order to exclude bonds, the Greek translation uses a larger term that encompasses every kind of fund. The doctrine therefore requires a strict approach to be taken by the Cypriot Courts in this area, as a broad definition of 'stocks' could potentially create some contradictions between the Sale of Goods Law and the Companies Law (Cap. 113).[417]

§4. CHATTELS PERSONAL AND CHATTELS REAL

334. The categories of chattels personal and chattels real are not officially established in Cypriot law. The categories of property which have been recognized are immoveable property (which is officially defined in Cap. 224) and personal or movable property (which is sporadically and inconsistently mentioned in different legislations and case law). *See* Part II, Chapter 1, §1. Additionally, the concepts of 'goods' and 'chattels' are also used. *See* General Introduction, §3, II, A.

In general, Cypriot law has been influenced by the methodological prototype of English law, where real property is distinguished from personal property. This division roughly corresponds to the division between immovables and movables in continental law.

The category of 'immoveable property', modelled on English law, includes 'incorporeal' components which are also considered as 'realty' and, par consequent, are distinguished from 'personalty' (personal or movable property). Personal property interests, which are also known as 'chattels', could be further subdivided into chattels personal (interests in tangible movables and in intangibles) and chattels real (personal property interests in land). Since Cypriot land law recognizes the Roman law concept of ownership, the significance of chattels real (mainly leasehold) is less

413. Indian Sale of Goods Act 1930.
414. *See Christodoulou v. Eurika Ltd* (2008) 1 CLR 1243.
415. *Christofi v. Kleanthous* (2010) 1 CLR 1050.
416. *R D Goyal and Anr v. Reliance Industries Ltd* (2003) 1 SCC 81.
417. Evripidis Hatzinestoros & Giorgos Charalampous, *Cypriot Sale of Goods Law and Consumer Protection* 28 (Nomiki Vivliothiki 2016).

important than in English law (*see* principally the limited-term ownership right arising from long-term lease registration: Part I, Chapter 4, §4). Chattels personal could be further distinguished into choses in possession (interests in tangible movables, including goods) and choses in action (interests in intangibles, including promissory notes and rights of action).

Chapter 2. Legal Interests

335. The classification into legal and equitable (beneficial) interests is only informally established in Cypriot legislation.

336. For legal interest in immovable property to lawfully arise, such interest must have been created under the provisions of Cap. 224 and the Immovable Property (Transfer and Mortgage) Law of 1965 (Law 9/1965) and the formalities (registration) for its formation must have been met. At the same time, the door has been left open for the introduction of certain legal tools of the law of equity in order to add some flexibility. Indeed, even if *a priori* the application of the law of equity is expressly excluded by section 4 of Cap. 224 in respect of the acquisition of real property, equity still has a role to play. Where formalities are not met, it is possible that a court will recognize an equitable proprietary interest on the basis of the mechanism of trust or proprietary estoppel. Legal interests bind all third parties, whereas equitable interests only bind third parties who are not bona fide purchasers for value of a legal estate without notice.

Chapter 3. Equitable Interests

337. The concept of equitable interests in movable and personal property has only sketchily been recognized by Cypriot case law. UK case law principles are applicable.

338. With regard to movable property, forms of equitable proprietary interest include trusts and floating charges over the assets, or a class of assets, of the grantor from time to time. For chattels, UK case law principles are applicable.

339. Any property whatever can form the subject matter of trust, whether that property be tangible ('chose in possession') or intangible ('chose in action'), while it is also irrelevant whether the interest subject to trust is legal or equitable. Property subject to trust must be capable of being identified.[418] Criminal law provisions related to theft are applicable to trust, as the beneficiary has an equitable interest on the good.[419] Furthermore, the notion is explicitly mentioned at section 64 of Commercial Shipping Law 45/1963, that states that the law does not forbids the recognition of equitable interests.

340. A mere delivery, on the condition that it is accompanied by the intent to transfer on trust, is sufficient for the establishment of an express trust.[420] In general, as it was noted in *Markidou v. Kilaris*, with reference to UK case law,[421] 'Whether a particular transaction amounts to an equitable assignment, is a matter to be gathered from the contents of the document relied upon as setting up an assignment.'[422] With regard to the assignment of a debt, it was held that an equitable assignment does not have to be in any particular form because equity looks to the intent rather than the form. Therefore, an equitable assignment of a debt, which is a chose in action (personalty), made between an assignor and an assignee, is complete even if no notice has been given to the debtor concerned.[423] Whether a particular transaction results in an equitable assignment is a matter to be decided on the basis of the documents relied upon as setting up an assignment.[424]

341. The concept of the beneficial owner has been established in case law. In *Papadopoulos v. Blue Emblem*, the Supreme Court held that the concept of '"ownership" in section 1(1)(a) of the English Administration of Justice Act, 1956 is not limited to legal ownership but it extends to "beneficial" or "equitable" ownership as well and that the aforementioned English Act is applicable in Cyprus by virtue of the provisions of section 29(2) of the Courts of Justice Law 14/1960.' Therefore, 'it

418. A.J. Oakley, D.B. Parker and A.R. Mellows, *Parker and Mellows: The Modern Law of Trusts* 17 (9th ed., Sweet & Maxwell 2008).
419. *Ioannidis Andronikou v. Cyprus* (2008) 2 CLR 486.
420. Oakley, Parker and Mellows, *supra* n. 418, 111.
421. *IRC v. Electric Industries* [1949] 1 All ER 120-6.
422. *Markidou v. Kilaris* (1983) 1 CLR 392. For equitable assignments, *see also Loukas Andreas v. Eurolife Ltd* (2009) 1 CLR 1524.
423. *Chrysostomou Chalkousi & Sons v. Chalkousi & Sons* (1978) 1 CLR 10.
424. *IRC v. Electric Industries* [1949] 1 All ER 120-6.

follows that the question whether the notions of "beneficial" or "equitable" ownership are known to the Law of Cyprus should be answered in the affirmative'.[425]

342. An old Cypriot case,[426] adopting the common law's relevant case law on this matter, held that a wife's rights in relation to occupation of the matrimonial home, where that was the property of her husband, were personal rights against her husband, deriving from her status as wife, and did not confer on her any equitable interest or right of property in the land. Nor was she, if she lived in the matrimonial home, there as licensee of her husband.

343. In the Cypriot case *Ayoub*,[427] the Supreme Court adopted all principles set out in the UK case *Independent Trustee Services Limited v. GP Noble Trustees Limited & Others* [2012][428] relating to the bona fide buyer. It means that, as a rule, where a bona fide purchaser subsequently transfers the property to a volunteer or even to persons with notice of a prior equitable interest, those transferees nevertheless take free of such interests and that the effect of a transfer of property to a bona fide purchaser is to extinguish any prior equitable interest.

425. *Papadopoulos et al. v. BLUE EMBLEM* (1985) 1 CLR 453 (1985) 1 CLR 453.
426. *Papasavva Theodoros v. Theodoros Papasavva* (1979) JSC 157.
427. Supreme Court, *Ayoub v. Director of land registrar*, No. 5165/2012, 20 November 2018.
428. *Independent Trustee Services Limited v. GP Noble Trustees Limited & Others* [2012] EWCA Civ 195.

Chapter 4. Security Interests (*See Also* Parts I, IV and V)

344. As a common law country, Cyprus recognizes all traditional forms of security interests. That includes mortgage ('true' legal, equitable or statutory), fixed equitable charge, or bill of sale, floating equitable charge, pledge, legal lien, equitable lien and hypothecation.

Part III. Acquisition of Property Rights

Chapter 1. Transfer of Property by Contract *Inter Vivos*

§1. General Principles Applying in the Transfer of Land

345. The conditions and the procedure of transfer of immovable property are defined in section 40 of Cap. 224, together with the Transfer and Mortgage Law 9/1965.

I. The Transfer of Immovable Property in Cap. 224 and the Transfer and Mortgage Law 9/1965

346. Under section 40 of Cap. 224, three elements are critical for the validity of transfer of immovable property. The first is the necessity of registration of transfer. No transfer of, or charge on, any immovable property shall be valid unless registered or recorded in the Districts Land Office. In this way, a system of formalities and transparency is established in relation to the registration of transfer and charges on immovable property, which are not evidential but constitutive in nature. The necessity of registration as a condition for the validity of transfer has also been consistently confirmed in Cypriot case law. For example, in *Rodothea Papagheorghiou v. Antonis Savva Charalambous Komodromou*,[429] the Court stated that 'a dowry that concerned immovable property, which did not comply with the conditions of section 40 of Cap. 224, that is a transfer which was not registered in the recipient's name and not recorded, is invalid'.

347. The rule established under section 40, along with the exclusion of the application of the law of equity, under section 4, regarding the acquisition of real rights, which nevertheless exempts trusts, places at the core of Cypriot land law the concept of the necessity of registration. The principle of the necessity of registration results in the following legal effect regarding: the extent of the transfer: the object of the transfer is everything that are mentioned in the title of ownership and does not include any other rights, which may exist due to adverse possession but which have not been registered.

429. *Georghiou v. Komodromou* (1963) 2 CLR 221. The principle of the necessity of registration concerns all the transfers which took place after the date that Cap. 224 came into force and not those which took place under 'the old law'; *Spanou v. Savva* (1965) 1 CLR 36.

348. The second important principle is that the transfer of land can be made only by the registered owner. Only the registered owner has the right to transfer. No transfer affecting any immovable property shall be carried out in the Land Registry by any person other than the registered owner of the property. The above principle stems from the fundamental principle of Roman law, *nemo plus juris ad alium transferre potest quam ipse habere.*[430] This rule is adopted by section 4 of the Transfer and Mortgage Law of 1965. In section 4 it is provided that the owner of the immovable property has the right to transfer it or mortgage it, while section 2 of the Law of 1965 defines 'owner' to mean 'the registered owner of the immovable property'. According to section 3 of Cap. 224 '"owner" means the person entitled to be registered as the owner of any immovable property whether he is so registered or not'.[431] The principle of transfer of immovable property only by the registered owner has been confirmed in the case *Ayios Andronikos Development Co. Ltd v. The Republic of Cyprus*, where the Court denied the application of common law and the law of equity rules in relation to a transfer of immovable property.[432]

349. Another fundamental principle that is established in section 12 of the Immovable Property (Transfer and Mortgage) Law of 1965 is that immovable property cannot be transferred unless it is free of any charge, encumbrance or prohibition (for an analysis, *see* section V. 'Transfer in Case of an Encumbered Immovable Property').

II. The Concept of Transfer of Immovable Property

350. Section 5 of Law 9/1965provides that '[n]o transfer of property or creation of a mortgage is valid, unless it takes place under the provisions of this law'. The law concerns only the transfer of immovable property and the creation and transfer of the real charge of mortgage. Thus, the law does not regulate the procedure of creating other real charges or other real rights in relation to immovable property. In this context, section 5(3) defines that the provisions of section 5 do not apply in relation to the acquisition of any right, privilege, liberty, easement or other advantage under sections 11 and 12 of Cap. 224. Nevertheless, the provisions of this law apply to transfers made in respect of granting shares of a company or to the capital account of a partnership (legal entity or partnership) or to transfers between a company and a consultant or a shareholder thereof or between a consortium and partners.[433]

---

430. That is the principle '*nemo dat quod non habet* rule'. *See* Alison Clarke & Paul Kohler, *Property Law, Commentary and Materials* 393 (Cambridge University Press 2005): 'no one can transfer to anyone a bigger interest over the land than the one he has'.

431. In *Michaelides v. Ttapoura* (1980) 1 CLR 610, the Supreme Court held that '"Entitled to be registered" is a term not confined only to cases of a claim by virtue of a prescriptive right but it includes, in our view, the case where all the formalities for an effective transfer under the law have been complied with and there only remains the recording of the registration by the appropriate Lands Clerk to complete it.'

432. *Ayios Andronikos Development Co. Ltd v. The Republic of Cyprus through the Minister of Interior, the Director of Lands and Surveys and the Minister of Finance* (1985) 3D CLR 2362.

433. Section 6 of Law 9/1965.

351. The acquisition of immovable property by legal entities is specifically regulated by the Legal Entities (Registration of Immovable Property) Law (Cap. 218). The Cap. 218 establishes that legal entities are equal to natural persons as regards the acquisition and possession of immovable property, while it explicitly provides that the legal entity in whose name an immovable property has been registered obtains the same rights given to natural persons in respect of the sale, disposition and mortgage of immovable property. The registration must be made in the name of the legal entity and immovable property registered in the name of the legal entity is considered to be collectively held by the legal entity, without taking into account the shares or the interests of the partners.[434]

352. As regards immovable property, transfer means the transfer of the title over the immovable property to another person. Subsequently, a prerequisite condition for the transfer of immovable property is the existence of a title deed, while the transfer of title is followed by the registration of the new owner in the Land Registry.

353. At the same time, the concepts of owner, transferor and acquirer are also defined. As already mentioned, the owner is considered to be the registered owner. The acquirer is defined as the person to whom the immovable property or the mortgage is willingly transferred, while the transferor is the owner who transfers the immovable property or the mortgaged lender who transfers the mortgage. The transfer of immovable property is considered to be completed after passing through three distinct but interdependent stages. These are: the submission of the declaration of transfer, the acceptance of the declaration by an officer of the Land Registry and the registration of the acquirer as the owner.

354. The Supreme Court in *Nicosia Race Club v. Republic*[435] examined whether section 5 of the Transfer and Mortgage Law of 1965 also the registration of property in the name of a nominee or agent or any other person holding otherwise than as an owner. In this case, the applicants passed a resolution authorizing their Committee to create 'a trust and appoint a trustee for the purpose of transferring the immovable property of the club into the name of such a trustee', appointed as trustee the Bank of Cyprus Ltd and authorized one of its members to transfer, on their behalf, 'free of charge' the immovable property of the club into the name of such trustee. Under the terms of a trust deed created for this purpose, the applicants retained absolute ownership and control of the property mentioned in the trust deed, and the trustee was appointed 'to hold the said property to be used, sold, leased, mortgaged or otherwise dealt with, as the appointers from time to time would direct' in accordance with the rules of the club. Then, the applicants applied to the Director of the Department of Lands and Surveys, requesting that the said property be registered in the name of Bank of Cyprus Ltd in its capacity as trustee of the property of the Club. The Director replied that for such registration, a written declaration of sale or gift had to be made in accordance with the provisions of section 18 of the

434. Section 6 of Legal Entities (Registration of Immovable Property) Law (Cap. 218).
435. *Nicosia Race Club v. The Republic (Minister of Interior et al.)* (1975) 3 CLR 73.

Immovable Property (Transfer and Mortgage) Law of 1965 (Law 9/1965), and the fees and charges provided by the Department of Lands and Surveys (Fees and Charges) Law had be paid. In this context, the applicants contended, *inter alia*, that what they asked for from the Director was not a transfer within the meaning of the said section 5, but a mere registration in the name of the said trustee without endorsing any conditions of servitude in the certificate to be issued, there being no legal obstacle in registering the property in question in the name of the trustee. They argued in this respect that section 5 does not mention that 'no transfer shall take place', but only that 'no transfer shall be valid'. Consequently, the applied registration could be effected, as the issue of the certificate of registration would not amount to either a sale or a gift, but a mere transfer. Furthermore, the fact that the Director can act in the present case and effect the transfer pursuant to section 18(1)(c) of Law 9/1965 as a trust, falls within the category of 'gratis' transfers envisaged by this sub-section.

355. The Court analyzed the meaning of the concept of 'transfer' in Law 9/1965 and dismissed the applicant's recourse. As it was explained, 'The question of registration of immovable property is regulated mainly by sections 39–65 of Part III of the Law. A consideration of these provisions together with the definition of "owner" to be found in section 2 of the Law, meaning, the person entitled to be registered as the owner of any immovable property, whether he/she is registered so or not, has led me to the conclusion that in Cyprus, registration can only be effected in the name of the owner of immovable property and a transfer, whether under Law 9 of 1965 or the Immovable Property (Tenure, Registration and Valuation) Law, Cap. 224 is a transfer of the title of the property and nothing else. Sub-section (2) of section 40 of the Law provides that no transfer or voluntary charge affecting any immovable property shall be made in the District Lands Office by any person, unless he is the registered owner of such property, the only exception being, the case of an executor or administrator of an estate of a deceased person, who, for the purposes of this sub-section, is deemed to be the registered owner of any immovable property registered in the name of the deceased. Sections 42, 43 and 44 which deal with the case of compulsory registration of unregistered property, general registration and procedure in individual cases, show that the registration to be made of immovable property is in the name of the respective owner.' On the basis of the above, it was held that 'there can be no registration in the records of the District Lands Office and no consequential issue of a certificate of registration, unless the person so registered is the owner of immovable property as defined in section 2 of Cap. 224. This being so, the registration in the name of a nominee or agent or any other person holding otherwise than as an owner thereof, is excluded by our Law, whether he is called a trustee or not … Therefore, in the absence of any provision by which the registration claimed by the applicants could be effected, there is no legal obligation in the administration to proceed to registration.'

III. Declaration of Transfer of Immovable Property

356. Section 8 of Law 9/1965 sets out the procedure of the declaration of transfer. The transferor and the acquirer must appear before the Land Registry and declare and sign the transfer.[436] The certificate of registration (i.e., the title deed) of the transferred property must also be attached to this declaration, given that, as already mentioned, transfer is considered to be the transfer of the title.

357. Section 18 defines the compulsory content of the declaration of transfer. It shall consist of an accurate description of the immovable property (location, registration number and date, value and portion or interest which will be transferred), a confirmation that the state of the property has not changed, a certificate for whether the property is under lease or not, a certificate of the transferor that he is the owner and has agreed to transfer the property as a grant or for consideration on a specific date, a certificate that this does not constitute a 're-transfer' back to the transferor for consideration or for any other reason, that they know each other and if they are relatives their degree of kinship, as well as a declaration regarding the existence or not of any encumbrance over the immovable property pursuant to section 11 of Cap. 224, such as an easement, which shall be declared and signed by both the transferor and the acquirer.

358. Therefore, it is obvious that the declaration of transfer must accurately reflect the state of the immovable property (description of the property, existence of any leases, restrictive covenants, encumbrances, easements), so that the subsequent registration be accurate. In this way, 'the mirror principle', as it is widely known, is manifested, according to which, the Registry shall reflect the all the real rights and charges concerning a title of ownership.[437] A search in the Registry must reveal the nature of the property and its restrictions. If the status of real rights is fully reflected, then the purchaser is protected. In fact, this is a rule that promotes commercial purposes and the security of transactions.

359. At the same time, when the declaration of transfer takes place before the Land Registry's office, a certificate of registration in the name of the transferor owner shall be submitted, along with invoices proving that all the rights, taxes and the disposition tax of the immovable property have been paid.[438]

360. In every transfer, there is an implied term that the transferor has the right to transfer and that the acquirer can enter, occupy, possess, use and enjoy all the profits from the immovable property without interruption and without any intervention from the transferor.[439] Subsequently, unless otherwise explicitly defined, the

436. This procedure takes place under the use of a specific form, namely the form no. 270.
437. Dixon, *supra* n. 82 at 38.
438. *See* s. 18(3)(a) and (b).
439. Section 20 of Law 9/1965.

acquirer obtains all the powers of the registered owner and he/she can enjoy the use and profits of the property, without the intervention from the transferor, who is alienated from the property.

361. The procedure of the acceptance of the transfer is considered to be complete, when the acquirer deposits to the Land Registry the registration fees. Thus, the procedure of the transfer is not completed with the acceptance of the declaration of transfer. Even after the acceptance of the declaration, but prior to registration, the Director may order an inquiry into the property.[440]

362. A refusal by the Registrar to accept and approve a declaration of transfer falls under the category of private law disputes.[441]

IV. Transfer of an Undivided Share in an Immovable Property

363. Section 25 of Cap. 224 introduces an estoppel as regards the transfer and registration in relation to the transfer of an undivided share in an immovable property to a non-co-owner, while at the same time provides a right of first purchase to the co-owner in order to buy the share that is being sold. According to section 25, when an owner of an undivided share in any immovable property makes a declaration before the District Lands Office, on the basis of section 18 of Law 9/1965 that he has agreed to sell the same to a person who is not a registered co-owner in the same property (i.e., the latter does not acquire a percentage of ownership in the immovable property), the transfer of such share shall not be registered, unless a specific procedure is followed, according to which all the registered co-owners must have been informed, and they do not wish the acquisition of the transferred undivided share in the immovable property. More specifically, the owner of the undivided share, who wishes to sell it, shall satisfy the Director in sixty days from the

440. Section 13(5) of Law 1965.
441. As it was held in *Hellenic Bank v. The Republic of Cyprus* (1986) 3 CLR 481 CLR: 'The particular decision of the Registrar to accept or refuse registration of a charge or mortgage is of no particular interest to either the public or any section of it. It is only of interest to the parties immediately affected thereby: The company of the mortgagee and its creditors. The decision to refuse registration is not taken by any reference to administrative policy or discretion, but in accordance with set principles of private law. As counsel for the applicants acknowledged, there is no lack of machinery to ventilate the dispute before the civil courts, the constitutional forum for the resolution of disputes affecting property rights. Moreover, the law has stipulated penal sanctions in the interest of its effective enforcement.' This is also the case as regards the declaration of transfer of a Turkish Cypriot property, which is under the special regime of state tutelage. *See* Torgut Yashar as proxy of *Yuksel Cemal Hudaverdi v. The Republic of Cyprus through the Director of Lands and Surveys*, No. 454/2002, 16 September 2004; *G. Spyropoulos Developments Ltd v. 1. Attorney General of the Republic, 2. Minister of Interior as Guardian of the Turkish Cypriot properties and 3. Director of Lands and Surveys*, No. 626/2005, 4 October 2006; *Molivo Ltd v. 1. Attorney General of the Republic, 2. Minister of Interior, 3. Director of Lands and Surveys*, No. 778/2005, 27 November 2006; *Altan Salih Niazi v. The Republic of Cyprus through the Minister of Interior*, No. 631/2005, 10 November 2006; *Andreas Pericleous (Ktimatiki) Ltd, v. 1. Attorney General of the Republic, 2. Minister of the Interior as Guardian of Turkish Cypriot Property, 3. Director of Department of Lands and Surveys*, No. 627/2005, 18 December 2006.

date of the advertisement of the proposed sale[442] that the rest of the registered co-owners do not wish to purchase his share at the price at which it is being sold.

364. The prospective purchaser shall advertise the proposed sale or bring it to the knowledge of the other owner(s) within sixty days from the date of the declaration of sale. The acceptance of the declaration and the registration of the purchaser as the new owner will only take place, if no other co-owner is interested in buying the proposed for sale share. The proposed sale is to be advertised in a form and in such newspaper or newspapers as the Director of the District Lands Office may require, or it can be brought to the knowledge of the other owner by serving on him a notice in writing that is in a form that the Director may require. The other registered co-owner may be registered for this share within thirty days from the date of the written notice or the publication, by lodging in the District Lands Office the price at which the interest is being sold, along with the registration fee, and this amount shall be paid to the party that participated in the declaration of sale as purchaser.

365. In fact, the purchaser is being alienated and replaced by the other registered co-owner in the transfer agreement. In other words, the acceptance of the declaration and the registration, if they have been conducted lawfully and if the relevant fees have been paid, will take place after the expiration of thirty days' time from the date of the receipt of the notice or the publication and provided that the rest of the undivided share co-owners do not show any interest in purchasing.

366. In case more than one co-owner pays the price and registration fee for the share that is being sold, the Director registers the seller's portion in the name of the co-owners in proportion to their shares. In addition, the declaration of transfer is annulled if no evidence of the written notice or notification to the other registered co-owners is submitted to the Director.[443]

V. Transfer in Case of an Encumbered Immovable Property

367. Under section 12(a) of the Transfer and Mortgage Law of 1965, the transfer of immovable property that is subject to encumbrances is prohibited, and a declaration of transfer in relation to such immovable property will not be accepted by

442. According to case law, s. 25 applies only in relation to the sale and not in relation to the exchange of immovable property, despite the fact that in the Explanatory Law the terms 'sell' and 'sale' include 'exchange, barter and offer, or demonstration for sale'. *See Georgios Iraklidis & Sia Ltd et.al v. Director of the District Lands Office et al.*, Application-Appeal No. 10/99, 26 January 2001; *Cantounas v. Ioannis N. Patsalides General Entreprises Ltd*, 2004 1C CLR 1876.

443. *See Palaiomylitou v. Panagiotou et al.* (2003) 1A CLR 407, where it was held that the inheritance right of a co-owner to an undivided share of immovable property and the right of first purchase, which is acquired by the co-owner on the basis of s. 25, outweigh the contractual right of a third party to whom immovable property was transferred under the specific performance of the contract between the latter and the co-owner who sold his share without following the procedure provided in s. 25.

the Land Registry. A list of charges which operate as encumbrances is established in Part I of the First Schedule to the Immovable Property (Transfer and Mortgage) Law 9/1965. It mainly comprises mortgages, memoranda, writs, the charge that is created by the deposit of a contract of sale of land etc.

368. In this respect, registration has a vital role to play, since the encumbrance cannot impede the transfer unless it is declared and registered at the Land Registry. This rule, which operates for the protection of the transferee, is subject to an important exception. In the case of mortgaged property, a transfer is permitted under certain conditions, such as the transferee's informed declaration that he is aware of the existence of the mortgage.[444]

369. As provided, no declaration of transfer of immovable property with an encumbrance thereon, or whose owner is under prohibition, shall be accepted. The same section defines also the concept of real charge.[445] Encumbrance is regarded to be the direct claim on land, lien or liability, which exists under any law. According to section 12(7)(a), the real charge has been notified to, or any document relating thereto has been declared, registered, produced or lodged, with the District Lands Office in order to have legal effects. In other words, the registration formalities must be followed and the registration fees paid. Thus, the rule prohibiting the transfer of immovable property subjected to an encumbrance is not absolute.

Pursuant to section 12A of Law 9/1965, a specific procedure was introduced in relation to the sale of any immovable property which is subject to an encumbrance or is affected by an interim order of the Court which prohibits the property's owner from alienating such property. This procedure is relevant to all encumbrances and not just to mortgages. Such immovable property may be transferred by a declaration of sale and by depositing the proceeds of sale with the competent Land Registry Office, which shall accept such declaration as long as the sale price referred to in the declaration is not less than the amount fixed by the Court as reflecting the market value of the immovable property and as long as no appeal has been filed against the decision of the Court fixing the market value. In order to follow this procedure, the owner of such immovable property must have filed an originating summons and served it upon those in whose benefit the encumbrance or aforementioned interim order exists, whereupon the Court shall determine the market value of the immovable property. Any interested person may, not earlier than four months from the date on which the decision of the Court was issued, apply to the Court for reconsideration of the market value of the immovable property as determined by the Court. If such appeal is exercised, the Land Registry shall not accept any declaration of sale in respect of the immovable property referred to in the application until the issue of a decision on such application. Finally, the proceeds of sale deposited at the Land Registry shall be disposed of in order of priority among the persons for whose benefit the encumbrance on the immovable property exists. The second exception concerns the transfer of an immovable property subject to mortgage. According to section 31 of Law 9/1965, the transfer by its owner of a mortgaged

444. Section 31 of the Immovable Property (Transfer and Mortgage) Law 9/1965.
445. Section 12(5)(a) of Law 9/1965.

immovable property. It must be emphasized that a mortgage arises out of a contract of mortgage. In particular, there are two cases. On the one hand, if the mortgage contract does not contain a clause that prohibits the transfer of the mortgaged immovable property, the transfer can take place without the permission of the mortgagee, provided that the acquirer confirms and signs that he is aware of the current mortgage. On the other hand, if the mortgage contract contains a prohibition clause in relation to transfer, the transfer can only take place upon the written permission of both the mortgagee and the rest of the guarantors. If the mortgage refuses to give his permission without a legitimate reason, the Court can order the transfer without his consent.

370. The registration of an easement is not considered as an encumbrance or charge that prevents the transfer, but the right of easement is considered as an attachment to the immovable property that is being transferred. Consequently, the transferee acquires the immovable property with the burden of the easement. In case the dominant tenement is being transferred, the easement is also 'part' of the immovable property that is being transferred. This principle is established in section 12 of Cap. 224 where it is stated that where any easement has been acquired in respect of an immovable property, this right shall be deemed to be attached to such property to be included in any dealing made with such immovable property.

VI. Acquisition of Immovable Property by Third-Country Nationals: Restrictions and Incentives

371. Cyprus has established some limits on land ownership in order to exclude foreigners from the land market. These limits, which are seen as an assertion of national sovereignty,[446] have been significantly affected by the accession of Cyprus to the EU.

372. Specifically, special restrictions are laid down in the Immovable Property Acquisition (Aliens) Law (Cap. 109), which provides that the acquisition of immovable property by a foreigner requires the granting of a special authorization by the Council of Ministers. This power was granted to the District Officers. Registration made without this authorization is invalid. For EU citizens, restrictions on the acquisition of immovable property in Cyprus continued to apply to those who did not have their habitual residence in Cyprus until 1 May 2009.[447] Since then, European citizens, whether or not they have a permanent residence in Cyprus, have been fully equated to Cypriots and can acquire real property under the provisions of Law 9/1965.

446. Peter Sparks, *European Land Law* 64 (Hart Publishing 2007).

447. This was possible because the Treaty of Accession of Cyprus to the European Union provided for a five-year extension period for maintaining certain restrictions on European citizens by way of derogation from Art. 39 of the EEC Treaty.

373. The Immovable Property Acquisition (Aliens) Law (Cap. 109) sets out a number of criteria on the basis of which it is presumed that the control of a company belongs to foreigners. In particular, a company is controlled by aliens if half or more than half of its directors are foreigners, or if half or more than half of the voting power is in the hands of persons who are aliens or persons exercising their voting powers on behalf of persons who are aliens, or if half or more than half of the shares are owned by foreigners, or if a foreigner at the time of the acquisition of ownership by the company has any of the powers conferred on him by the articles of association or other founding document to ensure that the operations of the company are carried out at his will; or if the interest in controlling the company is half or more than that of a foreigner or of a company controlled by a foreigner.[448]

374. The power of the District Officers is broad and includes the power to conduct on-the-spot investigations at discretion. If an on-the-spot investigation is not possible for practical reasons, and in particular because the land is located in areas not controlled by the Republic, permission to acquire the property may be refused. As held in *Jerusalem and the East Mission Trust (Cyprus) v. In the Republic of Cyprus*, permission may be refused if 'it is impossible to control the legal conditions for granting the permission to acquire the described property, due to the denial of access to the competent authorities because of the Turkish occupation. The Republic of Cyprus has legal jurisdiction throughout Cyprus, but the exercise of its jurisdiction over the occupied territories is effectively hampered by the presence of occupying invasion troops. Therefore, the Republic cannot, due to its occupation status and its genuine inability to control the application of the Law in the occupied areas, approve the application for the necessary permission to acquire the described property.'[449]

375. As regards the validity of the agreement of sale, this is not affected. The restrictions and the procedure of Cap. 109 concern only the registration of the transfer and not the ability of the foreigner to conclude the contract and the validity of the contract of sale under Cap. 149. Paradoxically, concluding a valid contract of sale in accordance with the requirements of Cap. 149 does not grant the foreigner the right to acquire the property without the required permission.[450] The foreigner may deposit the contract for the purpose of special performance under the terms of Law 81(I)/2011.

376. Furthermore, Cyprus has developed an ambitious investment program, which also comprises the acquisition of land as a means for obtaining Cypriot

---

448. It has been held that a company is not controlled by foreigners when two of its three directors are Cypriots, when more than half of the share capital is owned by Cypriots, the foreign shareholders and the foreign director have no special powers and none of them have never performed the duties of the Chairman of the Board of Directors of a company. *See Spartacos Estate Ltd v. The Republic of Cyprus through the Minister of Interior* (1978) 3 CLR 365.

449. *The Jerusalem and the East Mission Trust (Cyprus) v. Republic of Cyprus through 1. Council of Ministers 2. Minister of the Interior* (1998) 4 CLR 598.

450. *See Iosifakis Andriani A et al. v. Mohammed Abdul Ghani* (1967) 1 CLR 190; *Michel Saab, Mediterranean Paper Manufacturers Ltd v. The Holy Monastery of Ayios Neophytos* (1982) 1 CLR 499.

nationality. More specifically, the acquisition of Cypriot nationality on the basis of acquisition of land requires that the applicant must have made an investment of at least EUR 2 million for the purchase or construction or development of real estate for housing or commercial purposes, for tourism development or for other infrastructure projects. This criterion also includes investment in building land, provided that the application will include an investment plan for the development of the land.[451]

§2. General Principles Applying to Sales of Goods

I. Transfer of Property and Transfer of the Risk

377. The notion of transfer of the risk encompasses all situations whereas the goods have been damaged or even destroyed between the moment of the conclusion of the contract and the moment of the delivery of the goods, without apparent fault of the seller or the buyer. If the risk is transferred, then the buyer is deemed to be responsible for the goods. If not, the seller is liable for the damages.

378. In order to ascertain, on the basis of the Law 10(I)/1994 on Sale of Goods, whether the risk has been transferred or not, it is vital to analyze first the agreement between the parties and the object matter of the contract. Both existing goods as well as future goods are included in the definition of goods in the legislation. However, in this case, according to section 4(3) of Law 10(I)/1994, if the contract refers to a future transfer of goods (which includes the transfer of future goods), the contract is not a 'sale of goods' but 'an agreement to sell', which will automatically become a sale of goods when the conditions are met. The distinction is important, since if the goods are damaged while the contract is still an agreement to sell, then, according to section 8, there is no need to discuss the transfer of the risk. Instead, the contract is void. This applies only to the sale of specific goods.

379. Before calculating the moment of the transfer of the risk, there is a need to draw some distinctions. Specific goods mean goods identified and agreed upon at the time a contract of sale is made (section 2 of Law 10(I)/1994). Section 18 states that, when the contract concerns not specific goods but unascertainable goods, the transfer of property is delayed to the moment when the goods will become specific. In the classic English case *Kursell v. Timber Operators & Constructors (1927)*, merchantable timber was defined as 'all trunks and branches of trees but not seedlings and young trees less than 15cm in diameter at a height of 4 feet from the ground'. The buyer had fifteen years to cut the timber. The Court found that the goods were not specific, as it was too difficult to quantify and identify them.

380. Contrary to the general principle adopted in most continental countries, Cyprus follows the common law tradition of a transfer of the risk appreciated not at

451. *See* s. 111A of the Register of Population Laws of 2002–2019.

the moment of the delivery of the goods, but at the moment of the transfer of property. This follows the logic that the owner is responsible for the protection of the goods. Section 26 explains that the transfer of the risk does not intervene in cases whereas a liability is found, either due to a breach of the contract of sale of or on the basis of establishing liability under the principles of the law of bailment. On the same basis, the risk is transferred together with the property only, unless decided otherwise by the parties.

381. Section 19 of Law 10(I)/94 imposes three consecutive conditions to the transfer of property. In paragraph 1, it states that ownership is transferred when it is the intent of the contractual parties to transfer it. In paragraph 2, it adds that in determining the true intent of the parties, all the terms of the contracts but also the behaviour of the parties and the circumstances related to the contract must be taken into account. In paragraph 3, finally, it creates a simple presumption of transfer: if no clear intent is found in the contract, either explicitly or by way of interpretation, then the transfer of property is deemed to have occurred at the moment of the conclusion of the contract. Section 20 explains that in this situation, the transfer of ownership happens independently of the payment of the price or of the delivery of the goods. By exception, the transfer of ownership is delayed when the sale provides for an estimation of the goods (section 22). For instance, in a Cypriot case, the buyer had ordered a sofa but the delivery of the goods was delayed several times. The buyer finally asked for the contract to be rescinded. The court ruled that it was too late for that: as the sofa was in this case a specific good, its ownership had already been transferred at the moment of the conclusion of the contract.[452]

382. In conclusion, when the sale concerns a specific good and no intent as regards as the moment of the transfer of ownership can be construed from the contract or the behaviour of the parties, both the ownership and the risk are transferred at the moment of the conclusion of the contract. For unascertainable goods, it is necessary to wait for the goods to be in a 'deliverable state' (section 23). The deliverable state is not only a physical differentiation of the goods, that becomes specific as distinguished from similar goods, but must also be consented to by the buyer, pursuant to section 23. This consent may be either explicit or implicit and pure silence and acceptance of the goods will mean consent.

383. Neofytou v. Stylianou [453] may be seen as a landmark case law on this issue. A wine producer agreed with a farmer to buy grapes from a specific land. The harvest would be the responsibility of the wine producer and could occur at his/her discretion, after payment of the price. Before the conclusion of the contract, the wine producer had the opportunity to taste the grape and find it suitable. During the harvest a few days later, it appeared that the grapes were damaged. The Supreme Court ruled that it was a sale of specific goods. Therefore, the risk was transferred with ownership, after the payment of the price, when the wine producer had discretion to start harvesting the grapes.

452. *Krasa v. Ikeea G.S. Siakola Ltd* (2007) 1 CLR 532.
453. *Neophytou v. Stylianou* (1992) 1 CLR 541.

II. The Acquisition of a Good from a Non-owner

384. Another general principle stated by the Sale of Goods Law is the transposition of the classic *nemo dat quod non habet* rule. First, it has to be noted that the acquisition of a good from a non-owner may concern two different situations: the double sale from the owner to two distinct buyers or the sale from a third party to the owner (who could be the possessor) to a buyer. Section 14 creates some implicit statutory terms as regards these situations. First, there is an implicit condition that the seller has the right to sell the goods. It means that in case of the sale of goods from someone who is not the owner, the buyer can engage the liability of his/her counterparty, and the contract is voidable. Second, there is an implicit warranty that the buyer will peacefully enjoy the possession of the goods and that the goods are free from securities that have not been declared during the conclusion of the contract. For instance, in an English case, the court found liable the seller of a road marking machine on the basis that a third party possessed a patent on the machine, which would disturb the peaceful enjoyment of the goods by the buyer.[454]

385. The principle *nemo dat quod non habet* ('the buyer acquires no better title to the goods than the seller had') governs the situation of the third party who is the owner of the goods. Is he/she entitled to claim the goods from the hands of the counterparty of the seller? Section 27 states as principle that the third party does not acquire any kind of interest on the goods, which, therefore, should return to their owner. However, this principle recognizes a series of exceptions, namely the mechanisms of estoppel, bona fide buyer and market overt. These exceptions are welcome as they intent to protect the safety of the commercial transactions.

386. Estoppel by representation is a mechanism of the law of equity, but in this case its application is codified in the second limb of section 27. From the moment that the sale of goods is pursued through an agent, the buyer acquires a good title even if it appears at the end that the agent acted *ultra vires* or even without mandate.

387. The case of the bona fide buyer is governed by sections 28, 29 and 30 of the Sale of Goods Law. Section 28 deals with the specific situation of co-ownership. Sale by one of the co-owners will bind the other ones if it is proven that the buyer acted in good faith (in this case, the viable ignorance of the issue concerning the co-owner's capacity to sell). Section 29 states that when the seller of goods has obtained possession thereof under a contract voidable under section 18 or section 19 of the Contract Law (Cap. 149), – that is, on the grounds of false representation, fraud, coercion and undue influence – but the contract has not been rescinded at the time of the sale, the buyer acquires a good title to the goods, provided he buys them in good faith and without notice of the seller's defective title. Section 30 deals with the double sale, when the seller (who is by definition no longer the owner) has kept the possession of the goods. Here again, the buyer in good faith acquires a good title.

---

454. *Microbeads v. Vihurst Road Markings* (1975) 1 WLR.

388. The exception of market overt is not covered by the sale of goods legislation. However, it is a common law exception that traditionally applies when the buyer acquires the goods from a display in an open area, such as a (flea) market. The Cypriot case *A Pilottos ltd and others v. Houghton and others* [455] concerned the sale of a second-hand car from England by a commercial agent. When the car was destroyed during a fire, it was found that the car had in fact been stolen in the UK. It is noted that in case of stolen goods, none of the good faith exceptions are applicable. The Supreme Court considered that the good faith of the buyer, plus the fact that the conditions of acquisition of the cars were similar of the situation of market overt, meant that the buyer had acquired a title on the car.

III. The 'Guarantee'

389. Important legislation has been developed as regards consumer protection, with emphasis not only on the information right, the withdrawal right and the protection against unfair terms, but also on the legal guarantee against hidden defects of the goods. While an extended analysis of this legal framework would exceed the scope of the present work, it is worth noting that a similar mechanism already existed and is still valid on a more general level for all sales of goods.

390. Section 16 of the Sale of Goods Law states as a principle that there is no implied warranty or condition as to the quality or fitness for any particular purpose of goods supplied under a contract of sale. However, a series of exceptions applies. First, in the case of sale by description (section 15) or of sale by sample (section 17), the seller is bound by an implied condition as regards the description of the goods or the sample. That means that all of the goods have to correspond to the description in terms of quality and that the goods have to be free from all the hidden defects that could have not been apparent on reasonable examination.[456]

391. Furthermore, in section 16 it is stated that, when it is in the course of the seller's business to supply the goods in question, an implied condition is inserted in the contract that the goods shall be of merchantable quality. This means suitability for all purposes for which goods of this kind are usually supplied, appearance and finishing free from defects, free from micro-defects, security and durability of the goods (section 16.4). Furthermore, if the buyer has also informed the seller of his/her specific purpose, an additional implied condition is inserted, as the seller is liable that the goods shall be reasonably fit for such purpose.

455. *Pilottos Ltd et al. v. George Houghton et al.*, under the commercial name Sports Car Consultants (2007) 1 CLR 783.

456. *See* the landmark case *Grant v. The Australian Knitting Mills* [1936] AC 85. The buyer of a woolen garment claimed that it had caused him to get dermatitis. It was found to be defective due to the presence of excess sulphites, which were negligently left behind during the process of manufacture. For the judges, there was a sale by description even though the buyer was buying something displayed before him on the counter, as the good did not meet the implied description as regards the materials of the garment.

392. In *Palazi v. Elexif ltd and others*,[457] a manufacturer of solar water heaters constructed a series of devices using materials bought from a counterparty, who sold collectors suitable for the manufacture of open circuit water heaters (whereas the manufacturer needed collectors for closed circuit). While the first devices started to show signs of defect, the manufacturer continued buying the collectors for some time. The Court considered that in the first sales, the goods were not of a suitable quality for a reasonable use. However, as the problem had appeared, the defect was known to the buyer and all the subsequently sales were not covered by the guarantee.

393. Several Cypriot cases have dealt with defective products. *Magistrato Gardens Ltd v. Cyprus Republic*[458] concerned the water distribution towards a plantation during a drought. Due to the bad quality of the water, some plants died. The Court found that the water distribution company was liable. The goods were indeed not suitable for a reasonable use by a reasonable person. In another case, the sale concerned a defective system of cooling for cars,[459] and the Court considered that the buyer should have discerned the defect during the examination of the goods.

IV. The Unpaid Seller's Rights

394. The unpaid seller's rights are described in section 47 of the Sale of Goods Law. By definition, the non-payment of the whole of the price constitutes a substantial breach of contract and the seller is entitled to sue for the price. The term 'unpaid seller's rights' encompasses other prerogatives of the parties, some of them functioning as a security. Indeed, the most fundamental unpaid seller's right is the recognition of a 'lien' on the goods for the price while the seller is in possession of them. This lien corresponds to the physical closeness between the buyer and the goods, and it is automatically lost the moment the seller cedes the possession of the goods (section 50). The in rem nature of the lien is explicitly stated in section 54, which explains that the lien is not affected by potential resale of the goods by the buyer.

395. Additionally, in case of the bankruptcy of the buyer, the seller gains a right of stopping the goods in transit after he has parted with the possession of them. Similarly, where the property in goods has not passed to the buyer, the unpaid seller has a right of withholding delivery similar to and co-extensive with his rights of lien and stoppage in transit where the property has passed to the buyer.

396. Furthermore, in some circumstances explained below, he/she possesses a right of resale. This right has to be limited in specific circumstances, since, while justified in practice by the necessities of commerce, it is clearly a legal anomaly. Not only does it violate the *pacta sunt servanda* principle, but also the principle that

457. *Palazi v. Elefix (water and technics) Ltd et al.* (1997) 1 CLR 286.
458. *Magistrato Gardens Ltd v. Attorney General of the Republic*, Appeal No. 261/2008 (2012).
459. *A. P. Georgiades Ltd v. Space Bakery Plant & Equipment Ltd* (2001) 1 CLR 916.

the ownership of the goods has already been transferred to the buyer. Section 55(2) states that 'Where the goods are of a perishable nature, or where the unpaid seller who has exercised his right of lien or stoppage in transit gives notice to the buyer of his intention to re-sell, the unpaid seller may, if the buyer does not within a reasonable time pay or tender the price, re-sell the goods within a reasonable time and recover from the original buyer damages for any loss occasioned by his breach of contract, but the buyer shall not be entitled to any profit which may occur on the re-sale. If such notice is not given, the unpaid seller shall not be entitled to recover such damages and the buyer shall be entitled to the profit, if any, on the re-sale.' Therefore, a reasonable time must be given to the buyer as a prerequisite and two alternative conditions are set for the right to be available: either the goods are perishable or the seller has already exercised his lien or right of stoppage in transit. The notification of the buyer also plays a substantial role: with notification, the resale functions as if the goods were the property of the seller, while without notification, the seller actually works as an agent of the buyer.

Chapter 2. Transfer of Property on Death

§1. Introduction

397. Inheritance law is mainly governed by Wills and Succession Law (Cap. 195) and the Administration of Estates Law (Cap. 189), which deals with the execution of wills and the administration of estates respectively.

398. The Cap. 195 incorporates principles of both English and Roman laws. As Judge Josephides stated in the case *Anastassis Charalambous v. Alkis Demetriou,*[460] the part of this law concerning wills is based on English law and the sections relating to succession are based on Roman law. Succession to an estate may be either by will or by the operation of law or by will and by the operation of law.[461]

399. According to section 3 of Cap. 195, on the death of a person, his estate will pass as a whole to one or several other persons. According to Tsikkinis, the law establishes the rule of succession in *universitatem hereditatis of* Roman law, thus, the principle of universal succession according to which the estate of the deceased as a whole, and not in parts, passes to the successors (heirs) directly on the death of the deceased and the successors succeed the deceased not only in his rights but also in his liabilities.[462] The heirs are not liable for the debts of the deceased. The estate is liable for these debts and only when the debts are paid off can the property be distributed to the heirs.[463]

400. The Cap. 195 is applicable only to the legacy of persons who have domicile in Cyprus.[464] So, in the case of succession to the movable property of any person, Cap. 195 is applicable only in relation to the person who at the time of his/her death had his/her domicile in Cyprus. In relation to immovable property, Cap. 195 is applicable to the succession to any land located in Cyprus regardless of whether the owner of the property has domicile in Cyprus. In the case of *Siddika Mehmet Kochino v. Derenishe Irfan,*[465] the Court stated that Cap. 195 does not regulate the succession to property which is not located in Cyprus. Succession related to immovable property outside the Republic of Cyprus is governed by the *Lex Situs* (jurisdiction of the location of the property). The notion of 'estate' in Cap. 195 cannot, therefore, be treated as including immovable property outside Cyprus.

460. *Anastassis Charalambous v. Alkis Demetriou* (1961) 1 CLR 30.
461. Section 2 of the Wills and Succession Law (Cap. 195).
462. Lefkios Tsikkinis, 'Law of Succession', in *Introduction to Cyprus Law, Andreas Neocleous & Co* Ch. 15 (Yorkhill Law Publishing 2000) with reference to *National Bank of Greece v. Metliss* (1957) 3 All ER 612.
463. *See* ss 41(b) and 42 of Cap. 189.
464. Section 5 of Cap. 195.
465. *Siddika Mehmet Kochino v. Derenishe Irfan* [1976] 1 CLR 240.

401. Succession to movable property of persons dying in Cyprus but not domiciled there shall be regulated by the law of the country in which they had their domicile before the decease.[466]

402. The incapacity to succeed is regulated by section 17 of Cap. 195, where a series of grounds of incapacity are established. The incapacity is not absolute in the sense that it may be annulled and removed if the deceased has voluntarily and in express terms pardoned the otherwise incapacitated by a declaration made in writing or by provision made to that effect in his will.[467]

§2. Succession Through Will and Statutory Portion

403. Will is defined as the legal declaration in writing of the intentions of a testator with respect to the disposal of his movable property or immovable property after his death and includes codicil.[468] Section 23 of Cap. 195 provides the formalities of a will. Revocation of wills is regulated by section 37 of Cap. 195. Cypriot law establishes specific rules about the disposable portion of the estate (that can be freely disposed) and the statutory portion of the estate (that cannot be disposed by will).[469]

404. Similar to English law, in general the rights and liabilities attaching to the estate of the deceased are vested in the administrator of his estate or the executor of his will referred to in the law as 'personal representatives', except for certain deviations found in Cap. 189.[470] Renunciation to the estate is possible, and in that case, the heir will have no liability and will receive no benefit from the estate.[471]

405. Whether money is also included in the concept of 'mobile property' in the context of succession by will depends on the interpretation of the terms of the will. UK case law can be used as persuasive precedent.[472] In *Terzis v. Kekkou Petoufas,* the Supreme Court held that, according to the interpretation of the will and its whole spirit, a monetary sum found in the testator's home safe after his death is not included in the term 'movable property'.[473]

406. Cypriot succession law establishes the rule of a statutory portion of an estate under a will and intestate succession. The statutory portion is the portion of the testator's estate that is bequeathed to the testator's relatives or spouse despite the testator's intent or even though the testator has reduced the future legacy by

466. Section 12 of the Wills and Succession Law (Cap. 195).
467. Section 18 of Cap. 195.
468. Section 2 of Cap. 195.
469. Section 41 of Cap. 195.
470. Tsikkinis, *supra* n. 462.
471. Section 51 of Cap. 189.
472. *Walsh v. Walsh and Others* (1953) 1 All ER 1982 (movable property does not include money).
473. *Terzis v. Kekkou Petoufas* (2011) 1 CLR 336.

means of free handover to such an extent that the legal heir entitled to a statutory portion of the estate only receives a portion smaller than the one prescribed by law.

407. Specifically, where there is a child, the disposable portion of the inheritance may not exceed 25% of the net value of the estate. If there is no child but only a spouse or parents (father or mother) the disposable part must not exceed 50%, and in all other cases the entire inheritance can be disposed by will freely by the testator.[474] If the testator disposes more than the disposable portion, the will shall not be considered null and void as a whole, but the disposal of the estate will be reduced according to the provisions of the law.[475] The provision of section 51 of Cap. 195 is also relevant. According to this provision, any child or other descendant of the deceased who becomes entitled to succeed to the statutory portion and to the undisposed portion, if any, shall in reckoning his share bring into account all movable property and immovable property that he has at any time received from the deceased by way of advancement or under marriage contract or as a dowry or by way of gift made in contemplation of death. It is understood that no such movable property or immovable property shall be accounted for if the deceased left a will containing a special provision for the non-calculation of such movable property or immovable property.

408. The reasoning and the interpretation of Article 51 were analyzed by the Supreme Court in the case *Kyriakidis et al. v. Dikigoropoulos et al.*[476] As it was stated, 'the legislator, in establishing the provisions at issue, as the Court of First Instance points out, aims at the safeguarding of the equality of the inheritance right. However, the implementation of the redistribution of property upon this provision does not aim at achieving a posteriori equality between the descendants. The aim is not to place the child that during the life of the heir received less property than the property received by another child in equal measure with the one who received the most, but to prevent the child that received more valuable property to receive equal part with the least favored child. Accordingly, the law aims to redistribute the inheritance shares in a way that does not cause injustice to those children that received less property. So, if the benefits that one of the children has received during the life of the heir exceed the inheritance share to which he/she is entitled by the statutory portion of the inheritance, then he/she is under no obligation to repay any additional sum to be found that has been given to him/her. The favored child is simply excluded from the share of the inheritance to which he/she would normally have been entitled.' Concerning the time when the value of the benefits given to the heirs during the lifetime of the deceased and the value of the property which is inherited, the value must be calculated in money, and this evaluation will take place after the deceased's death. Thus, the date that will be used to calculate the inheritance share is the date of death.[477]

474. Section 41 of Cap. 195.
475. *Papanasiliou v. Papafedia* (1975) 1 JSC 96.
476. *Kyriakidis et al. v. Dikigoropoulos et al.* (2012) 1 CLR 1164.
477. *See also Odysseos v. Papadouri*, No. 217/12, 10 September 2018.

§3. Intestate Succession

409. If a person dies intestate, or to the extent that the deceased's right to dispose by will is restricted because of the existence of statutory heirs, the estate shall be distributed in accordance with the provisions of Cap. 195.[478] Intestate succession can only occur if the testator did not dispose of his estate in a disposal of property on death. Furthermore, if the testator disposed of only a portion of his estate by will, the rules of intestate succession will apply to the remaining portion of the estate.[479]

410. In the absence of a will, succession shall be made in accordance with the provisions of sections 44 et seq. of Cap. 195. Section 46 of Cap. 195 states that after the deduction of the share of the surviving spouse the remaining property is distributed between the remaining kin of the deceased in the manner provided for in the First Schedule of Cap. 195 (Appendix A). The surviving spouse is always entitled to a share in the statutory portion and in the undisposed portion of the estate (therefore, irrespective of whether the deceased had made a valid will or not[480]). The surviving spouse's share is defined on the basis of the existence of other heirs under the provisions of section 44 of Cap. 195. If there is a spouse and children, the net value of the inheritance is distributed between the spouse and children in equal parts. In the absence of children or descendants thereof, the spouse's share increases, depending on the existence of other relatives up to a fourth degree of kindred. In particular, if there are siblings or parents of the deceased (ancestor or descendant thereof within the third degree of kindred to the deceased), the spouse's share is 50% of the net value (of the statutory portion and the undisposed portion). If there are no such relatives but there are other relatives (ancestor or descendant thereof) of the fourth degree of kindred to the deceased, the spouse is entitled to three-fourth of the inheritance. In all the other cases, the spouse is entitled to the whole of the estate. Persons of first degree of kindred will exclude persons of a subsequent degree of kindred.[481]

478. Achilleas Emilianides, *Family and Succession Law in Cyprus*, *supra* n. 12.
479. Section 50 of the Wills and Succession Law (Cap. 195).
480. Achilleas Emilianides, *Family and Succession Law in Cyprus*, *supra* n. 12.
481. Section 46 of Cap. 195.

Chapter 3. Possession

§1. The Place of Possession in Cypriot Land Law

411. In land law theory, the distinction between ownership, occupation and possession is fundamental. Thus, the attempt to categorize and theoretically analyze these concepts, which are sporadically encountered in Cypriot legislation and jurisprudence, seems to be unorthodox in as much as Cypriot land law appears to be predominantly pragmatic and is characterized by the absence of an abstract legal analysis in parallel with English common law.[482] This observation is further enhanced by the fact that the protection of real rights in Cypriot law does not take place through the legislative provision of a series of specific actions, but mainly through the provisions on torts, which have been structured similarly to English common law.

412. The significance of the above theoretical distinction in Cypriot land law is also undermined by the historical institutional role of the functioning of the Land Registry. In a legal system, such as the Cypriot one, where the acquisition of ownership is substantially connected with the registration of property to the Land Registry, it could be said that the recognition of the legal consequences and legal protection in the real state of the physical power over the property is *a priori* incompatible with the system of acquiring real rights through registration in the Land Registry. In this context, Cap. 224, which is the basic legal source of Cypriot land law, does not define or especially provide for the concepts of ownership, use and possession, except for the general mention in the title of Cap. 224 in 'tenure' of immovable property and the provisions for the adverse possession.

413. The concept of possession, in addition to the existence of a corpus element of the physical power and control over the property, focuses on the existence of an animus (psychological) element, which comprises the will of the possessor to exercise its power over the thing, as if were the owner, irrespectively of whether or not he believes that he is exercising that power on the basis of a right or whether he knows that he is exercising it without being entitled to it (*animus domini, animus rem sibi habendi*).[483]

414. The concept of possession seems to be significant within the scope of Cap. 224 only in the context of the concept of adverse possession. Furthermore, the concept is critical in the context of tort, since the right to bring a claim for trespass to immovable property and private nuisance is provided in principle to the tenant of the immovable property and the owner. The civil wrong of 'trespass to land' is an

482. In common law, the concept of tenancy developed as a precondition of the civil wrong of trespass or private nuisance and not through an independent, structured, theoretical mechanism. That was the result of the trend of defining the legal fields in relation to the type of claims and not in relation to the type of rights. *See*, Pollock Frederick & Robert Wright, *An Essay on Possession in Common Law* 4 (Oxford at the Clarendon Press 1888).

483. *See* Gray & Gray, *supra* n. 99 at 161.

offence against the possession-tenancy and not against the ownership of the property.[484] As a result, the owner of the immovable property has the right to bring a claim only in exceptional cases, when the vibrations of the land cause damage to the foundations of the rented house or the interference is of a permanent nature.[485]

415. The increased protection of possession in tort law is also in line with the particular position adopted in the English legal system in relation to the concept of 'possession', where the central point of reference in the field of property law was the physical power over the land and not the concept of ownership.[486] This is also the case in relation to the tort of private nuisance, where the possessor-tenant is eligible for bringing a claim, while the owner can be the plaintiff only in specific cases, such as when the nuisance causes a permanent damage to his property. The bare licensee, whose legal status has its parallels in the status of 'bare possessor', has no right to bring a claim.[487]

§2. The Protection of Possession of Movable Properties

416. The Civil Wrongs Law (Cap. 148) provides three different torts protecting the possession of movable properties, inherited from the common law tradition: detention, conversion and trespass to movable property. These multiple of torts protecting the same legal interests can be considered counter-productive, and it must be noted that in the UK, the tort of detention was abolished on 1 January 1978 by the Torts (Interference with Goods) Act 1977. However, the tort of conversion was extended at the same time to cover circumstances that had previously been covered only by detinue.

417. The tort of unlawful detention is governed by section 37 of Cap. 148: '(1) Unlawful detention consists of the unlawful withholding of any movable property from any person entitled to the immediate possession thereof. (2) any action brought in respect of any unlawful detention the onus of proving that the withholding was lawful shall be upon the defendant.' The tort possesses two main uses. First, it is used to recover possession (and damages) after breach of contract, for instance after non-payment of annuity in case of a leasing purchase of a car. In this case, the tort may be invoked concurrently with the tort of conversion, if the previous party to the contract continued to use the car.[488] Second, the tort could be used against the finder of lost goods who would want to keep them. Unlawful detention is a continuing offence and is enforceable from the first day of the defendant's refusal to return the goods to their legitimate possessor. The offence continues until the thing has been delivered or a judgment has been issued. The offence involves an interference

484. *Rhondda Cynon Taff County BC v. Watkins* (2003) 1 WLR 1864; Artemis and Erotokritou, *Cap 148, Civil Wrongs, Law and Case Law* 131 (Nicosia 2003).
485. Artemis and Erotokritou, *ibid.*, with reference to *Georgiou v. Andrea* (1998) 1 CLR 2311.
486. As it is mentioned in *Hunter v. Canary Wharf Ltd* (1997) AC 655 at 733, 'Exclusive possession de jure or de facto, now or in the future, is the bedrock of English land law.'
487. Artemis and Erotokritou, *supra* n. 484 at 144.
488. *Elliniki Trapeza Ltd and Trapeza Barkleys Plc v. Tsartelli* (2003) 1 CLR 246.

with the right of possession and thus the right to sue belongs to the person who either owns the object or has the direct right to own it. Ownership of the item is not a prerequisite.

418. As highlighted by Cypriot case law,[489] in an unlawful detention, the court's judgment can take three forms: (1) the value of the item and compensation for its retention; (2) return of the item or payment of its value and (3) return of the item and compensation for its retention. The market value of a product must be proven. If there is no market value, the compensation is calculated by estimating the replacement cost of the property.

419. A very interesting case of unlawful detention concerned the refusal by an architect working previously for a company to give the draft schemas of the building to the company that was working on. Based on intellectual property principles, the schemas were the property of the company and the architect was condemned on the basis of the unlawful detention tort.[490]

420. The tort of unlawful detention does not extend to situations where the legitimate possession of the goods is compromised by physical intervention. Indeed, this situation belongs to the tort of conversion. The tort of conversion is stated in section 40 of Cap. 148: 'Conversion consists of an unlawful physical act which affects any movable property and asserts a claim to deal therewith in a manner inconsistent with the rights of any person entitled to the immediate possession thereof.' In conformity with common law principles and with the tort's philosophy of protection of the immediate possession of the goods, Cap. 148 adds that *jus tertii*, that is a claim that a third party possesses a better title to the goods, is not to be a defence to action for conversion.[491] The tort of conversion is a strict liability tort. The mere act of putting in danger the possession of the plaintiff is enough to raise the liability of the defendant, even if he/she acted in error.

421. Lastly, the tort of trespass to movable property is defined in section 43 as '(1) Trespass to movable property consists of- (a) the unlawful disturbance of or interference with, or (b) any unlawful act directly causing damage to, any such property, such disturbance or interference being caused by or such act being done by some person. (2) In any action brought in respect of any trespass to movable property the onus of showing that the act of which plaint is hade was not unlawful shall be upon the defendant.' This tort differs from the tort of conversion as definitive loss of possession is not a prerequisite for bringing an action. In contrast, the main application of the tort concerns the case of damages caused to the goods or the case of temporary loss of possession (interference). For the tort of trespass to movable property, the intent to interfere with or damage the property must be proven, or else the case will be dealt with under the general tort of negligence.

489. *Tribunal of Limassol, Louimar Fisheries Lt v. 5 Oceans Food Ltd*, No. 470/2008, 16 June 2014.
490. *Papachrisostomou v. Kosta Grigoriadi & Synetairoi et al.*, Civil Appeal No. 118/2010, 16 December 2015.
491. Section 41 of Cap. 148.

Chapter 4. Accession

422. The concept of accession refers to the situation when the owner of a good becomes the owner of everything that attaches or is incorporated to it. In this context, accession is a method of acquisition of property by material incorporation of another good, either immovable or movable, which is deemed less important from a good considered more important. As regards immovable goods, the accession may be either natural or be a result of human intervention.

423. In relation to immovable property the general principle is that everything permanently annexed to the land is acceded to the land, since the land is the principal thing. Cypriot land law regulates the issue of accession mainly through this doctrine and case law on 'fixtures/chattels'[492] (*see* Part II, Chapter 1). Subject to the doctrine of accession, personal property can become immovable property through its transformation into a fixture. The law of fixtures is founded on the principle that whatever is attached to the land becomes a part thereof. Chattels are items of personal property, but if they are so affixed to the land as to become a part of it, they lose the character as chattels and pass with the ownership of the land. Buildings and structures that are firmly attached to earth are 'fixtures', while attachments that are not firmly connected with the earth are 'chattels'. Furthermore, special provisions in Cap. 224 govern the ownership of buildings, structures, plants and trees[493] and specific cases of natural accession of immovable goods.[494]

424. There is no reference in Cypriot legislation or case law to the accession of a movable to a movable. UK law principles fill the gap. The general rule when two chattels are firmly attached is also that the owner of the principal thing becomes the owner of the attached thing.[495] If two movables were combined but detachment can be effected with relative ease and without damaging the movables, accession does not occur.[496] In general, as it is noted by Knobel, the criteria to determine whether accession has taken place have not been comprehensively defined since problems

492. As regards accession of a chattel to land, the relation of the party making the accession with the land shall be taken into account. A person who attaches a chattel to his own land is usually assumed to have done so permanently and meant it to become part of the land. In case of a lease, the duration of the lease might also be relevant. In the case of *O' Brien Loans Limited v. Missick* (1977) 1 BLR 40, Georges J.A. stated, that in the case that a yearly tenant erects a wooden house to a column anchored in the ground, there would be no reason why it would lose its characteristic as a chattel and become a fixture; however, a long-term lease holder who erects such a structure would be reasonably held to have done so for the purpose of improving the land.

493. According to the definition of immovable property in s. 2 of Cap. 224, '"immovable property" includes: buildings and other erections, structures or fixtures affixed to any land or to any building or other erection or structure; trees, vines, and any other thing whatsoever planted or growing upon any land and any produce thereof before severance; springs, wells, water and water rights whether held together with, or independently of, any land.'

494. According to s. 7 of Cap. 224, any land from which the sea or the water of any such lake, river, stream or watercourse has receded, with the exception of any such land as is privately owned at the date of coming into force Cap. 224 shall be vested in the Republic of Cyprus.

495. McFarlane, *supra* n. 311 at 163.

496. S. Worthington, *Personal Property Law Text and Materials* 504 (Hart Publishing 2000).

relating to personal property are addressed mainly through the law of torts.[497] In relation to specification (i.e., where a new movable is made out of material belonging to another), the rule is that the ownership of the new movable vests prima facie with the creator.[498] The creator can, however, be exposed to liability under conversion,[499] although he/she may benefit from a statutory allowance if he/she has acted in good faith.[500]

497. Ina Knobel, *Accession of Movables to Movables and Inaedificatio – South Africa and Some Common Law Countries, Journal of Contemporary Roman-Dutch Law, 74.* 296 (2011), https://ssrn.com/abstract=2016868.

498. *Borden (UK) Ltd v. Scottish Timber Products Ltd* [1981] Ch 25, CA; *Re Peachdart Ltd* [1984] Ch 131.

499. N. Palmer and A. Hudson, 'Improving Stolen Chattels' in *Interests in Goods* 935 (2nd ed., N. Palmer & E. McKendrick eds., LLP Reference Publishing 1998).

500. Andreas Rahmatian, *A Comparison of German Movable Property Law and English Personal Property Law*, https://germanlawarchive.iuscomp.org/?p=340.

Chapter 5. Appropriation

425. Modalities of appropriation of property (acquiring ownership) belonging to another person vary depending on whether we are talking about immovable or movable property. The main modalities of appropriation for land belonging to another person are adverse possession, accession, incorporating construction, building on land owned by someone else. For movables the common law principles of appropriation through finding are applicable. Furthermore, special legislations regulate *bona vacantia*.

§1. Appropriation of Immovable Property Through Adverse Possession

426. Original acquisition of ownership through adverse possession is expressly provided in section 10 of Cap. 224. Acquisition by usucaption is one of the areas of real property law that has been scrutinized considerably by Cypriot courts, and it therefore deserves a more detailed analysis.

427. According to section 10 of Cap. 224, uninterrupted and undisputed adverse possession of land for a full period of thirty years grants the possessor the right to be registered as the owner of the land.[501] Cap. 224 has no retroactive effect. This is also expressly stated in the second limb of section 10 which reads as follows: 'Provided that nothing in this section contained shall affect the period of prescription with regard to any immovable property which began to be adversely possessed before the commencement of this Law, and all matters relating to prescription during such period shall continue to be governed by the provisions of the enactments repealed by this Law relating to prescription, as if this Law had not been passed.'

428. Section 9 of Cap. 224 provides that there can be no adverse possession against the State or a 'registered owner'. This rule was introduced in 1946 by Cap. 224, while in the past *usucaption* against a registered owner was possible too. The prohibition significantly diminished the scope of application of adverse possession in Cyprus, at least as regards the period after 1946, since the law has no retroactive effect, as previously mentioned.

429. However, the interpretation of the term 'registered owner' raised a number of controversies. In fact, the rule was interpreted by the Land Registry as protecting only the person of the *living* registered owner of the land and not the registered land itself. As a consequence, if the registered owner died and his heirs did not re-register the land in their own names, the land could be acquired by a possessor if the conditions of adverse possession were fulfilled. This interpretation was reversed in

501. 'Subject to the provisions of section 9 of this law, proof of undisputed and uninterrupted adverse possession by a person, or by those under whom he claims, of immovable property for the full period of thirty years, shall entitle such person to be deemed to be the owner of such property and to have the same registered in his name.'

2007 by the Supreme Court in *Theodosiou v. Kramvia.*[502] The Court clarified that if a parcel of land was registered, it would be protected even after the death of the registered owner and transferred by law to his/her heirs. Therefore, in the case of inheritance, the protection of section 10 also extends to the heirs of the deceased registered owner. This decision dramatically diminished the scope of application of adverse possession.

430. In addition to the need to prove uninterrupted and undisputed possession *animus domini* for thirty years,[503] it is also a prerequisite that possession be exercised without the landowner's consent, whether express or implicit.[504]

431. Cypriot case law has established very specific rules on this point. In cases of co-ownership following succession it is presumed that possession of the immovable property by one of the co-owners is deemed to be exercised with the consent of the other co-owners. Consequently, such possession will not be deemed adverse against the co-owners who are not in possession.[505] If the co-owners of land have not derived their title from the former owner by succession but are each purchasers and strangers, the consent of the co-owner not in possession cannot be presumed, and therefore the co-owner's possession is adverse to the other co-owner.[506] Nonetheless, even in the case of co-owners by succession, the presumption of possession with the co-owners' consent is rebuttable. Therefore, if the possessor proves that the legal basis for possession is not succession but another cause, for example a transfer by dowry contract that has not been registered, the presumption is reversed.[507]

432. As far as the manner of adverse possession is concerned, this is proportionate to the use or enjoyment that this property may be subject to. As noted in *Andreas Constantinou as administrator of the estate of Maria Charalambous Stylianou v. Andrea Ioannou Kourides,*[508] 'the most important criterion is the substantiveness of the possession … possession must be substantial and actual. There must also exist animus domini, that is, it must be exercised in a manner that shows the existence of the right of ownership thereon. The whole behavior of the person exercising possession must be the behavior of an owner. Possession must be obvious and continuous.'[509]

502. Supreme Court, *Margarita Charalambous Theodosiou v. Andrea Kramvia and others*, 27 November 2007.
503. *Diplaros v. Nicola* (1974) 1 CLR 198.
504. *See* s. 2 of Cap. 224.
505. *Eleni Angeli v. Savvas Lambi and others* (1963) 2 CLR 274.
506. *Diplaros v. Nicola* (1974) 1 CLR 198.
507. *Ioannou et al v. Georghiou* (1983) 1 CLR 92; *Eystathiou v. Panayi* (1992) 1B CLR 1297.
508. Action 3011/08, 13/3/2013.
509. *See Soteriou v. Heirs of Despina Hadjipaschali* (1962) CLR 280; *Yiangou Aradippioti v. Christos Kyriakou et al.* (1971) 1 CLR 381 and *Diplaros v. Nicola* (1974) 1 CLR 198. In this case, it was held that the erection of buildings on the property at issue by the person who is exercising possession without a building permit is an offence, but does not constitute the possession of the property illegal so as to make it impossible to be for the benefit of the possessor for the purposes of

433. Another delicate issue that has been clarified by case law is instances where the periods of possession by a successor and a predecessor-in-title can be added together in order to complete the thirty-year period of adverse possession. The periods of possession of an area of land by successor and predecessor-in-title can be added up in cases of devolution by inheritance and in transfers where the title deed is not related to a survey plan excluding the area in question, and in such a case the proviso to section 50 (*supra*) will operate and the period of adverse possession by transferor and transferee will then be added up.[510]

434. If the conditions of section 10 are fulfilled, the possessor has the right to be deemed the owner of the immovable property and to be registered as such. Nevertheless, the protection of the possessor cannot be exercised against a bona fide purchaser for value without notice. More specifically, Cypriot case law, following the principles of equity, has established that a person who has acquired a prescriptive claim to be registered in respect of immovable property, but who delays in obtaining registration, is prohibited from asserting his claim against a bona fide purchaser for value, who without notice of his claim has acquired the property from the registered owner.[511] The purchaser is not considered bona fide if he knew about the adverse possession or he would have known about it, had he had made reasonable enquiries and inspections.[512]

§2. Appropriation of Movables Through Finding

435. Cypriot legislation regulates the ownership of movables that are found in Cap. 149 (Contracts Law). Section 71 of Cap. 149 states that a person who finds goods belonging to another, and takes them into his custody, is subject to the same responsibility as a bailee. Therefore, the duties and rights of a bailee are applicable to the finder of goods (duty to take care of goods found,[513] duty not to make unauthorized use of goods,[514] duty not to mix the goods,[515] duty to return the goods to whom they belong[516]). If the finder refuses to return the goods, he could be made liable for the tort of conversion.

436. As regards the rights of the finder, according to section 126 of Cap. 149, the finder of goods has no right to sue the owner for compensation for trouble and expense voluntarily incurred by him to preserve the goods and to find out the owner;

prescription. The illegal building act on the property does not change the fact that the person possesses the property *nec vi, nec clam, nec precario*, i.e., not as a result of violence, not in secret and not with the permission of the owner.

510. *Papagheorghiou v. Komodromou* (1963) 2 CLR 221.
511. *Haji Haralambo Michael and others v. Haji Stilli Nikoli and others* (1909) VIII 1 CLR 113; *Akil Hussein Arnaout v. Emine Hussein Zinouri*, Civil Appeal No. 4012, 1953.
512. *Akil Hussein Arnaout v. Emine Hussein Zinouri*, Civil Appeal No. 4012, 1953.
513. Section 109 of Cap. 149.
514. Section 112 of Cap. 149.
515. Sections 114 and 115 of Cap. 149.
516. Section 118 of Cap. 149.

but he may retain the goods against the owner until he receives such compensation; and, where the owner has offered a specific reward for the return of goods lost, the finder may sue for such reward and may retain the goods until he receives it. Furthermore, section 127 of Cap. 149 states that when a thing which is commonly the subject of sale is lost, if the owner cannot with reasonable diligence be found, or if he refuses upon demand, to pay the lawful charges of the finder, the finder may sell it when the thing is in danger of perishing or of losing the greater part of its value or when the lawful charges of the finder, in respect of the thing found, amount to two-thirds of its value.

437. Common law precedents are applicable to finders' rights. The basic rule as highlighted by case law is that the finder has the right to acquire property over the movable that he has found *erga omnes*, except for the real owner. This principle was affirmed in *Bridges v. Hawkesworth.*[517] In this case, which was concerned with whether the finder or the owner of the shop had better title to an envelope with money found on the floor of the shop, it was held that the finder of a lost article is entitled to it as against all, except the true owner. The fact that the property was discovered on premises owned by another does not constitute an exception to the general rule that a finder has the superior claim of right to possession of lost property. However, when the chattel has a connection with the land or was found inside the land, the owner of the land has a better claim to the object.[518] In *Waverley Borough Council v. Fletcher*[519] a brooch was found by the defendant with the use of a metal detector in a park owned by the claimant Council. The issue was who could claim the brooch. It was held that the Council had a better right to the brooch because the brooch had been found within or attached to the land rather than on the surface of the land.

§3. PRINCIPLES FOR *BONA VACANTIA*

438. Bona vacantia is the legal status of a property found without an owner. There are special provisions for assets of dissolved companies that have failed to be distributed, assets of dissolved unincorporated associations that have failed to be distributed and assets of the estates of deceased persons that have failed to be distributed due to intestacy and a lack of known persons entitled to inherit.

---

517. *Bridges v. Hawkesworth* (1851) 21 LJQB 75, 15 Jur. 1079. *See also Hannah v. Peel* (King's Bench Division, K.B. 509 (1945)).
518. *Elwes v. Brigg Gas co* (1886) 33 ChD. In relation to a prehistoric boat that was found by a tenant six feet below the surface of the land, Judge Chitty noted about the claim of the owner of the land (plaintiff) that 'he was in possession of the ground, not merely of the surface, but of everything that lay beneath the surface down to the centre of the earth, and consequently in possession of the boat … The plaintiff then, being thus in possession of the chattel, it follows that the property in the chattel was vested in him. Obviously the right of the original owner could not be established; it had for centuries been lost or barred … The plaintiff, then, had a lawful possession, good against all the world, and therefore the property in the boat. In my opinion it makes no difference, in the circumstances, that the plaintiff was not aware of the existence of the boat.'
519. *Waverley Borough Council v. Fletcher* [1995] 4 All ER 756.

439. Section 328 of Cap. 113 establishes a *bona vacantia* rule for the property of a company that has been dissolved. According to this provision, 'Where a company is dissolved, all property and rights whatsoever vested in or held on trust for the company immediately before its dissolution (not including property held by the company on trust for any other person) shall, subject and without prejudice to any order which may at any time be made by the Court under sections 326 and 327 be deemed to be bona vacantia and shall accordingly belong to the Republic, and shall vest and may be dealt with in the same manner as other bona vacantia accruing to the Republic.'

440. For associations and institutions, section 25 of Law 104(I)/2017 provides some rules for the transfer of property of a dissolved society to another entity. Such property shall be transferred to another entity whose purposes are consistent with the purposes of the dissolved society, as such purposes were set out in its articles of association. In the event that the dissolution of the society is not voluntary, the Registrar of Societies shall have the power to intervene in the process for the purpose of better distribution of the society's assets for public benefit.

441. Section 47 of the Wills and Succession Law (Cap. 195) provides that if there is no person of kin to the deceased within the sixth degree of kindred living at his death he shall be taken to have died without heirs, and no one of his kin beyond the sixth degree of kinship shall on his death become in any matter entitled to the statutory portion and to the undisposed portion if any. On failure of heirs and subject to the share of a surviving wife or husband, if any, the statutory portion and the undisposed portion shall become the property of the Republic of Cyprus.

Chapter 6. Expropriation

442. Deprivation of property and restrictions on the power of disposal of the owner may be effected by a number of mechanisms in both private and public law. The analysis of these mechanisms goes beyond the scope of this book insofar as they are governed by the law on civil procedure or by the specific laws on forced expropriation (compulsory acquisition[520]) and requisition[521] that have been adopted under Article 23 of the Constitution. The following paragraphs will provide a brief overview of the relevant legislation and the procedure.

§1. By Means of Public Law: Compulsory Acquisition and Requisition of Property

443. According to Article 23 of the Constitution, expropriation is only allowed for public purposes and with just compensation. Specifically, restrictions or limitations which are absolutely necessary in the interest of the public safety or the public health or the public morals or the town and country planning or the development and utilization of any property to the promotion of the public benefit or for the protection of the rights of others may be imposed by law on the exercise of such right. Just compensation shall be promptly paid for any such restrictions or limitations which materially decrease the economic value of such property and such compensation is to be determined in case of disagreement by a court.

444. An acquiring authority authorized by law to carry out a compulsory acquisition is the Republic, the Municipal Corporations, the Communal Chamber, Public Corporations and Public Utility Bodies. Article 23 of the Constitution states that compulsory acquisition can be done only: (a) for a purpose which is to the public benefit and shall be specifically provided by a general law for compulsory acquisition which shall be enacted within a year from the date of the coming into operation of this Constitution; and (b) when such purpose is established by a decision of the acquiring authority and made under the provisions of such law stating clearly the reasons for such acquisition; and (c) upon the payment in cash and in advance of a just and equitable compensation to be determined in case of disagreement by a civil court. Section 3 of Law 15/62 provides a list of public purposes which can justify a compulsory acquisition. Specifically, these purposes are: (a) national defence or security; (b) public safety, public order, public health, or public policy; (c) the fulfilment of international obligations; (d) the supply, maintenance or development of supplies and services which are necessary in life or promote the well-being of the public; (e) rural reform; (f) the production or development of agriculture, industry, commerce or tourism; (g) the production or development of mining or any other,

520. The Compulsory Acquisition of Property Law of 1962 (Law 15/62).
521. Requisition is subject to the provisions of the Requisition of Property Law 21/62 and may refer both to movable and immovable properties.

similar nature, industrial production; (h) archaeological excavations or the preservation or restoration of ancient monuments or archaeological sites or the development of surrounding texts; (i) town planning, land surveying or residential development (j) the creation, maintenance or development of land, sea or air transport; (k) soil conservation or the conservation or development of natural water resources, including forests and water, and water distribution; (l) the use and development of property in the best profitable way for the public benefit; (m) the creation or maintenance or development of leisure centres; (n) the creation or the maintenance or the development by the Republic of public buildings and public works; (o) the achievement or production of the aims of the cooperative institutions; (p) the achievement or promotion of any purpose of an educational, religious, charitable, or athletic institution; (r) the achievement or promotion of public authority, public law, or public benefit organizations, specially provided for therein; (s) the creation or maintenance or development of a place of burial.

445. According to section 8 of Law 15/62, the acquiring authority shall within twelve months from the date of publication of the notice of compulsory acquisition to enter into negotiations for the acquisition of the property, by a private agreement[522] and the determination by agreement of the compensation. If no agreement is reached within twelve months, the acquiring authority shall promptly offer the amount of compensation assessed. The owner may choose to accept the compensation offered by the acquiring authority and by his consent in writing that the acquired property be promptly registered in the name of the acquiring authority. In such a case, the owner has the right within the period of seventy-five days, from the date of receiving the compensation to apply to the court for the determination of the compensation. If the period of determination has lapsed, it is deemed that an agreement has been reached. If, until the date of the publication of the order of acquisition, no agreement has been reached, the acquiring authority or the interesting parties shall apply to the court for the determination of the compensation.[523] Section 10 establishes rules for the assessment of compensation. The compensation to be paid for property compulsorily acquired should be equivalent to the loss suffered by the party deprived of his property. District courts have a broad discretion in relation to the calculation of the 'just and equitable' compensation and to accept every testimony for that purpose.[524]

---

522. As it was held in *Oroklinis v. Georgiades* (1999) 1 CLR 335, this agreement constitutes a contract in the sense of private law. Therefore, the obligations and rights of the parties are governed by the usual rules of private law.
523. Section 8 of Law 15/62.
524. A. Symeou, *The Protection of Property and Compulsory Acquisition of Property in Cyprus*, 183–184 (2003), with reference to: *Rashid Ali et al. v. Vassiliko Cement Works Ltd* (1971) 1 CLR 146; *Republic of Cyprus v. Petsa*, Appeal No. 9284, 18 December 1996 ('while giving the parties considerable scope for both their placement and testimony, the court still has statutory investigative capabilities … The court may, on its own initiative, require a party to provide further and better details of the reasons for the referral. This character is also consistent with the provision in Article 23.4 (c) of the Constitution for the determination of the just and equitable compensation. Putting the burden entirely on the parties, through a process of pure confrontation, would make the outcome too much dependent on the manipulations they would make … ').

446. Any immovable property or any right over or interest in any such property compulsorily acquired shall only be used for the purpose for which it has been acquired. If within three years of the acquisition such purpose has not been attained, the acquiring authority, after the expiration of the said period of three years, shall immediately offer the property at the price it has been acquired to the person from whom it has been acquired. Such person shall be entitled within three months of the receipt of such offer to signify his acceptance or non-acceptance of the offer, and if he signifies acceptance, such property shall be returned to him immediately after his returning such price within a further period of three months from such acceptance.

447. The acquiring authority shall cause a notice of the intended acquisition to be published in the Official Gazette of the Republic, containing the description of the property, the purpose of acquisition, the reason of acquisition and calling upon any person interested in such property to submit to such authority not less than thirty days of the date of publication, an objection which it may wish to raise.

448. The person entitled to compensation is the owner of such property and where the property is pledged or charged with the payment of any sum secured by a mortgage, registration of judgment or any other encumbrance or charge, the whole or such portion of the compensation shall be paid to the respective pledgee, mortgagee, judgment creditor or other person in whose favour such encumbrance or charge operates in order to satisfy, in whole or in part, the sum due thereunder. Where any property is under any lease, hiring or hire-purchase agreement, there shall be paid to the lessee, tenant, hirer or hire-purchaser such portion of the compensation payable as shall be sufficient to compensate him for the termination of his lease, tenancy, hiring or hire-purchase agreement, as the case may be.

449. The requirements of proper administration and the proper use of the relevant discretionary powers render it imperative that a compulsory acquisition should not be ordered if its object can be achieved in any less onerous manner. It must be absolutely necessary to do so and after exhausting the alternative possibility of achieving its object by means of purchasing other suitable property which is voluntarily offered for sale by its owner. Moreover, before resorting to compulsory acquisition of a particular immovable property, the acquiring authority must exhaust the possibility of acquiring compulsorily other suitable immovable property the acquisition of which will entail a deprivation less onerous than the deprivation entailed in the proposed acquisition.[525]

450. There is an obligation of the acquiring authority to return the expropriated property if it does not, within the period provided by the Constitution, take substantive measures to make the purpose of the expropriation feasible, that is, feasible within a reasonable time. In case of delay, the owner of the property shall prove that

525. *Venglis and The Electricity Authority* (1965) 3 CLR 252; *Chryssochou Bros v. 1. The Cyprus Telecommunications Authority 2. The Republic of Cyprus through the Council of Ministers (1966) 3 CLR 482; Agrotis v. Electricity Authority* (1981) 3 CLR 50.

the administration has not taken such actions as would reasonably be necessary on the basis of its objective data of any case for the implementation of the acquisition.[526]

§2. By Means of Private Law

451. The compulsory deprivation of property by means of private law takes various forms: forced sales of immovable property by public auction made as a result of the application of a relevant legislative provision or of the execution of a judicial order or judgment of a competent court and the sale of co-owned 'non-divisible' land for the purpose of removing the condominium under section 28 of Cap. 224.

452. In particular, with regard to the latter provision, the main purpose of the procedure provided for in section 28 of Cap. 224 is to eliminate co-ownership of immovable property which cannot be divided under section 27 of Cap. 224.[527] Any co-owner may apply to the Director for a certificate to the effect that partition of the property is impossible by reason of the aforementioned provisions, and upon being furnished with such certificate, such co-owner may serve a notice on the other co-owners in Cyprus together with a copy of such certificate informing them that, unless within thirty days after service they can agree to an arrangement, whereby the property is allocated to one person or divided in a manner which does not contravene any of the said provisions, he will apply to the Director to put up the property for sale by auction. The Director, upon proof of such service and upon being satisfied that no arrangement as hereinbefore has been agreed upon, may, at his discretion and without any further notice and notwithstanding the absence of any co-owner from Cyprus, proceed to sell the property by auction, and distribute the proceeds, after deducting the expenses of such sale, among the persons entitled thereto according to their respective rights in the property.

---

526. *Zenon Efthimiadis Estates Ltd v. The Republic* (2006) 3 CLR 166.
527. Specifically, it is certified that a particular land cannot be distributed or separated between the co-owners without violating the provisions of the law establishing minimum acreage for real estate.

Chapter 7. Insolvency

§1. Bankruptcy and Insolvency of Natural Persons

453. The legal provisions for bankruptcy of a natural person are found in the Bankruptcy Law (Cap. 5), as amended, which has followed closely the UK Bankruptcy Act 1883. Furthermore, the Insolvency of Natural Persons (Personal Repayment Plans and Debt Relief Orders) Law of 2015 (Law 65(I)/2015) is applicable. The Insolvency Advisors Law of 2015[528] and the related Regulations, establish and regulate the profession of the Insolvency Consultant in Cyprus. The institutionalization of the profession was deemed necessary to ensure that the implementation of the procedures and projects envisaged in the whole of insolvency laws is sound and effective.

454. A bankruptcy petition can be made either by the creditor or the debtor himself for debts of more than EUR 15,000. The act of bankruptcy must have been done in Cyprus and the debtor must have been personally present in Cyprus, or ordinarily resided, or was carrying out business in Cyprus, or was a member of a partnership that carried out business in Cyprus.

455. After the issuance of a bankruptcy order, the Official Receiver becomes the Administrator of the bankrupt estate. At any later stage any licensed Insolvency Consultant may be appointed as such Administrator. The duty of the Administrator is to dispose of the bankrupt estate and distribute it to its creditors. Once the Official Receiver or any Insolvency Consultant assumes the duties of Administrator, the debtor continues to retain ownership of all of his/her property which, however, shall be entirely managed by the Administrator from the date of the bankruptcy.

456. A necessary condition for the issuance of an order is that efforts have been made for a debt restructuring upon compromise with the creditors according to the provisions of the Insolvency of Natural Persons (Personal Repayment Plans and Debt Relief Orders) Law of 2015. Specifically, the bankruptcy order cannot be issued at the request of the debtor, unless the petition is accompanied by an affidavit declaring that the debtor has made reasonable efforts to compromise with the creditors by submitting to them a Personal Repayment Plan, provided that the debtor's circumstances would allow him to proceed to such a submission. Furthermore, no bankruptcy order shall be issued unless a certificate is presented, either by the creditor or the debtor, that no application has been made for a Personal Repayment Plan or a protective decree or no Personal Repayment Plan or a protective order is in force in accordance with the provisions of the Insolvency of Natural Persons (Personal Repayment Plans and Debt Relief Orders) Law of 2015.

457. The Insolvency of Natural Persons (Personal Repayment Plans and Debt Relief Orders) Law of 2015 provides for personal repayment plans (conditional and

528. The Insolvency Advisors Law of 2015 (64(I)/2015), as amended.

mandatory), that can guarantee under certain conditions the main residence of the debtor, coordinated repayment plans, which safeguard both natural persons and businesses, and debt relief orders.

458. The Personal Repayment Plan is a mechanism that allows an insolvent debtor, provided certain criteria are met, to achieve, under conditions, debt restructuring. Debt restructuring can ensure the repayment of creditors and the maintenance by the debtor, if possible, of his/her main residence. It is a debt restructuring plan for repayment which shall be prepared by an Insolvency Consultant[529] in form of a proposal. The duration of the plan can be up to five years, with the possibility of extension in some cases for another one year. The plan is also addressed to debtors who meet the eligibility criteria of the Personal Repayment Plan and have a decisive influence on a very small business which employs less than ten people ('Coordinated Repayment Plan').

459. On the basis of a Personal Repayment Plan, the debtor will apply to a licensed Insolvency Consultant who, if the criteria are met,[530] applies to the Court for a ninety-five-day protective order, during which the Consultant will submit a personal redemption plan. This type of plan requires the consent of the creditors.[531] Special majority is required for the approval of the proposal at the assembly of the creditors. It is then referred to the court, either by the Insolvency Service or a lawyer appointed by the debtor. In case the creditors' assembly does not approve the proposal, but the specific criteria and conditions for its approval are satisfied, the debtor can ask from the court the enforcement of the plan (Non-consensual Personal Repayment Plan). The repayment plan is for a maximum of sixty months and stipulates that payments will be made if the debtor is provided with reasonable living expenses issued by the Insolvency Bureau and for a transitional period by the Ministry of Finance. A basic requirement of this plan is to keep the creditors in the same or better position as they would have been if they had sold a property that was put up as collateral.

460. If the Personal Repayment plan is rejected by the creditors' assembly, the debtor may unilaterally apply to the court for an order imposing on all creditors the Personal Repayment Scheme which they have rejected. In this case, an application to the court for the enforcement of the plan is possible only if the total outstanding debt (including secured and unsecured debt) does not exceed EUR 350,000 and certain criteria and conditions are met, such as that the main residence of the debtor which is located in the Republic of Cyprus is mortgaged and has a market value of up to EUR 300,000 and the total value of the debtor's other assets, excluding the debtor's main residence, does not exceed EUR 250,000. Apart from the fulfilment

529. Sections 23 and 24 of the Insolvency of Natural Persons (Personal Repayment Plans and Debt Relief Orders) Law of 2015 (65(I)/2015).

530. For the criteria, *see* s. 35 of the Insolvency of Natural Persons (Personal Repayment Plans and Debt Relief Orders) Law of 2015 (65(I)/2015).

531. *See* ss 51–56 of the Insolvency of Natural Persons (Personal Repayment Plans and Debt Relief Orders) Law of 2015 (65(I)/2015).

of the basic requirement that with the plan the creditor should be in the same or better condition as he/she would have been in case the property has been sold, it should also be ensured that any additional income of the debtor, in addition to the expenses for covering the reasonable living expenses of both himself and his dependents, is used for the payment of his/her debts.

461. The main eligibility criteria for a debt relief order are that the debtor still be insolvent and will continue to be for a period of one year after the submission of the application, with monthly income (other than reasonable living expenses, income tax payable by the debtor, social security contributions payable by the debtor) not exceeding EUR 200 and his assets not exceeding EUR 1,000.[532] The procedure has two steps. An application is submitted to the Insolvency Service. If the latter is satisfied that the conditions of the application are met, a claim is filed with the court for the issuance of a Debt Relief Order. If the order is issued, the debtor and any guarantor are exempted from the specified eligible debt (up to EUR 25,000) and from all liabilities, accumulated arrears, charges and interests in relation to the debt from the date on which the debtor's application was filed with the Insolvency Service until the issuance of the order by the court. Furthermore, creditors cannot initiate any judicial proceedings against the debtor for the payment of the debt, communicate with the debtor asking the payment of the debt or demand that the debtor be declared bankrupt.[533]

§2. Liquidation of Companies

462. Unlike the individuals who, as mentioned above in the event of their insolvency, are subject to bankruptcy, companies in Cyprus are liquidated. The provisions relating to liquidation are set out in Cap. 113 (Companies Law) in sections 203–344 and the Companies (Winding-up) Rules and the Civil Procedure Rules.

463. There are two main ways in which a company can be liquidated: (1) by order of the Court; (2) voluntarily either by the members of the company or by creditors or voluntary liquidation under the supervision of the Court.

464. In relation to the voluntary liquidation by creditor, it is an out-of-court procedure which can take place in the event that the company is insolvent and the Board of Directors of the company decides to liquidate it. Voluntary liquidation by creditors begins with the convening of a creditors' meeting presenting the company's extraordinary general meeting with its voluntary liquidation. Voluntary liquidation by members is also an out-of-court liquidation procedure, which is triggered by a special resolution of the general meeting of shareholders when the company is solvent. In the case of voluntary liquidation under the jurisdiction of the court, the

532. Section 12 of the Insolvency of Natural Persons (Personal Repayment Plans and Debt Relief Orders) Law of 2015 (65(I)/2015).
533. Section 19 of the Insolvency of Natural Persons (Personal Repayment Plans and Debt Relief Orders) Law of 2015 (65(I)/2015).

company will have adopted a resolution for voluntary liquidation and the court may issue a decree to continue the liquidation under the jurisdiction of the court.

465. Furthermore, the Companies Law (Cap. 113) provides for company arrangements and reconstructions and insolvency procedures, such as receivership and the examinership scheme.

466. The purpose of receivership is recovery of the secured creditor's debt. The appointment of a receiver can be made by the court (debenture holders or other creditors of a company can make an application to the court[534]) or alternatively, a secured creditor may appoint a receiver under a specific power contained in the charge.[535] In this context, a contract of mortgage may give explicit authority to a creditor/mortgagee to appoint a receiver and a trustee in the event of a breach of the mortgagor's obligations. A creditor holding a charge over assets may appoint a receiver to realize the assets subject to the charge and discharge the debt out of the proceeds. According to Article 340 of Cap. 113, where a receiver or manager of the whole or substantially the whole of the property of the Company is appointed on behalf of the holders of any debentures of the company secured by a floating charge, the receiver shall forthwith send notice to the company of his appointment. The company shall, within fourteen days after receipt of the notice, or such longer period as may be allowed by the Court or by the receiver, submit to the receiver a statement in the prescribed form as to the affairs of the company. On the basis of this statement, the receiver shall decide whether to realize assets in a piecemeal fashion.[536]

467. The Companies Law was amended in 2015 (and several times since), with the aim of modernizing the legal framework and for the purpose of introducing an examinership scheme. This procedure is largely based on the corresponding Irish legislation. Examinership is a debt restructuring procedure for insolvent companies or companies that are likely to be insolvent. The scheme permits the creditors of a company to reach a formal settlement that will enable the company, which would have otherwise been wound up, to continue its operations for the purpose of paying all its creditors. For an examinership order to be granted, the court must be convinced that the company has a 'reasonable prospect of survival'.[537] The petition can be made by a creditor of the company, shareholders who hold at least 10% of the company's share capital or every guarantor of the company for the company's debts. The court shall evaluate the prospect of viability/rescue of the company, and if such a prospect reasonably exists, it will appoint an examiner. For the court to order the appointment of an examiner, certain conditions have to be met: the company must be unable or likely to be unable to pay its debts, no resolution has been passed for

---

534. Section 336 of Cap. 113.
535. E. Neocleous & M. Kyriacou, *Multi-jurisdictional Guide 2011/12, Restructuring and Insolvency*, Andreas Neocleous & Co LLC (Practical law company: 2012), https://www.neocleous.com/publications/plc_restructuring_chapter_cyprus-pdf.
536. *Ibid.*
537. C. Christodoulou, *The Insolvency Review*, (7th ed., December 2019), https://thelawreviews.co.uk/edition/the-insolvency-review-edition-7/1211464/cyprus, last visited on 24 December 2019).

the winding-up of the company and no order has been made for the company to be wound up. After the filing of the petition together with an Independent Expert's Report, the company gains the protection of the court for four months. This period can be extended up to six months. During this period the creditors are prohibited from bringing any action against the company and a compromise with regards to the debts and obligations of the company is expected to be concluded between the company and its creditors. When the appointment of an Examiner is approved by the court, the Examiner shall inspect the company's affairs and to develop a rescue plan for approval.[538] However, the implementation in practice of the examinership scheme has not been successful. Given the very lengthy court procedures in Cyprus and the possibility of objection which is provided to all interested parties which can further delay the process, examinership petitions cannot be processed within the strict timescales provided.[539]

538. For an overview of all the stages of the process, *see* S. Christou & S. Christofides, *Examinership: A Process of Saving Jobs while Taking Care of Creditors' Interests* (July 2017), https://www.gzg.com.cy/media/filer_public/62/26/62264990-bf61-4068-838f-0579a4c35a39/examinership.pdf.

539. A. Antoniou, *Examinership: A Missed Opportunity*, http://www.crigroup.com.cy/wp-content/uploads/2018/10/Examinership-A-missed-opportunity.pdf.

Part IV. Trust and Fiduciary Mechanisms

Chapter 1. Administration of Property: *Fiducia Cum Amico*

468. *Fiducia cum amico* broadly refers to the situation where a fiduciant (settlor) and fiducarius (amicus, trustee) agreed that the fiduciant will transfer his/her property to the fiducarius who is obliged to use it according to the terms of the agreement and subsequently give it back to the fiduciant.[540] Although the concept, which originates in Roman law, has not directly influenced common law jurisdictions, such as in Cyprus, the fiduciary mechanisms of Roman law and the common law trust share the fundamental common element of a fiduciary nature. In this context, the situations covered by *fiducia cum amico* are addressed in Cypriot law by the law of trusts.

469. Without doubt, the most significant contribution of the law of equity to English law was the concept of trust. In the Cypriot legal system, the concept of trust is characterized by the following particularity. The Cap. 224, in section 65IE, defines that no trust concerning immovable property is valid, unless it is established by a document signed by the person entitled to it or by a will, both of which, a trust deed or a will, are registered in the Register of Registration of the relevant District Lands Office. The above provision, along with section 4 of Cap. 224, which defines that no interest or real right over immovable property is acquired in any other way than according to the provisions of Cap. 224, excluding the application of English common law and the law of equity,[541] could be interpreted as leading to a refusal in recognizing the concept of trusts, which have not been created on the basis of the conditions of section 65IE. Thus, section 4 introduces an explicit proviso in relation to the application of the trusts law, and in this way creates an exception from the rule of exclusive regulation of proprietary rights over immovable property by section 4 of Cap. 224.

470. In this context, even if the legislation does not expressly refer to resulting and constructive trusts, the Supreme Court of Cyprus has affirmed that in appropriate cases, if the necessary evidence is available, it is possible to claim immovable

540. P. Stec, 'Fiducia in an Emerging Economy', in *Modern Studies in Property Law*, Vol. 2, 44 (Elizabeth Cooke ed., Hart Publishing 2003).
541. *See Cyprus Cinema & Theatre Co. Ltd. v. Karmiotis* (1967) 1 CLR 42.

property rights on the basis of such trusts despite the absence of a document.[542] In this respect, except for express trusts which are established by a trust deed or a will and are registered in the Land Registry according to section 65IE, the recognition of resulting or constructive trusts is possible.[543]

471. The Supreme Court dealt with the interpretation and the scope of application of section 65IE in a series of cases. In *Charalambides v. Constantinou et al.*,[544] it was held that section 65IE provides for the creation of a trust by document and its registration in the Land Registry for the commitment of property for the purposes of the trust and that, regardless of the law in England, in Cyprus the issue of what constitutes a valid trust is regulated by section 65IE. In order to be able to register a document in the Registry of the competent Land Registry, it must have been drafted in the manner provided for in section 65IE. This section leaves no doubt that in order for a document to be regarded as a trust, it must be explicitly stated that it creates a trust. This requirement arises from the wording in paragraphs (1) and (2) of section 65IE. Both passages refer to a 'trust deed'. If a document does not explicitly refer to the creation of a trust, it follows that it has not been established in the manner provided for in section 65E of Cap. 224.[545] It could not, therefore, be registered in the Registry specified in section 65IE(2). In *Eliadis et al. v. Papakyriakou et al*,[546] the Supreme Court elaborated further on the significance of the section 65 E by stating that the registration of the document founding the trust in the Land Registry is not a constituent or condition for the validity of the trust. Section 65IE provides only the possibility of registration of the document for any purpose deemed necessary by its founder: for the purposes of the trust and for the purpose of specific performance. Furthermore, it was held that even if a trust is not established in the manner provided by section 65IE of Cap. 224, so as to be considered a valid express trust, this does not preclude the creation of a constructive trust, if this is required by the circumstances of the case.[547]

542. *Charalampidis v. Konstantinou*, Civil Appeal No. 85733 (1996) CLR; *Tsangari v. Gavriilidou et al.* (2003) 1 CLR 472. For the recognition of trusts in Cypriot land law, *see Miltiadous v. Miltiadous* (1982) 1 CLR 797; *Pentavkas v. Pentavkas* (1991) 1 CLR 547; *Constantinou v. Dimosthenous* (1992) 1 CLR 621; *Orphanides v. Orfanides* (1998) 1 CLR 179; *Clerides v. Stavrides* (1998) 1 CLR 521.

543. Thus, the discharge of the legal owner from the obligation to pay taxes for renting the property which constitutes the subject of the trust, presupposes the existence of a valid trust according to ss 4 and 65IE of Cap. 224. *See* in relation to this: *Fili et al. v. The Republic of Cyprus et al.* (1997) 4B CLR 1257 ('According to Cypriot case law the income generated by the rent of immovable property is considered to be income of the legal owner and for that reason, he has to pay personally the tax, unless where there is an alienation of the income from the owner in favor of another person. The simple disposal of income is not enough. As a result, in case there is a transfer and registration of property in the name of a third party, the income is considered to belong to the new owner, unless there was an alienation which shall be a valid trust in accordance with ss 4, 40 και 65IE of the Immovable Property (Tenure, Registration and Valuation) Law Cap. 224.')

544. *Charalampidis v. Konstantinou*, Civil Appeal No. 85733 (1996) CLR.

545. As regards the language which creates a trust, common law principles are applicable. In general, the trust is not required to be phrased in a particular formula and any words which clearly show the intention to create a trust are sufficient. *See Cowcher v. Cowcher* (1972) 1 WLR 425 at 430.

546. *Eliadis et al. v. Papakyriakou et al.*, Civil Appeal No. 220/2012, 27 November 2018.

547. *Konstantinou Tsillara v. Spyrou Kyriakou*, No. 13/2016, 1746/2011, 13 October 2016.

472. Moreover, the Supreme Court safeguards the application of a wide exception regarding trusts in section 4 and rejects the argument for an implied abolishment of the exception by section 65IE. As underlined in *Christophorou v. Christophorou,* 'since the legislator chose not to explicitly abolish the exception of section 4 as regards trusts, the exception is applicable since it is not possible to tacitly abolish the law, unless it is so contradictory or incompatible with a later law, that it is impossible for these two to coexist. Thus, in sections 4 and 65 IE, such incompatibility does not exist. In section 65 IE, the wording "no trust" does not refer to resulting and constructive trusts. As a result, their validity or voidness is not judged, according to whether they were founded in the way they define. This would be incompatible with their nature. The first ones are created or function primarily on the basis of an assumed from the facts of each case intention. The latter are imposed in line of a state of affairs, regardless of intent, explicit or implied, especially where a retention of property is attempted for private profit, non-fraudulent or consciously unacceptable exploitation or abuse of legislative provisions or other fundamental principles of law.'[548]

473. For the definition of the concept of trust, Cypriot courts follow the corresponding definitions of English law. In this context in *Nicosia Race Club v. Republic,*[549] it was held that 'the most satisfactory definition of a trust is that by Professor Keeton (*The Law of Trusts*, 8th ed., 1963, p. 3, quoted in Snell's Principles of Equity, 26th ed., p. 97) which reads: "A trust is the relationship which arises wherever a person called the trustee is compelled in Equity to hold property, whether real or personal, and whether by legal or equitable title, for the benefit of some persons (of whom he may be one and who are termed cestuis que trust) or for some object permitted by law in such a way that the real benefit of the property accrues, not to the trustee, but to the beneficiaries or other objects of the trust".' Similarly, it was held that 'Difficult, however, though it may be to give a simple yet satisfactory definition of a trust, it is easy enough to grasp the general idea of it, which is that one person in whom property is vested is compelled in equity to hold the property for the benefit of another person, or for some purposes other than his own. Thus it has been said, somewhat broadly, that "all that is necessary to establish the relation of trustee and cestui que trust is to prove that the legal title was in the plaintiff and the equitable title in the defendant". It is not, however, always accurate to say that the trustee is the legal while the cestui que trust is the equitable owner, for the interest of the trustee may be (and often is) equitable only, as where a beneficiary under a settlement himself makes a settlement of his interest while the legal ownership is still in the hands of the trustees of the former settlement, or for some other reason the legal estate is outstanding. It is therefore better to say that the trustee is the nominal, while the cestui que trust is the beneficial, owner of the property.'[550]

474. The recognition under case law of the application of constructive and resulting trusts necessitates the further analysis of the basic trust categories. There

548. *Christophorou v. Christophorou* (1998) 1 CLR 1551.
549. *Nicosia race Club v. Republic* (1975) 3 CLR 73.
550. *Ibid.*

are three main categories of trusts: express or declared trusts, constructive trusts and resulting or implied trusts.[551] Express trusts arise directly from the intention of the parties to create a trust, such as a trust deed, on the basis of which is defined that specific ownership is transferred to the trustee for the benefit of the beneficiary. The constructive and the resulting trusts arise either through tacit intent, which is recognized by the court, or their recognition is imposed by the court when certain facts have arisen. With regard to resulting or implied trusts, these arise when a settlor or testator carries out some intentional act other than the creation of a relationship of trustee and beneficiary from which the court infers a relationship of trustee and beneficiary. Specifically, there are two sets of circumstances in which resulting trusts are recognized. First, resulting trusts arise when a person either pays, wholly or in part, for the purchase of property which is vested on the name of another (or in the joint names of him and another) or gratuitously transfers property to another person. In this case, in the absence of any evidence countervailing intention, a financial contribution towards the acquisition of a property in the name of another person normally generates a resulting trust in favour of the contributor.[552] The second case is when a settlor or testator who is creating an express trust fails to dispose of the whole of the beneficiary interest in the property in question. It is then implied that so much of the beneficial interest as is undisposed of is held on trust for the settlor or his estate, or for the testator's residuary beneficiaries or intestate successors.[553] Constructive trusts have a broader scope of application since they are not concerned so much with a financial contribution but with expressly or implicitly bargained commitments. In this context, a constructive trust is created when it would be unconscionable not to give effect to a common intention which was provided on the basis of the mutual expectations of the parties.[554] The Court recognizes constructive trusts independently from the intent of the owner of the property, explicit or implied, in cases where it would be unfair to recognize a proprietary interest to a certain person or to refuse this person the proprietary interest of somebody else or in cases where it would constitute an abuse of confidence on the part of the legal owner to retain property for his own benefit.[555] An informal agreement or the acceptance in common that the assignor would enjoy some kind of right or interest to the property, which later on the trustee rejects, is usually presupposed. In this context, we could say that the constructive trust is similar to the concept of proprietary estoppel.[556] Their main resemblance is that they both provide a means for a person to

551. The majority of commentators consider the terms 'implied trust' and 'resulting trust' as synonymous. The two alternative names appear to stem from the fact that such a trust is not only implied by the court but also often causes the beneficial interest arising thereunder to 'result' to the settlor or his estate, or to the testator's residuary beneficiaries or intestate successors. *See* Oakley, Parker and Mellows, *supra* n. 418, 292.
552. Gray & Gray, *supra* n. 99 at 825, 826.
553. Oakley, Parker and Mellows, *supra* n. 418, 293.
554. Gray & Gray, *supra* n. 99 at 825, 826.
555. *Clerides v. Stavrides* (1998) 1 CLR 527.
556. Gray & Gray, *supra* n. 99 at 866. For the application in Cyprus of proprietary estoppel stemming from the law of equity, pursuant to s. 29 of the Courts law, despite the explicit exclusion of s. 4 of Cap. 224, *see Stylianou v. Papacleovoulou* (1982) 1 CLR 542; *Tsialis v. Hatziiandreou et al.* (2000) 1(B) CLR 1250; *Chrysostomou v. Fragkou et al.* (2000) 1 CLR 622. ('A minimum precondition for the existence, at least, of a cause for the estoppel, is the promise of the owner of the land to the

claim a property right over someone else's land without the formality that is normally required and, therefore, they both result in the informal creation of property rights.[557] Furthermore, if a beneficial interest on the land cannot arise on the basis of trusts, it may still arise on the basis of proprietary estoppel.[558]

475. In *Tsillara v. Kyriakou*, the court referred extensively to the principles applying to constructive trusts. As it was held, a condition of a constructive trust is that the property which is the object of the trust must have fallen into the hands of the trustee as a result of unconscionable dealing or an infringement a duty of confidence ('fiduciary obligation'). Such a fiduciary obligation exists in any case a person trusts his property to another person and relies on that other person to treat the property for his own benefit or for the purposes that he/she has authorized. If the trustee allows the property of the trust to fall into the hands of a third party, the trustee shall be personally liable for the abuse of confidence and shall bear the consequences provided for by the law of equity. However, as a general rule, a third party may not be held liable if it demonstrates that he/she is a bona fide purchaser for a consideration without knowledge of the trust. However, there is also a case where the beneficiary of the trust can recover treatment (known as the 'propriety remedy'), whenever the property of the trust can be located 'in the hands' of the third party (known as 'innocent volunteer') who has acquired the property without giving any consideration and in good faith (i.e., without knowledge of the breach of trust). In this case, the trustee (as mentioned, the second trustee) may be called upon to return the property to the beneficiary. Additionally, other equity remedies may apply where, in addition to the above-mentioned treatment, the trustee will be held accountable for any damage to such property, whether or not the property is still in his possession or control. As regards, in particular, the case of a seller of immovable property who sells it under an agreement, the law of equity has recognized that the buyer becomes the owner in equity and that the seller of immovable property becomes, from the moment of the agreement, the property's trustee for the buyer. Indeed, in the case where the price for the purchase of the immovable property has been fully paid and the buyer has no other obligation to implement under the relevant agreement, the seller of the immovable property is its custodian ('trustee without qualification' or 'naked, bare or mere trustee'). In any other case – for example, where the price for the purchase of the immovable property has not been paid, or where a condition remains to be fulfilled – the seller shall become a quasi-custodian immediately upon the conclusion of the relevant agreement ('quasi trustee'). The seller (trustee) is not just a mere inactive custodian. He is a custodian with a personal and substantive right to immovable property, with a right to protect that right and with an active right to seek it when, in any way, it is affected. Consequently, the seller (trustee), on the one hand, has a duty to use reasonable diligence to maintain the property in a reasonable manner and, on the other hand, has the right to own

promisee, that he waives his rights over the land and that the promisee can regard the land as his own fortune. The wrong impression of the owner for the boundaries of the property does not confer to him a basis for claiming a right.')

557. Dixon, *supra* n. 82 at 204.

558. Diane Chappelle, *Land Law* 84 (8th ed., Pearson Education 2006), *See Baker v. Baker* (1993) 25 HLR 408.

and reap any benefits arising from its ownership (such as collect rents) until the conclusion of the agreement by paying the sale price or otherwise.[559]

476. Similarly, according to *Christophorou v. Christophorou*, a recognized aspect of the constructive trusts is the case where the retention of property for private benefit is attempted with fraudulent or consciously unacceptable exploitation or abuse of legal provisions or other fundamental principles of law.[560] A distinctive example of judicial recognition of a constructive trust in Cypriot land law is the case *Saint George's Car hire Ltd κ.a. v. Macedonia Gavriilidou et al.*, which concerned the purchase of apartments in a building. Due to the financial difficulties of the construction company, the building remained incomplete and the buyers of the apartments completed it at their own expense. The landlords, who were the registered owners of the immovable property on which the building was built, refused to recognize ownership rights for the buyers who suffered damages. But, the Supreme Court supported the creation of a constructive trust in favour of the buyers. According to the Court, 'the law of equity imposes, under these circumstances, the creation of a constructive trust in favor of the buyers and deters the owners from giving rise to their proprietary rights and deprive in this way the buyers from the rights that acquired, as right-holders over the apartments that bought from the company, but also as persons who completed the building at their own expense, for the benefit of the land-owners as well. Even if there is no contractual relationship between the land-owners and the buyers, the law of equity provides substantial proprietary rights to buyers, before which the proprietary rights of the land-owners collapse.'[561]

477. On the contrary, a typical example of rejecting the recognition of a construction trust comes from the *Holy Monastery of Machera v. Maria Papasavva*. The case concerned the transfer of a monk's immovable property to his blood relatives, despite provisions to the contrary in the Charter of the Church of Cyprus and the Regulation of the Monastery, which provide that the property of a monk belongs to the Monastery. The Supreme Court rejected the argument of the Monastery asking for recognition of a constructive trust in favour of the Monastery in the transferred immovable property. According to the Court, the facts of the case did not show that the property had been retained by the deceased monk in order to deceive the monastery, nor could it be concluded that the property was held unacceptably or unlawfully, while the fact of the transfer of immovable property into the name of his relatives does not in itself lead to a result contrary to what was positively expressed by the deceased, namely his desire to transfer his immovable property to his relatives.[562]

478. As already been mentioned, resulting trusts concern mostly cases of transfer of property into the name of a person (trustee), in which part of the price or even the entire price has not been paid by the settlor but by the trustee. In this case, a

559. *Konstantinou Tsillara v. Spyrou Kyriakou*, Nos 13/2016, 1746/2011, 13 October 2016.
560. *Christophorou v. Christophorou, ibid.*
561. *Saint George's Car hire Ltd et al. v. Macedonia Gavriilidou et al.* (2006) 1A CLR 47.
562. *Holly Monastery of Machera et al. v. Maria Papasavva Kouvatzia et al.* (2007) 1A CLR 436.

resulting trust is recognized in favour of the person who paid the price, which is also based on the implied absence of intent to enrich the right-holder and lawful owner.[563]

479. The beneficiary of the trust acquires a contractual right against the trustee as regards the obligations of the latter, that is in case of infringement of the trust. However, the interest is not completely deprived of a real power, as the beneficiary of the trust can bring a claim against third parties who possess the property, and can also bring a claim against the right-holder to whom the trustee transferred property, provided that the right-holder is not a good faith purchaser for consideration.[564] In Cypriot law, the application of the above rule has been confirmed in *Pirillos v. Konari*.[565] The case concerned the transfer of immovable property for securing a debt and there was an explicit mention in the written agreement of the parties for a re-transfer of property to the transferor after the payment of the debt. The court ruled that this agreement, which was not registered in the Land Registry and was not explicitly referred to a trust, does not give rise to an express trust, given that the conditions of section 65IE of Cap. 224 were not met, but did give rise to a constructive trust. In this context, the sale from the trustee of an immovable property to a third party, knowing the substantial proprietary interest of the beneficiary of the trust, constituted the purchaser trustee of the constructive trust, of its rights, for the benefit of the plaintiff and he/she is not considered to be a good faith purchaser without notice. As a result, the purchaser had no right to charge the immovable property, which is subject to a pre-existing trust in favour of the plaintiff, and the beneficiary of the trust has the right to ask the annulment of the submission and registration of the contract of sale in the Land Registry for the purpose of specific performance.

480. A constructive trust can be recognized, even when the registration of property in the name of a person took place for the convenience of the right-holder of the immovable property, who was incapable of going to the Land Registry to make the registration. Thus, the recognition of a constructive trust does not simultaneously confer a registration right, if pursuant to Cap. 224 the right to register the property presupposes its division.[566]

481. As regards the liability of the trustee in case of fraud, section 310 of the Criminal Code provides that any person who, being a trustee of any property, with intent to defraud destroys or converts the property to any use not authorized by the trust, is guilty of a felony, and is liable to imprisonment for seven years. For the purposes of this section the term, 'trustee' includes the following persons: trustees

563. Gray & Gray, *supra* n. 99 at 839–840. An example of claiming the establishment of a resulting trust in relation to immovable property, which nevertheless dismissed by the court is *Crestar (overseas) Ltd et al. v. Tatiana Visotskagia. See Crestar (overseas) Ltd et al. v. Tatiana Visotskagia* (2008) 1B CLR 942.

564. John Mowbray, Lynton Tucker, Nicholas Le Poidevin, Edwin Simpson, *Lewin on Trusts* I 13 (17th ed., Sweet & Maxwell Ltd, 2000).

565. *Pirillos v. Konnari* (2000) 1B CLR 1153.

566. *See Papaioannou v. Andreou* (2001) 1B CLR 903.

upon express trusts created by a deed, will, or instrument in writing, whether for a public or private or charitable purpose; trustees appointed by or under the authority of a law for any such purpose; person upon whom the duties of any such trust as aforesaid devolve; executors and administrators.

Chapter 2. Security: *Fiducia Cum Creditore* (*See also* Parts I, II and V)

482. *Fiducia cum creditore* broadly refers to the transfer of ownership or possession as security with the obligation of the acquirer or possessor to transfer them back when the claim is satisfied. 'Fiducia cum creditore includes two relations: (i) the initial transfer of dominium (full ownership), which causa is to secure debt by way of title transfer (ii) the subsequent transfer (pactum fiduciae) back transfer of the dominium, which transfer is under condition and depends on debtor's performance of obligation.'[567]

483. With regard to immovable property, the equitable mechanism of trust also applies.[568] In relation to movables, security interests are satisfied through various mechanisms of transfer of possession, further analyzed below. For instance, bailment, guarantee and bond in customary form are valid contracts recognized by Cap. 149 that can be used as security. In the same way the mechanism of lien (agent's lien, unpaid seller's lien, banker's lien or bailee's lien, for instance) works as a security. However, no legislative disposition regarding movables concerns the mechanism of *fiducia cum creditore* per se.

484. On this topic, it has to be noted that the Directive 2002/47/EC of the European Parliament and of the Council of 6 June 2002 on financial collateral arrangements, which was implemented in Cyprus by Law 43(I)/2004, recognizes the possibility of transfer of ownership as a security. The financial collateral to be provided shall consist of cash, financial instruments (primarily shares) or credit claims. It is possible to have either full ownership of the collateral[569] or simply security in the sense that the taker has security over collateral, but the full ownership of the financial collateral remains with the collateral provider when the security right is established[570] (the latter encompasses mortgages, pledges, fixed charges, floating

567. Ivan P. Mangatchev, *Fiducia cum creditore contracta in EU*, 6 (Electronic copy), https://www.academia.edu/3496659/Fiducia_cum_creditore_contracta_in_EU_law, last visited on 23 December 2019.

568. *See Pirillos v. Konnari* (2000) 1B CLR 1153. The case concerned the transfer of immovable property for securing a debt and there was explicit mention in the written agreement of the parties for a retransfer of property to the transferor after the payment of the debt. The court ruled that this agreement, which was not registered in the Land Registry and was not explicitly referred to a trust, does not give rise to an express trust, given that the conditions of s. 65IE of Cap. 224 were not met, but conferred the creation of a constructive trust. In this context, the sale from the trustee of an immovable property to a third party, knowing the substantial proprietary interest of the beneficiary of the trust, constitutes the purchaser a trustee of the constructive trust, of its rights, for the benefit of the plaintiff and he/she is not considered to be a good faith purchaser without notice. As a result, the purchaser had no right to charge the immovable property, which is subject to, in favour of the plaintiff, a pre-existing trust and the beneficiary of the trust has the right to ask the annulment of the submission and registration of the contract of sale to the Land Registry for the purpose of specific performance.

569. *See* Art. 2(1)(c) of the Directive 2002/47/EC and s. 6(1) of the Law 43(I)/2004.

570. Article 2(1)(c) of the Directive 2002/47/EC.

charges and liens). The collateral-taker under a security financial collateral arrangement will have the right to 'appropriate' collateral without a court order for foreclosure – provided that this has been expressly agreed by the parties. Furthermore, no formalities have to be met for the validity of the agreement.[571] The law is applicable to financial collateral arrangements where one of the parties is either a supervised financial institution, a public authority, a central bank or a central counterparty which are evidenced in writing.

571. Section 5 of the Law 43(I)/2004.

Part V. Security

Chapter 1. Securities in Immovable Property (*See Also* Parts I and IV)

§1. Privileges, Liens and Charges

485. The term 'charges on immovable property' refers to the creation of a real burden or encumbrance on a property belonging to another person. The charges are mainly established in order to secure the payment of a claim, such as a debt, through the commitment and the divestiture/sale of the charged immovable property from the person in favour of whom, the charge has been established.

486. The general category of charges consists of the encumbrances, which are defined under the Transfer and Mortgage Law 9/1965, and which include the encumbrance of mortgage, which is the security most commonly granted over an immovable property. While all encumbrances of third parties on the immovable property of another person constitute a burden or restriction on the property, for the purposes of this analysis, the term charges is defined *stricto sensu*, putting aside the legal interests of easement, habitation, usufruct and restrictive covenants, which charge the alien immovable property *in corpus* by restricting the use, profit-making and development by the registered owner, without though restricting the power to dispose of it.

487. In this context, the analysis focuses on the charges that are created in order to secure a claim against the registered owner or for the fulfilment of one's obligation. The basic legal effect from the creation of these charges is the commitment of the property in order to secure a claim or an obligation.

488. In section 12(5)(a) of Law 9/1965 the definition of charge is provided (but is referred to as an 'encumbrance'). Subsequently, a charge is regarded as the direct claim over immovable property, right of retention or lien over immovable property or obligation or where it lies, on the basis of any provisions.

489. In fact, the above definition is quite wide. The creation of a charge does not confer the transfer of a proprietary right, nor does it confer the transfer of the possession of the immovable property to the beneficiary of the charge. In contrast to easements, a dominant and a servient tenement are not presupposed. The beneficiary of the real charge acquires a sui generis real right, which consists of its preferential satisfaction from the charged property, in the event of non-fulfilment of the claim or the obligation against which the charge is created.[572]

490. Charges are either wilful or unintentional. Wilful charges are those which are created under the will of the registered owner of the charged immovable property, such as the mortgage. Unintentional charges are those which are created under the will of another person, for example, through the deposit of the contract of sale for specific performance by the buyer or through a legislative provision, such as the real charge that is created in relation to the payment of fees on the basis of section 5 of the Department of Lands and Surveys (Fees and Charges) Law (Cap. 219) or the charge that is created by the registration of a court order on the registered immovable property of the judgment debtor.

491. The provisions of any law may give rise to a charge. Under Law 9/1965, the most usual charges (encumbrances) are defined. These are the mortgage, the Memorandum or Memo (sections 53–62 of the Civil Procedure Law, Cap. 6),[573] the application for registration of immovable property in the name of the debtor (sections 63–71 of the Civil Procedure Law, Cap. 6), the order of sale of immovable property, known as a writ, the registration of a bond relating to a loan to a member of a Cooperative Society, the registration of a supplementary bond for a further loan relating to a loan to a member of a Cooperative Society, the deposit of a contract of sale of immovable property, the conditional charge by the Registrar of Cooperative Companies, the court's judgment or order to alter or cancel the registration of a property, the publication of a apportionment of expenses for the construction of a road, the charge on an immovable property in respect of charges or fees payable to the Land Registry and a court's judgment or order for the sale of a mortgaged property.

492. According to the above list, easements do not constitute charges that can result, upon registration, in the legal effects, which are described in Law 9/1965, that is the commitment of the immovable property, the restriction in disposition and the possibility of divestiture in order to secure the satisfaction of a claim or an obligation, which is being guaranteed by the registration of the real charge.

493. According to section 40 of Cap. 224, the charge is valid, provided that it is registered in the Land Registry. No transfer or charge over immovable property is valid, unless it is registered or recorded in the Land Registry. The principle of *nemo data quod non habet* continues to apply even in the case of the wilful charge over

572. Alison Clarke & Paul Kohler, *supra* n. 430 at 664.

573. When the lender obtains a Court's order, according to which the defendant is ordered to pay an amount ('judgment debtor'), he can register in the Land Registry a charge against immovable property that is registered (there are titles) in the name of the debtor, in order to make this property a guarantee for the payment of the judgment debt. During the registration, the property is charged by the payment of the debt on the basis of the Court's decision in priority of any other debt or obligations of the debtor, with which the property was not charged before the submission of the note.

immovable property. Subsequently, no wilful charge affecting any immovable property is registered in the Land Registry by any person unless he/she is the registered owner of the property.

494. The same rule is reasserted in section 12(7) of Law 9/1965, where it is provided that a charge, lien or encumbrance which is not or has not been notified to, or any document relating thereto has not been declared, registered, produced or lodged to the Land Registry is not valid. At the same time, all the necessary formalities must have been complied with and all fees and charges payable in respect of the acceptance or registration thereof have been paid.

495. The legal effect of the registration of the charge is the commitment of the immovable property in order to divest it for the preferential satisfaction of the claim or the obligation against which the charge was created. According to section 12 of Law 9/1965, no declaration of transfer or mortgage of immovable property with charge thereon shall be accepted by the Land Registry. Still, an exception to the above rule is introduced under section 12A of Law 9/1965 regarding all charges, while more specific exceptions are provided by sections 29 and 31 of Law 9/1965 in relation to mortgage. That is the case of transfer of a mortgaged immovable property, as will be further analyzed.

496. According to section 12A, the owner of the charged immovable property may, under a declaration of sale and payment of the full price to the competent District Lands Office. The latter shall accept the declaration if the declared price is not lower that the amount which was defined by the competent court as the amount corresponding to the market value of the property and if there is no pending appeal against this decision of the court.

497. In order for the court to define the market value, an originating summons is brought, which is served on the beneficiaries of the charge. The deposited sale proceeds are distributed in order of priority among the persons for whose benefit the charge on the immovable property exists (principle of temporal priority).

§2. Mortgage

I. Legal Nature and Creation of Mortgage

498. The mortgage is the main category of a real security. The term security is referred to the placement at the disposal of the creditor – that is, the person who finances, who gives credit – the appropriate assets, to which he/she can resort, if the credit relationship takes an abnormal course.[574]

499. The modern mortgage law is considered to be in line with the main principle of natural law and the law of equity, which recognizes that the main right of

574. Papasteriou, *supra* n. 66 at vol. III, 246.

the mortgaged lender concerns the payment of a debt and that his right on the immovable property refers only to the security of the debt.[575]

500. The Cypriot Supreme Court has declared in the past that a mortgage is not considered to be a real right over an alien immovable property, but as security and an encumbrance. This shall be interpreted in the sense that a mortgage means nothing more than a charge on land which does not transfer any estate or interest in the land to the mortgagee.[576] It is created under a mortgage contract and is registered in the Land Registry. As provided in section 22 of Law 9/1965, a mortgage can be created as security for the fulfilment of an existing, future or a conditional obligation, including the obligation relating to a cash amount paid in instalments or as a balance of a current account.

501. The procedure of creating a mortgage is similar to transfer of immovable property, while at the same time, Law 9/1965 introduces some basic rules regarding the transfer and mortgage of immovable property. The conditions and the procedure of creating a mortgage are set out in section 21 of Law 9/1965. The procedure requires the conclusion of a mortgage contract between the mortgagor and the mortgagee, in which the debtor takes over the obligation to pay the debt to the lender, while a declaration of mortgage shall be submitted to the Land Registry. Similar to the case of transfers, the declaration of mortgage shall be accepted by a Land Registry officer.[577] In fact, the deposited with the Land Registry document constitutes at the same time a contract and a declaration of mortgage, and as a result the deposit of a separate mortgage contact is not considered necessary.

502. Nevertheless, if there is a separate mortgage contract, its validity is subject to the conditions of concluding a valid contract according to contract law,[578] while its terms are checked for unfairness, provided that the conditions of the Unfair Terms in Consumer Contracts Law (Law 93(I)/1996) are met.

503. Thus, the form of the mortgage provided in the First Schedule of Law 9/1965 is not binding and, subsequently, the mortgage is not considered invalid, if there is not a substantial differentiation from it, since according to section 3(1)(b) of Law 9/1965 'the Director may authorize such other form to the like effect to be used

575. *Thornborough v. Baker* (1675) 36 ER 1000.

576. *Spyros Michaelides v. Chrysses Demetriades etc* (1968) I CLR 211. *See also Nicola v. Sofocleous* (1955) 20 CLR. Part II, 49, at p. 50: 'To prevent confusion of ideas it should be stated at once that the word "mortgage" as used in our Cyprus statutes and in these proceedings means nothing more than a charge on land which does not transfer any estate or interest in the land to the mortgagee.' This finding, however, shall be revised, since in recent case law some district courts have referred to mortgages as 'real rights' with regard to their protection as property by the Constitution in cases related to the 'enclaved buyers' protection vis-à-vis the mortgagee's rights. For instance, *see Alpha Bank Cyprus Ltd v. District Land Officer of Limassol*, No. 53/16, 17 May 2017. For the question of enclaved buyers, *see* VI. Transfer of Property into the Name of the 'Enclaved' Buyer of Land.

577. Section 8 of Law 9 of 1965.

578. *See Aggelidis v. Cooperative credit company of Palouriotisa* (1997) 1C CLR 1771: null contract of mortgage which is connected to fake bill notes. The independence of mortgage contract does not protect it from the consequences of a violation of another with which is functionally connected.

and such alteration of any form set out in the Second Schedule to be made, as the circumstances of any case may render necessary; and any variation of such other form or altered form from the respective form set out in the Second Schedule, not being in matter of substance, shall not affect its validity or regularity.'[579] If the mortgagor is a company, the mortgage shall also be registered with the Registrar of Companies.[580] In case of a default the mortgage will be considered void against the liquidator or creditor of the company but the mortgage would remain valid and enforceable between the mortgagor and the mortgagee.

504. The mortgage of the immovable property may be considered to be a guarantee in favour of a third person, so that the guarantor, and not the primary debtor, would appear as a mortgaged debtor. Indeed, as held in *Ioanni Nicola Hadjioikonomou v. Hellenic Bank Ltd*, the appropriate meaning of sections 21 and 22 of Law 9/1965 results in the fact that the mortgage of immovable property may be considered as a guarantee in favour of a third person, so that the guarantor would appear as the mortgaged debtor.[581]

505. The contract-declaration of mortgage is accepted, once the existence of barriers has been investigated, and the land to be mortgaged is free and the debtor is not under a prohibition. If the property is charged, the declaration of mortgage will not be accepted, unless the pre-existing charge is a mortgage.

506. In relation to the submission and acceptance procedure of the declaration, the same rules as with the declaration of transfer apply regarding the formalities, the submitted documents and the discretion of the Director of the Land Registry. Similarly, there are also three stages: the declaration, the acceptance and the registration stage.[582]

507. Section 21 of Law 9/1965 defines in detail the components that the declaration of mortgage shall contain: a precise description of the immovable property; a statement on whether or not there is any change in the condition of the immovable property proposed to be mortgaged as described in the registration therefor and on the nature of any such change and a statement on whether or not there is any subsisting tenancy of such immovable property. In addition, the mortgaged debtor shall present the mortgaged contract duly stamped, upon which his obligation against the lender would be defined (date of debt, a specified or ascertainable amount or, costs and expenses in case of legal proceedings for the payment of the debt). If the mortgage concerns any future or a conditional liability, the maximum amount of the potential liability shall be specified.

579. *Hadjioikonomou v. Hellenic Bank Ltd* (1992) IB CLR 949.
580. Section 90 of Cap. 113.
581. *Hadjioikonomou v. Hellenic Bank Ltd, supra* n. 579.
582. *See* ss 13 και 14 of Law 9/1965.

508. The Director may order an enquiry once the declaration is accepted and before its registration.[583] Provided that the fees are paid, the mortgage registration will follow. Subsequently, the Director issues to the lender the certificate of the registration of the mortgage in his name endorsed on the contract and declaration of mortgage, and accompanied by the certificate of registration, in the name of the mortgagor, of the immovable property mortgaged, and a copy thereof to the debtor.[584]

509. It is however possible for the declaration of transfer and mortgage to take place simultaneously. In this case, both declarations are considered to be legally binding from the moment that the declaration of transfer took place.[585] Furthermore, it is also possible for a subsequent mortgage to be created on a mortgage-charged property, if the subsequent mortgagee, before the acceptance of mortgage, declares that he is aware of the existing mortgage[586] and the subsequent mortgage consists of any property included in the existing mortgage and nothing else.[587] Section 30 of Law 6/1965 provides for the principle of temporal priority, in accordance with the registration order, which regulates the classification/range of mortgages and the charges law in general.

II. Legal Effects of Mortgage

510. From the moment the mortgage is accepted, the immovable property is charged for the payment of the amount secured thereby, in priority to all other debts and obligations of the mortgagor or of the owner thereof for the time being, other than a debt already secured under a previous mortgage or any charge, that has priority over all other charges and encumbrances.[588]

511. The mortgage creates a particular legal situation, where the interests of the mortgagor and the mortgagee come into balance. The immovable property continues to remain in the ownership and physical power of the mortgagor, who, nevertheless, is obliged under the charge, unless there is an agreement to the contrary, to exercise his ownership in such a way as the interests of the mortgagee are not affected, in line with the principle of reasonable and usual management. In particular, he/she has to pay the taxes and any expenses related to the property and to repair and maintain in good condition all the buildings on the property without, however, being obliged to act or make improvements that would put the building in better condition than it was at the date of the declaration of mortgage. In addition, as far as cultivable land is concerned, he must continue to cultivate the land, as a good farmer, and he cannot cut trees without the consent of the mortgage lender, unless this is necessary under good husbandry. The law also grants the lender the right to

583. Section 13(5) of Law 9/1965.
584. Sections 16(4)(β) and (c) of Law 9/1965.
585. Section 17 of Law 9/1965.
586. Section 29(1)(α) of Law 9/1965.
587. Sections 29(2)(α) and (β) of Law 9/1965.
588. *See* ss 22 (2) and 23 of Law 9/1965.

visit the mortgage property, upon reasonable notice to the debtor, in order to examine the property's situation. Subsequently, despite the fact that the physical possession of the property remains with the debtor or guarantor, that is to say the registered owner, a statutory right of control is granted to the lender to ensure that the property's condition will not deteriorate and its value will not be reduced due to the inappropriate exercise of the usufruct right by the debtor.

512. The lender also acquires certain other rights, such as the right to demand from the debtor and keep the certificate of registration of the property for himself and, where insurance against loss of, or damage to, such property is effected or to be effected by the mortgagor, to demand and keep the policy of insurance and the receipts for the payment of the premiums in respect thereof.[589] Regarding the protection of the property, the lender has equal rights with the lawful owner and possessor of the property, since according to section 26 of Law 9/1965 it has concurrent and equal powers with the mortgagor for the purposes of taking any action, whether by civil or criminal process, against any person for the protection of such immovable property against destruction or damage. The above rights are granted in order to satisfy in priority the debt by the charged property through the disposal of the latter. As underlined in *Olga Ioannou Polycarpou et al. v. Laiki Bank et al.*, it is self-evident that if the debt by judgment is paid before the disposal, the disposal does not proceed, and it is also self-evident that in case of disposal, any remaining balance, after the debt is paid, is returned to the debtor.[590]

513. The real interest of the mortgaged lender is also guaranteed by the Compulsory Expropriation Law (Law 15/1962), which secures the payment of the debt from the amount of compensation. According to section 11(1)(a), when property for which compensation is paid for compulsory expropriation is subject to pledge or charged for payment of any sum secured by mortgage, registration of a court order or any other relevant security or charge, pledge, mortgage to a pledged, mortgaged or judgment lender or, as the case may be, to any other person in favour of whom a charge or security exists, the aforementioned compensation is given towards the complete or partial payment of the debt, in accordance with the existing priority of pledge, mortgage, registration of court's order or any other security or charge.

III. Transfer of Mortgage

514. Section 32 of Law 9/1965 provides for the possibility of transfer of mortgage. The mortgaged lender can transfer the mortgage, unless the contract of mortgage forbids it. The case of the transfer of the mortgage by the mortgagee should be distinguished from the case of the transfer of the mortgaged property from the debtor to a third party, who either acquires the charge of the mortgage until the mortgagor pays the debt or undertakes himself the obligation of payment by substituting the mortgagor, if the most secure process of payment of the debt from the

589. Section 25 of Law 9/1965.
590. *Ioannou Polycarpou et al. v. Laiki Bank et al.* (2002) 1 CLR 1688.

sale price is not followed in order to obtain the transferred property free from the burden of the mortgage. A typical case of transfer of mortgage is when the bank transfers its mortgages to a third party (known as 'mortgage book').[591]

515. The Credit Agreements for Consumers relating to Residential Immovable Property Law (Law 41(I)/2017) transposing Directive 2014/17/EU of the European Parliament and of the Council of 4 February 2014 in the Cypriot legal system provides as part of the pre-contractual information provided by means of the European Standardised Information Sheet (ESIS) that some flexibilities should be mentioned in the loan agreement, e.g., where appropriate the conditions under which the loan may, at the consumer's initiative, be transferred to another creditor or to another property. Other provisions include the borrower's rights, e.g., the right of withdrawal or examination and, where appropriate, other rights such as transferability of the loan.[592]

516. Additionally, the national legislator has adopted a separate legal framework under the Law for the Sale of Credit Facilities and Other Related Issues of 2015 (Law 169(I)/2015), where the sale of a credit facility is also regulated.[593] Before the sale of all or part of its credit facilities, a credit or financial institution or a credit acquiring company shall: (a) either notify its intention to sell or dispose of all or part of its portfolio of credit facilities; or (b) call the borrower concerned and its guarantors, within a period of forty-five days, to submit a proposal to purchase the credit facility under sale. Any credit facility transferred by a credit institution shall be deemed to have been transferred to the buyer at the time of the transfer; and all rights and obligations arising from the credit facility agreement are automatically transferred to the relationship between the borrower and the buyer relationship and are still valid between these two parties.

517. As soon as the transfer is registered, the Director of the Land Registry shall notify the mortgagor and the mortgagee of any subsequent mortgage over the property that the mortgage has been transferred and supply the details of the transferee.[594] The transfer has no effect on the priority of the mortgage transferred as between such mortgage and any other encumbrance on the same immovable property.[595] As already underlined, the transferability of the mortgage strongly suggests the attribution of a real right in the mortgage, beyond its characterization only as real security and charge. In fact, it is a real interest, non-proprietary, over an immovable property, which constitutes the subject of transfer and transactions, like other real rights, provided that this is not explicitly forbidden by the contract establishing the mortgage.

591. Dixon, *supra* n. 82 at 448.
592. Section 14(2) *see* Index II, s. 10 of the Law 41(I)/2017.
593. Section 18(1) and (2), Law 169(I)/2015.
594. Section 32(7)(b) of Law 9/1965.
595. Section 32(8) of Law 9/1965.

IV. Discharge, Judicial Annulment of Mortgage and Release from Mortgage

518. In Law 9/1965, two ways of discharge of a mortgage are provided. In principle, the mortgagee has a duty to proceed with the discharge of the mortgage as soon as the debt is paid or otherwise satisfied, and as a result, all the mortgaged immovable properties are released from the mortgage. The discharge takes place with the deletion of the note related to the mortgage from against the registration of the immovable property in the Land Registry's records.[596]

519. Thus, where the mortgagee refuses or neglects to take action for the discharge of the mortgage, despite the fact that the liability secured thereby has been satisfied or has ceased to exist, or if the mortgagee refuses to accept payment of the amount secured by the mortgage, after it has become payable, or if the mortgagee is of unknown residence, or is a company or partnership which is no longer in existence, or has died and his personal representative or heirs are unknown, and in any of these cases either the liability secured by the mortgage has been satisfied or has ceased to exist, or the mortgagor is for any of these reasons unable to pay the amount secured by the mortgage, after such amount has become payable, to the person who is entitled to this amount, the mortgagor can apply to the court for an order cancelling the mortgage. If the court makes such a cancellation order, the Director of the Land Registry shall give effect to it and cancel the mortgage.[597]

520. At the same time, there is the option of release of the immovable property from a mortgage. If two or more immovable properties are included in a mortgage, or if there is a share in immovable property which is less than the mortgagor's interest in such immovable property included in a mortgage, any of such immovable properties, may be released from the mortgage by the mortgagee, provided that there has been a part payment made by the mortgagor or otherwise. Such release requires the written consent of the mortgagee and of every guarantor.[598] For the partial release of mortgaged properties, the consent of all the co-owners/mortgaged debtors is necessary.[599]

---

596. Section 35 of Law 9/1965.
597. Section 36 of Law 9/1965. The principle 'once a mortgage always a mortgage' applies. In this context, Cypriot courts have recognized the concept of 'equity of redemption' with reference to UK case law and doctrine. As it was noted by the District Court of Larnaca (*Bank of Cyprus Plc v. ALENTIA LIMITED et al.*, Claim No. 4763/2013, 17 May 2019): 'It is a settled rule of equity that any agreement which interferes with the mortgagor's equitable right to redeem is ineffectual. The rule is an application of the principle "once a mortgage, always a mortgage". Where a mortgage fixes a contractual date for redemption and then provides that the right shall not be exercised by the mortgagor for a substantial period thereafter, this is void as a fetter on the right to redeem. On the same basis, a provision to the effect that the right to redeem is exercisable only by particular persons or until the expiry of a particular period of time is ineffective. Such provisions are said to be void as "clogging" the equity of redemption. This doctrine applies to all types of mortgages, whether legal or equitable, or by way of floating charge or otherwise. While it has been criticised as ((an appendix to our law which no longer serves a useful purpose and would be better excised the Privy Council has more recently accepted that it remains "an old-established but not obsolete doctrine of equity".'
598. Section 34 of Law 9/1965.
599. *See Stavrou Christophorou et al. v. Bank of Cyprus Ltd* (2003) 1B CLR 1205.

V. Auction Sale of the Mortgaged Property by the Mortgagee

521. This procedure is governed by Part VIA of Law 9/1965 together with the Regulations of 2015 on Law on Sale of Immovable Property pursuant to the Part VIA of the Law on Transfer and Immovable Property No. 9/1965. Part VIA, which is entitled 'Sale of a Mortgage by a Mortgagee', was introduced into Law 9/1965 in 2014. This amendment modified the previous regime by simplifying the auction procedure provided for in sections 44A to 44AA and differs from the disposal provisions of Chapter 6 and Part VI of Law 9/1965.

522. Part VIA provides for the process of forced sale of real estate which is carried out by the mortgagee himself. The whole procedure is based on a series of notices which are sent by the mortgagee (the lender) to the mortgagor (borrower). If the debtor does not comply with the notice within the time limit set, the mortgagee can apply to the Land Registry and request the sale of the property, adducing sworn evidence that the amount specified has become payable, and that the amount specified or some part thereof remains unpaid.

523. The procedure has been subject to significant modifications following the Memorandum of Understanding that Cyprus concluded with its international creditors in 2013, on the basis of which the Cyprus government was required to introduce a new 'foreclosure law'.[600] According to section 44B, in the event of a default, as a result of which the whole debt secured by the mortgage is rendered payable, and in the further event that the default is for a period of not less than 120 days from the date on which it has been rendered payable in accordance with the terms of the mortgage agreement or the provisions of this Law, the mortgage creditor may initiate proceedings for the sale of the property unless the process of enforced sale of the mortgaged property by the mortgage creditor is suspended on the basis of the provisions of any other laws, or regulations, or directives. In particular, a notice of default (notice of type 'Θ')[601] and a notice whereby a mortgagee is required within thirty days to pay mortgage debt (notice of type 'I')[602] accompanied by a statement of account regarding the mortgage debt are sent to the mortgagor. According to section 44C(2), if the mortgagor or any other interested person fails to comply with the notice of type 'I', then the mortgagee may serve a second notice on the mortgagor and any other interested person, to the effect that the property will be sold by auction. Furthermore, according to section 44A(4), nothing excludes the right of the mortgagee to proceed with a civil action to obtain a court order for the sale of the mortgaged property.[603]

---

600. *See* Law 142(I)/2014 which amended Law 9/1965.
601. Section 44B(2).
602. Section 44C(1).
603. This is not an abuse of process since the lender seeks the same effect provided by the relevant law, but in another way. The issuance of a judgment or an order for the sale of a mortgaged property shall confer only rights on the lender and no obligation. Nor does it restrict the lender's right to pursue another method of executing the mortgage or selling the mortgaged property when the law so permits. *See Kounounas et al. v. Bank of Cyprus Public Company Ltd*, District Court of Paphos, Request for Appeal No. 195/2016, 7 November 2016; *Linos Junior Ltd et al. v. Bank of Cyprus*

524. According to section 44C(3), as amended by Law 87(I)/2018, the mortgagor, and any other interested person may, within thirty days from the date of receipt of the notice file an appeal before the District Court to set aside the notice of intended sale, only by virtue of a series of grounds: (a) that the notice does not comply with the required form and content; (b) that the notice was not duly served; (c) that the time period to make the payment given by the mortgagee had not ended at the time this notice was sent; (d) that an interlocutory injunction has been issued in favour of the mortgagor in accordance with section 32 of the Courts of Justice Law; (e) that a protective order has been issued in favour of the mortgagor under the provisions of the Insolvency of Natural Persons (Personal Repayment Plans and Debt Relief Orders) Law; (f) the mortgagor whose participation in the 'ESTIA' scheme for non-performing loans or to any other State aid plan for credit facilities has been approved, provided that he/she accepts and complies with the agreement and his/her credit obligations resulting from that plan. The above reasons need not be cumulative in order to set aside a notice of Intended Sale of a Mortgaged Property, and if even one of them is present, the Court may dismiss the said Notice.[604]

525. One of the main aims of the new provisions introduced by the amending Law 87(I)/2018 was to stop the abuse of the system at the time which allowed debtors to delay the sale of mortgaged property for years by means of strategic applications to the Courts for orders to cancel auctions, by objecting to the reserve price set by the Department of Lands and Surveys or on a number of procedural grounds. The result was that the average time taken to enforce a mortgage was ten years, while a mortgagor could extend the delay well beyond that.[605] Indeed, one of the reasons the mortgagor previously had the right to register an application/appeal for the purpose of cancelling the Auction Notice (notice under type I), was where an action was brought before the Court and concerned the Notice. In this context, one of the most significant amendments brought by the new law is that today the mortgagor has no right to register an appeal by invoking the argument that an action is pending before a Court of Justice, since Law 87(I)/2018 has deleted section 44IV of Law 9/1965 and amended section 44C of Law 9/1965 by enabling the mortgagee to proceed with commencing a procedure for the auction of the mortgaged property even in the case where an action is pending. So, under section 44C(3) of the Law 9/1965, a pending legal action no longer constitutes a ground on which a mortgagor

---

Public Company Ltd, District Court of Limassol, Request for Appeal No. 51/2018, 3 May 2018; *Frostin Limited v. Bank of Cyprus Ltd*, Request for Appeal No. 204/2016, District Court of Paphos, 14 November 2016; *Sprekelia Properties Limited v. Bank of Cyprus Public Company Ltd*, Request for Appeal No. 256/2016, District Court of Paphos, 17 February 2017; *Totalpack (Cyprus) Ltd et al. v. Bank of Cyprus Public Company Ltd*, Request for Appeal No. 1/2017, District Court of Nicosia, 22 March 2017.

604. *Pavlou v. Bank of Cyprus Ltd*, District Court of Ammochostos, Appeal No. 25/2018, 19 February 2019.

605. C. Vezouvios & L. Tsikkinis, 'Cyprus', in *The International Comparative Legal Guide to: Real Estate, A Practical Cross-Border Insight to Real Estate Law* Ch. 9 (10th ed. Global Legal Group Ltd 2015).

can file a court application to suspend an auction procedure. Instead, now an interlocutory injunction shall be issued in favour of the mortgagor in accordance with section 32 of the Courts of Justice Law.

526. The Nicosia District Court applied the new legislation in *Kyriakos Papavasiliou (Trading) Ltd v. Hellenic Bank Public Company Limited.*[606] This case concerned an auction procedure which had been initiated by the sending the relevant notices to the mortgagor. The mortgagor filed an action against the creditor (a bank) in order to suspend the foreclosure procedure. The District Court of Nicosia confirmed the retroactive effect of the law, clarifying that the wording of the provision about this effect was clear and unambiguous and, therefore, not open to an alternative interpretation.

VI. Transfer of Property into the Name of the 'Enclaved' Buyer of Land

527. On 3 September 2015, the House of Representatives enacted the Immovable Property (Transfer and Mortgage) (Amendment) Law 139(I)/2015[607] which entered into force on 4 September 2015 with its publication in the Official Gazette of the Republic. At the same time, the House of Representatives enacted the Immovable Property (Transfer and Mortgage) (Protection of Buyers) Regulations of 2015. The aim of the law was to offer protection to 'enclaved buyers'. The term 'enclaved buyer' is used to describe the case where a buyer of an immovable property paid the full price and/or fully complied with his obligations under the contract of sale, he/she submitted the contract of sale to the Land Registry for specific performance purposes, but nevertheless did not receive a title. Despite some existing possibilities of protection for those buyers by previous legislation (mainly by Articles 5(2) and 7(4) of the Law 81(I)/2011 which enables the buyer to obtain priority for the encumbrance which is created in his favour by the deposit of the contract of sale over the mortgage in favour of the vendor's lender), their number in 2015 was high, since, according to the Land Registry, they were about 70,000.

528. The new legislation introduces provisions for the transfer of property to the property buyers who have fulfilled their contractual obligations under the contract with the seller, who is however unable or neglects or fails to transfer the property

606. No. 385/18. For an overview, *see* George Ioannou & Achilleas Christophorou, *Amendments to Transfer and Mortgage of Immovable Property Law introduced* (2018).

607. Immovable Property (Transfer and Mortgage) (Amendment) Law 139(I)/2015. The enactment of law which deals with the question of the 'enclaved buyers' was an obligation of the Republic of Cyprus upon the Memorandum of Understanding on Cyprus' Macroeconomic Program and the Loan Agreement of 2013. Both the initial and subsequent updated memoranda contained provisions relating to the issue of those buyers and the obligations imposed on the Republic of Cyprus to deal with it. As mentioned by Yialourou, the number was such that the issue was approached by lenders as a systemic problem in the Cypriot real estate market, which was a blow to the country's development and competitiveness and, therefore, had to be addressed. *See* S. Yiallourou, *Enclaved buyers: The Problem, Regulation and Constitutionality* (2019), available at: https://www.academia.edu/40671133.

in their name, because the property or part of it is subject to mortgage and/or encumbrance and/or prohibition. The new procedure which is introduced by the law aims to facilitate the issuance of title deeds to buyers of immovable property in Cyprus, notwithstanding problems that may exist on the part of the seller, such as mortgages or house and planning inconsistencies. In particular, it was very common for land sellers/developers who had borrowed from credit institutions in order to develop the property to be reluctant to secure separate title deeds for the properties under sale. Therefore, the registration of the contract of sale according to the provisions of the law on the specific performance did not provide any priority in favour of the buyers of those properties since the mortgage in favour of the credit institutions preceded the deposit of the contract of sale. The consequence of this situation was that the buyer had to pay the mortgagee (credit institution from which the seller/developer has borrowed) part of the mortgage, in order to be able to release any part of the property that belonged to him/her from any encumbrance. Specifically, sections 44IH–44KZ are applicable to buyers who have fully paid off the seller and who are consistent with their contractual obligations or are in the process of redemption and are willing to pay the remaining amount in respect of mortgaged real estate.[608]

529. According to the provisions of Law 139(I)/2015, the following conditions for the transfer of the title deed into the name of the buyer must be fulfilled: (a) the full payment of the purchase price; (b) the existence of the registered title deed of the property which is the object of the contract; and (c) the fulfilment of the contractual obligations of the buyer to pay the taxes on the property which is the object of the contract. Second, for the transfer of the title deed into the name of the buyer there must be a registered title of the property which is the object of the contract. If there is no registered title for the object of the contract, the applicant has the right to apply to the Department of Lands and Surveys for the compulsory acquisition of title pursuant to the provisions of Part VI of Cap. 224. Lastly, the Land Registry will proceed to examine the third requirement, namely the payment of taxes, provided that their payment is a contractual obligation of the buyer.

530. Where all these conditions have been fulfilled, the Land Department will proceed to send all interested parties a relevant notice of the transfer of the property into the name of the buyer, giving a period of forty-five days to any interested person (holders of registered encumbrances on the property which is the object of the contract) to submit an objection and/or application for the transfer of the encumbrance. In case of an objection and/or application for the transfer of the encumbrance, such objection and/or application shall be examined and subsequently a decision will be issued. Upon completion of the above, a relevant notice will be sent to the buyer and the seller, calling upon them within sixty days from the date of service of the notice, to proceed with the transfer of the property into the name of the buyer. Additionally, the buyer will be called upon within the above period, to pay the fees for the transfer of the property into his name.

608. For an analysis of the aims of the law, *see National Bank of Greece (Cyprus) Ltd v. Director of Department of Land and Surveys*, Request-Appeal 279/16, 07 November 2017.

531. Law 139(I)/2015 also provides for the rights of the stakeholders to oppose or object to various decisions. On 8 September 2015, the Department of Lands and Surveys announced the acceptance of applications for the transfer of Cyprus property into the buyer's name in accordance with the new provisions of Law 9/1965.

532. The non-compliance of this law with the rights of property[609] and freedom of contract,[610] as the latter are safeguarded by the Constitution of the Republic of Cyprus, has been invoked by mortgagees before the Cypriot Courts. Specifically, credit institutions have argued that the transfer of property to the buyers notwithstanding the existence of a mortgage is a violation of their rights derived from the mortgage and of the contract of loan between them and the sellers of land. Indeed, the legislator was required to choose between two concurrent rights in rem – the mortgagee's mortgage and the right (encumbrance) which is created by the deposit of the contract of sale in the land registry in favour of the buyer – after both parties have substantially fulfilled their contractual obligations. The law gives priority to the interests of the buyers of land by enabling the issuance of a title deed without the burden of the mortgage. It has been put forward that the protection of the buyers of land is justified by the need to safeguard their interests vis-à-vis the credit institutions which should be seen as entities possessing a special economic power. This argument was rejected in the case *Alpha Bank Cyprus Ltd v. District Land Officer of Limassol*,[611] where it was noted that the law does not refer specifically to persons having a special economic power and that any lender could be in the place of the credit institutions. The Court also rejected that argument that without the law being enacted a serious, if not unavoidable risk exists that the interests of the enclaved buyers will be jeopardized and, therefore, a legislative intervention that restricts the mortgagee's rights is needed.

533. Furthermore, even if it were possible for a mortgage to be transferred to another property owned by the seller of land, it was held in *Alpha Bank Cyprus Ltd v. Limassol District Land Officer* that this is only a theoretical possibility. Specifically, as it was noted by the Court 'the reference in section 44KB (4) that the mortgagee may requested that the mortgage be transferred to another immovable property of the same seller can only be of theoretical importance. How easy is it for a mortgagee to force the seller to transfer the mortgage to another property when neither the mortgagee nor the seller is part of the process of Article 44BB? Furthermore, how this will be fulfilled if there is no other immovable property of the seller? Article 23 of the Constitution imposes limitations on the right of property on grounds of public interest. There is no public benefit in this case. There is only a need to protect the rights of a group of people.'[612] Additionally, it was noted that any transfer of a mortgage to an unknown property of the seller burdened with other liens, without specifying the extent that the transferred mortgage will receive, is a

609. Article 23 of the Constitution.
610. Article 26 of the Constitution.
611. *Alpha Bank Cyprus Ltd v. District Land Officer of Limassol*, No. 53/16, 17 May 2017.
612. *Ibid.*

deprivation and/or total restriction of the right of ownership.[613] On the basis of the above, it was decided that the sections of Law 9/1965 on which the Director's contested decision was based were contrary to the provisions of Article 23 of the Constitution, because they resulted in the deprivation of ownership without applying the procedure of compulsory acquisition laid down in Article 23 paragraph 4 of the Constitution and without providing a fair and reasonable compensation to the mortgagee.[614]

534. It was also held that the restriction of the credit institution's right to the mortgage for the purpose of enforcing the right of the buyer constitutes discrimination against the mortgage lenders, whose right in rem had preceded against that of the buyer.[615] Another argument invoked by the mortgagees was that the contractual freedom is also violated. The justifications of the constitutional protection of contractual freedom was defined by the Supreme Court in the case *Republic of Cyprus through the Commissioner of Income Tax v. Charalambos Menelaou*, where it was held that 'it would be contrary to common sense and the rules of justice to allow the foundations of a contractual settlement to be demolished and thereby to create uncertainty and mistrust in the rights and obligations of citizens'.[616] As regards the concept of the freedom of contract, Cypriot case law has evolved to adopt a broad understanding of this concept which comprises not only the freedom to conclude a contract[617] but also the freedom to form the terms of the contract.[618] Furthermore, in the case *President of the Republic v. House of Representatives (No. 2)*,[619] the Supreme Court emphasized that the meaning of contractual freedom of Article 26 of the Constitution may be restricted only to the conditions, restrictions and commitments provided for by the general principles of contract law. On the basis of the above, sections 44ΙΘ, 44Κ, 44ΚΒ, 44ΚΓ and 51 of the Law 9/1965, as the latter was amended by the Law 139(I)/2015, constitute an intervention in the content of the contracts between the lenders and the sellers of property and violate Article 26 of the Constitution.[620] Similarly, it was held that the legislation also violates Article 25 of the Constitution which safeguards the right to practice any profession or to carry on any occupation, trade or business, because it is an

613. *Alpha Bank Ltd v. Director of the Department of Land and Surveys of Paphos*, No. 71/16, 24 May 2017.
614. *Ibid.*
615. *Ibid.*
616. *The Republic of Cyprus through the Commissioner of Income Tax v. Charalambos Menelaou*, 3 CLR 419, 11 May 1982.
617. *Chimonides v. Manglis* (1967) 1 CLR 125. In that case the full bench of the Supreme Court was not unanimous on the content of the right. The majority held that the right vested is the right to conclude a contract and not the rights created under the contract. The minority considered that the above provision protects the full freedom of the 'contract', subject only to such conditions, restrictions or commitments as are based on the general principles of contract law.
618. *Lextalionitis Investments Ltd v. Hellenic Bank Ltd* (2010) 1 CLR 1833; *President of the Republic v. House of Representatives*, Petition No. 4/14, 31 October 14; *President of the Republic v. House of Representatives*, Petition No. 9/2016, 26 January 2017.
619. *President of the Republic v. House of Representatives (No. 2)* (2011) 3 CLR 683.
620. *Alpha Bank Cyprus Ltd v. District Land Officer of Larnaca of the Department of Land and Surveys of the Ministry of Interior*, Request for Appeal No. 24/2017, 8 March 2019.

unauthorized interference with the credit institution's right to freely organize its business for profit and impedes and restricts its free exercise.[621]

535. While the unconstitutionality of the new regime on 'enclaved buyers' has been declared by first instance courts, the issue is not settled, since there are pending appeals concerning these cases and a decision of the Supreme Court is awaited to clarify the situation. In the meantime, on July 2019, Part VIB of Law 9/1965 was amended by the Law 118(I)/2019. The amending law, in its preamble, explains that the 'enclaved buyers'' protective regime aimed to reply to a pressing social need, which is still present. The new law modified certain procedural rules of the initial provisions of 2015, but maintained the core of the 'enclaved buyers'' protection, its underlying reasoning and its justifications.

621. *Ibid.*

Chapter 2. Securities in Movable Property

§1. Privileges, Liens and Charges

I. The Agent's Lien

536. There are in Cypriot law multiple manifestations of specific liens, and the legal framework of the unpaid seller's lien has been analyzed above (*see* Part III, Chapter 1, II). One of the most important cases in practice concerns the agent's lien. The agent may work for remuneration. In addition, the employer of an agent is bound to indemnify him against the consequences of all lawful acts done by such agent in exercise of the authority conferred upon him or against the consequences of all acts done in good faith that may harm a third party. Therefore, the agent may possess an interest against the principal (i.e., the person for whom such acts are done, or who is so represented by the agent). To protect this interest, section 177 of Cap. 149 states that 'An agent may retain, out of any sums received on account of the principal in the business of the agency all money due to himself in respect of advances made or expenses properly incurred by him in conducting such principal's business, and also such remuneration as may be payable to him for acting as an agent.' Furthermore, section 181 refers to a lien and specifically states that 'in the absence of any contract to the contrary, an agent is entitled to retain goods, papers and other property, on whether movable or immovable, of the principal received by him, until the amount due to himself for commission, disbursements and services in respect of the same has been paid or accounted to him.'

II. The Bailee's Lien

537. According to section 106 of Cap. 149, bailment 'is the delivery of goods by one person to another for some purpose, upon a contract that they shall, when the purpose is accomplished, be returned or otherwise disposed of according to the directions of the person delivering them'. This definition corresponds to the Indian concept of bailment,[622] which is based on common law. Five distinct contracts have to be distinguished under the general category of bailment.

538. In this context, first, a deposit (*depositum*) is a bailment contract that can be defined as the relationship with a person, called a depositor, who delivers to another, called a depositary, a movable property for safekeeping without consideration. Second, the mandate (*mandatum*) is the relationship by which the mandator entrusts the other party with the accomplishment of a specific action, without consideration. Third, a loan (*commodatum*) is defined as the relationship by which the possessor of the goods provides to the other party the use of a mobile thing without consideration. Fourth, the pledge (*pignus*) is the relationship by which one of the parties, called a pledgor, delivers to the other, called a pledgee, a movable thing to

622. Pollock and Mulla, *supra*, 13.

secure a claim. Fifth, the lease (*locatio conductio*) is the relationship by which one of the parties, called a lessor, undertakes to give the other, called a lessee, the use of a movable property in lieu of a certain sum of money which is called rent.

539. The general principles of bailment apply, which means that the bailor has to disclose to the bailee any unusual danger related to the possession of the goods that exposes the bailee to 'extraordinary risks' (section 108) and the bailee is bound to take as much care of the goods as 'a man of ordinary prudence would take' (section 109). If the bailor has no title to the goods, and the bailee, in good faith, delivers them back to, or according to the directions of, the bailor, the bailee is not responsible to the owner in respect of such delivery (section 124[623]).

540. In certain circumstances, bailment contracts do give a security to the bailee. Section 128 of Cap. 149 states that 'Where the bailee has, in accordance with the purpose of the bailment, rendered any service involving the exercise of labour or skill in respect of the goods bailed, lien he has, in the absence of a contract to the contrary, a right to retain such goods until he receives due remuneration for the services he has rendered in respect of them.' As mentioned, a condition for the recognition of the bailee's lien is the rendering of services. The Courts traditionally interpret this condition strictly. For instance, in a classic UK case, a mere car wash was not deemed to be a service that would create a lien on the car.[624] It means that no general lien exists in favour of the bailee. Only upon realization of a substantial service may the issue arise.

541. As a general exception, however, the legislator does recognize a general lien, but for specific categories of bailees only: bankers, factors and wharfingers. Specifically, section 129 states that 'bankers, factors and wharfingers, may, in the absence of a contract to the contrary, retain, as a security for a general balance of account, any goods bailed to them; but no other persons have a right to retain, as a security for such balance, goods bailed to them, unless there is an express contract to that effect'.

III. Bond in Customary Form

542. The bond in customary form constitutes a specificity of Cyprus Contract Law. Even if this agreement is called a 'bond', it is a contract, not a security. According to section 78 of Cap. 149, 'A "bond in customary form" is a promise in writing made by one person to another signed by the maker in the presence of at least two witnesses themselves competent to contract, engaging to pay, on demand or at a fixed or determinable future time, a sum of money to a person specified therein, together with interest at a rate fixed therein not exceeding nine per centum per annum and, in the event of any legal proceedings thereon, the costs thereof, and

623. *See also Merkis v. Intertobacco (Cyprus) Ltd* (2003) 1 CLR 1091.
624. *Hatton v. Car Maintenance co Ltd* [1915] 1 Ch 621.

stating therein the consideration for which it is given. The person who makes the promise is called the "debtor"; the person to whom the promise is made is called the "creditor".'

543. The bond in customary form is characterized by rigid formalities. Mention must be made of the consideration, the debt must be clearly indicated, and not only the debtor but also two witnesses must sign the document. This formality is essential since this contract possesses a substantial particularity, as stated in section 80 of Cap. 149: the content of the bond (the debt) is protected by an irrefutable presumption of validity. As an exception, only two situations are permitted where the debtor may doubt the validity of the debt: forgery of the signature or coercion/fraud. Of course, a third defence is allowed: the debtor may invoke the invalidity of the bond in customary form (for instance, because instead of two witnesses, the creditor himself signed the document).[625]

544. The bond in customary form is therefore used in practice as an acknowledgement of debt from the debtor, requested by the creditor to ensure the validity of the debt. Therefore, even if the content of the bond in customary form is strictly defined – for instance, no conditions may be inserted in the bond, as it would undermine its certainty[626] – it is permitted to add some securities to the bond. Specifically, as stated in section 79 of Cap. 149, the bond may be secured by a pledge, a guarantee or a mortgage of immovable property.

IV. Mortgage of Ships and Aircrafts

545. Special provisions exist for the mortgage of specific assets, namely ships and aircrafts.

546. Section 31 of the Merchant Shipping (Registration of Ships, Sales and Mortgages) Law (Law 45/1963) provides for the creation and registration of mortgages over Cyprus-registered vessels. If the ship-owner is a Cyprus company, the ship mortgage (and the deed of covenants) must be registered both in the Cyprus Ships Registry, as a charge over the vessel, under section 31 of Law 45/1963 and at the Cyprus Registrar of Companies, as a charge against the ship owning company, under section 90 of Cap. 113.[627]

547. Aircraft mortgages are registered as a charge against the mortgagor company at the Registrar of Companies under section 90 of Cap. 113. Furthermore, the Civil Aviation Law of 2002 (Law 212(I)/2002) provides also that if the aircraft is registered in Cyprus, registration in the Cyprus Aircraft Register is also required.

625. *See* cases *Papastratis v. Economou* (1970) CLR 11 and *Paulou et al. v. Greek bank Ltd* (1990) 1 CLR 483.

626. *Hadkinson Charles R. v. Top Kinisis Travel Public Ltd* (2010) 1 CLR 897.

627. Lia Iordanou Theodoulou, Angeliki Epaminonda, Elena Georgiou and Stylianos Trillides, Patrikios Pavlou & Associates LLC, *Lending and taking security in Cyprus: overview*, https://uk.practicallaw.thomsonreuters.com/, last visited on 23 December 2019.

§2. PLEDGE

548. As seen above, only a specific case of bailment, the pledge, works as security. In this peculiar form of bailment, the bailee is called 'pawnee' and the bailor 'pawnor'.[628] The pawnee's right of retainer is acknowledged by the legislator in section 131 of Cap. 149, interestingly, not only for the payment of the pledge but also for the interest of the debt and all necessary expenses related to the possession and preservation of the goods. In case where the pawnor makes default, this right of retainer becomes a collateral security. Section 134 of Cap. 149 explains that '(1) If the pawnor makes default in payment of the debt, or performance, at the stipulated time of the promise in respect of which the goods were pledged, the pawnee may bring legal proceedings against the pawnor upon the debt or promise, and retain the goods pledged as a collateral security; or he may sell the thing pledged, on giving the pawnor reasonable notice of the sale. (2) If the proceeds of such sale are less than the amount due in respect of the debt or promise, the pawnor is still liable to pay the balance. If the proceeds of the sale are greater than the amount so due, the pawnee shall pay over the surplus to the pawnor.'

549. The pawnee's lien is not general but related to the specific debt. It is not possible for the pawnee to use the lien in relation to a debt arising out of another contract. In case where multiple contracts have been made with the same person and multiple debts contracted, a simple presumption is proposed by the legislator in section 132 of Cap. 149 that each payment concerns subsequent debts. In other words, older debts are considered to be paid first and the pawnee may retain the goods until payment of the debt. If he/she has only a limited interest to the goods, the pledge is valid to the extent of that interest.[629]

550. As mentioned in section 134 of Cap. 149, the pawnee may also sell the goods. In a case that concerned a pledge upon shares, the pawnor complained that since the pawnee did not sell the shares in time, they lost much of their value (to the detriment of the pawnor's debt, obviously). The court, however, dismissed the argument: the sale of the goods is a privilege of the pawnor when the pawnor defaults on his obligations, not an obligation.[630]

551. It is worth noting that this protective (for the pawnee) legal framework of the pledge extends to various situations whereas no explicit pledge has been agreed. Section 136 of Cap. 149 asserts that 'A person who is in possession of any goods, or of any bill of lading, dock-warrant, warehouse-keeper's certificate, wharfinger's certificate, or warrant or order for delivery, or any other document of title to goods, may make a valid pledge of such goods or documents: Provided that the pawnee acts in good faith, and under circumstances which are not such as to raise a reasonable presumption that the pawnor is acting improperly: Provided also that such

628. Section 130 of Cap. 149.
629. Section 137 of Cap. 149.
630. *Dionisiou v. Cyprus Bank Ltd*, No. 450/12, 26 June 2019.

goods or documents have not been obtained from their lawful owner, or from any person in lawful custody of them, by means of an offence or fraud.'

552. As a general rule, bailment as any kind of contract, is not subject to formalities and the contract can be agreed upon in writing, orally or even by conduct.[631] However, as regards pledge of bills of exchange, promissory notes, bonds or shares, the legislator requires more formalities.[632] Specifically, the contract needs to be in writing, signed by the pawnor, and by two witnesses that were present during the conclusion of the contract. For shares, it is additionally required that the company has been put on notice.

§3. Retention Right, Compensation

553. In a Cypriot case, it has been ruled that a bank, in the absence of any other agreement between itself and the clients, was entitled to calculate interest until the date on which payment was made for a particular debt and to repay the interest first after the capital.[633] The ratio of the decision is that interest is the return or compensation for the use or retention by one person of a sum of money belonging to or owed to another.

§4. Delegation, Direct Claim (Possibility Created by Statute Law to Claim Payment Directly from the Debtor of One's Debtor)

554. First, it is necessary to examine the creditor's direct claim against the guarantor. Guarantee is the contract whereby the guarantor promises to the creditor the enforcement of the obligation of the principal debtor. The contractual relationship between the creditor and the principal debtor may be of varying nature and may concern immovable property. In practice, a guarantee is often requested by banks within the framework of loans. Guarantee is not a security per se, as it does not give the creditor any real property privilege over the possessions of the guarantor. In Cyprus, guarantee is ruled by Part 11 of Cap. 149 (sections 82–105). No consideration is needed for the guarantee contract to be valid.[634] The contract is based on the implied statutory term that the guarantor is entitled to be indemnified by the principal debtor for any sum 'rightly paid'[635] to the creditor. Upon payment of the debt, the guarantor is invested in all prerogatives of the creditor and is entitled to the benefit of all securities that the creditor had against the principal debtor.

631. Section 10 of Cap. 149.
632. Section 138 of Cap. 149.
633. Supreme Court, *Loukos Ltd a.o. v. National Bank of Greece AE* (2005) 1 CLR 38.
634. Section 85 of Cap. 149.
635. Even if the debt was limited (time elapsed), the payment by the guarantor is seen as rightly made, in the light of the Indian case law on this topic. *See* Pollock and Mulla, *Indian Contract and Specific Relief Acts* (16th ed., Lexis Nexis 2019).

555. The contract terminates in five situations. First, in case of continuous guarantee, such as guarantee on the future credit of a bank account, the guarantor can normally revoke the contract anytime as regards future obligations.[636] However, this possibility is restrained by the courts, as they require that the existence of the guarantee is not an essential part of the contractual relationships. In other words, if it is the intent, expressed or implied, of the parties to place the guarantee at the heart of the contractual mechanism, the guarantor cannot revoke his/her participation.[637] Furthermore, in this case, the revocation may be invoked by the guarantor only and not by the principal debtor.[638]

556. Second, Cap. 149 states four cases whereas the guarantor may leave: substantial variation of the terms and conditions of the principal contract without consent of the guarantor (section 91), discharge of the obligations of the principal debtor through a new contract (section 92), or agreement between the principal debtor and the creditor that ensures the creditor will not sue or will give more time to the principal debtor (section 93), and any act or omission of the creditor incompatible with the rights of the guarantor (section 97). The courts, however, interpret the issue of time strictly for the guarantor. It has been ruled, for instance, that an extension of the contract for three years does not mean substantial variation of the contract and therefore the guarantor is still bound by the guarantee.[639] Section 97 has been used for instance in cases where the principal contract contained terms incompatible with the original purpose of the guarantee (the State was the guarantor of a loan for investment, while the company did not invest the money).[640]

636. Section 88 of Cap. 149.

637. *Georgiou v. Cyprus Bank* (2009) 1 CLR 862.

638. *Director of customs v. Pop life electric shops Ltd et al.*, Nicosia District Court, No. 4941/2008, 19 December 2014.

639. *Argiri v. Chrysostomou as an Administrator of the estate of Chrysanthos Chrysostomou* (2006) 1 CLR 1362.

640. *Laiki Kypriaki Trapeza Ltd v. The Attorney General of the Republic* (2004) 1 CLR 83.

Chapter 3. Fixed and Floating Charges over the Assets of a Company

§1. Privileges, Liens and Charges

557. The Cap. 113 governs the procedure for the registration of charges created over the assets of a company. Charges can be fixed or floating.

558. A fixed charge is created over a specific and identified asset of the company, such as immovable property, ships, shares, etc. The company cannot deal with the charged asset unless it has permission from the charge.[641] A fixed charge, such as a mortgage, grants contingent proprietary rights to the right-holder entitling the right-holder to take full proprietary rights over the charged property, the contingency being that the charger must have defaulted in some defined obligation.[642] A floating charge is a security interest, generally over all the identifiable assets of a company, which 'floats' until an event of default occurs or until the company goes into insolvent liquidation, at which time the floating charge crystallizes and attaches to all the relevant assets. The main characteristic of the floating charge is that the company is free to deal with the charged assets in the ordinary course of its business. There are two main powers conferred to the security holder by the floating charge. First, the creditor can crystallize the charge and realize any assets as if it were a fixed charge. In general, the floating charge crystallizes when, upon the non-payment by the company of the secured debt when it is due, the chargee appoints a receiver.[643] Second, if the charge includes all of the assets of the company, the

641. Derek French, *Mayson, French & Ryan on Company Law* 289 (Oxford University Press, 2018–2019).

642. Alastair Hudson, *Equity and Trusts* 809 (4th ed., Cavendish Publishing 2005).

643. Derek French, *supra* n. 640. The question of the powers and duties of the receiver is not regulated by the Cypriot legislation, but by case law. Cypriot courts analyzed the powers and the duties of a receiver in a series of cases. As held by the District Court of Larnaca in the case *Electricity Authority of Cyprus v. Milk and Ice Cream Zumaras Industry*, No. 2734/15, 27 July 2017, the Recipient/Administrator has an obligation, during the exercise of his/her duties, to protect the rights primarily of the bank which appointed him/her and secondarily of the interests of the company and all its creditors (*see: In re Chatzirousou (*2011) 1 C CLR 1703, pp. 1712–1713). The directors of the company retain a residual power that includes the ability to sue the holders of the bonds who appointed the Administrator/Receiver (*see Newhart Developments Ltd v. Co-op Commercial Bank Ltd [1978] 2 All ER 896).* Furthermore, although the Administrator/Receiver is essentially a representative of the company, his/her primary task is to liquidate the assets of the company to the interest of the holder of the bond under which he/she was appointed and his/her powers of management of the company are essentially subsidiary to that task (*see Gomba Holdings UK Ltd v. Homan* [1986] 3 All ER 94). The powers of the Administrator/Receiver are so broad in relation to his/her primary duty to liquidate the property of the company for the benefit of the creditor who appointed him, that he/she may even apply for an injunction to sell the company shares and appoint a receiver to deal with the sale, under the provisions of Law 31(I)/92, provided that it does so in good faith and sufficiently establishes the necessity for their sale (*see Eleni L. Ioannou (Siarmatta) et al. v. Emporiki Bank of Greece SA* (2000) 1 CLR 1463).

creditor can appoint a receiver to take control of the business with a view to discharging the debt out of income or selling the entire business.[644] A powerful creditor, such as a credit institution, will often take a charge on all or, substantially all, of a company's assets (composite charge which is a fixed charge on specific assets and a floating charge on other assets which are not covered by the fixed charge).[645]

559. The concept of the 'floating charge' was analyzed in Cypriot case law with reference to English doctrine. In this context, the District Court of Nicosia held that 'The terms "floating charge" and "floating security" mean a charge or security which is not to be put into immediate operation, but is to float so that the company is to be allowed to carry on its business. It contemplates, for instance, that book debts may be extinguished by payment, and other book debts may come in and take the place of those which have disappeared. While a specific charge is one which without more, attached to ascertained and definite property or property capable of being ascertained and defined, a floating charge moves with the property which it is intended to affect until some event occurs or some act is done which causes it to settle and fasten on the subject of the charge within its reach and grasp. It is of the essence of a floating charge that it remains dormant until the undertaking charged ceases to be a going concern, or until the person in whose favor the charge is created intervenes. His right to intervene may be suspended by agreement, but if there is no such agreement he may exercise his right whenever he pleases after default.'[646]

560. Section 90 of the Cap. 113 establishes the conditions to establish a validly created charge that will be recognized in law by any liquidator or any creditor of the company. According to this provision, 'every charge as well as every amendment, assignment or other change to it created after the fixed date by a company registered in the Republic and being a charge to which this section applies shall, so far as any security on the company's property or undertaking is conferred thereby, be void against the liquidator and any creditor of the company, unless the prescribed particulars of the charge together with the instrument, if any, duly stamped by which the charge is created or evidenced, are delivered to or received by the registrar of companies for registration in manner required by this Law within twenty one days after the date of its creation, but without prejudice to any contract or obligation for repayment of the money thereby secured, and when a charge becomes void under this section the money secured thereby shall immediately become payable.'

644. Elias Neocleous and George Chrysaphinis, 'Cyprus', in *International Secured Transactions* Ch. 11 (Thomson Reuters 10/2015), https://www.neocleous.com.

645. Derek French, *supra* n. 640.

646. Callia in his capacity as Receiver and Administrator of *Pak Estates Limited and Andri Georgiou (Coiffure) Limited v. 1. Georgiou 2. Andri Georgiou (Coiffure) Limited et al.*, No. 3587/10, 16 July 2010.

561. Section 90 applies to the following charges: (a) a charge for the purpose of securing any issue of debentures; (b) a charge on uncalled share capital of the company; (c) a charge on book debts of the company; (d) a floating charge on the undertaking or property of the company; (e) a charge on calls made but not paid; (f) a charge on a ship or any share in a ship; (g) a charge on goodwill, on a patent or a licence under a patent, on a trade mark or on a copyright or a licence under a copyright; (h) a charge on any other movable property created or evidenced by an instrument, where the company retains possession of such property; (i) a charge on immovable property, wherever situate, or any interest therein. The law specifically excludes from the scope of this provision a pledge of shares in companies and all the rights emanating from and agreements for the provision of financial collaterals within the meaning of the Financial Collateral Arrangements Law, as may be amended and apply from time to time.

562. Section 91 of Cap. 113 provides for the duties of companies with regard to mortgages and charges created by the company. According to this provision, It shall be the duty of a company to send to the Registrar of Companies for registration the particulars of every charge created by the company and of the issues of debentures of a series requiring registration under section 90, but registration of any such charge may be effected on the application of any person interested therein.

563. In relation to mortgages, it shall be the duty of a company to send to the Registrar of Companies within twenty-one days after the date of every mortgage effected by the company on its immovable property under any Law relating to the registration of mortgages of immovable property in force for the time being, particulars thereof for recording, as well as particulars of any cancellation thereof in whole or in part, within twenty-one days after the date of such cancellation.

564. In case of default by the company to comply with the duties, the company and every officer of the company who is in default shall be liable to a default fine of EUR 427.

565. Furthermore, section 92 establishes the duty of the company to register charges existing on property acquired. Specifically, where a company registered in the Republic acquires any property which is subject to a charge of any such kind as would, if it had been created by the company after the acquisition of the property, have been required to be registered under Part III of Cap. 113, the company shall cause the prescribed particulars of the charge, together with copy (certified in the prescribed manner to be a correct copy) of the instrument, if any, by which the charge was created or is evidenced, to be delivered to the Registrar of Companies for registration in manner required by Cap. 113 within twenty-one days after the date on which the acquisition is completed.

566. With the regard of the publicity of charges, Cap. 113 provides that the Registrar of Companies shall keep, with respect to each company, a register and a record in the prescribed form of all the charges requiring registration and of all the mortgages requiring recording. The Registrar shall give a certificate under his hand of the registration of any charge registered, stating the amount thereby secured, and the certificate shall be conclusive evidence that the requirements as to registration have been complied with.[647] A mechanism of rectification of the register of charges or the record of mortgages by the court is also provided. Accordingly, the court, on being satisfied that the omission to register a charge or to record a mortgage within the time required by Cap. 113 or that the omission or misstatement of any particular with respect to any such charge or mortgage or in a memorandum of satisfaction or cancellation of mortgage, was accidental, or due to inadvertence or to some other sufficient cause, or is not of a nature to prejudice the position of creditors or shareholders of the company, or that on other grounds it is just and equitable to grant relief, may, on the application of the company or any person interested, and on such terms and conditions as seem to the Court just and expedient, order that the time for registration or recording shall be extended, or, as the case may be, that the omission or misstatement be rectified.[648]

567. A charge may be invalidated on the grounds of certain provisions of Cap. 113 during the bankruptcy procedure. Section 301 establishes invalidity in case of fraudulent preference. According to this provision, any conveyance, charge, mortgage, delivery of goods, payment, execution or other acts relating to property made or done by or against a company within six months before the commencement of its winding up which, had it been made or done by or against an individual within six months before the presentation of a bankruptcy petition on which he is adjudged bankrupt, would be deemed in his bankruptcy a fraudulent preference, shall in the event of the company being wound up be deemed a fraudulent preference of its creditors and be invalid accordingly. Furthermore, section 303 provides that where a company is being wound up, a floating charge on the undertaking or property of the company created within twelve months of the commencement of the winding up shall, unless it is proved that the company immediately after the creation of the charge was solvent, be invalid, except to the amount of any cash paid to the company at the time of or subsequently to the creation of, and in consideration for, the charge, together with interest on that amount at the rate of 5% per annum or such other rate as may for the time being be prescribed by order of the Accountant General.

647. Section 93 of Cap. 113.
648. Section 96 of Cap. 113.

Selected Bibliography

Alikakos, P. *Abuse of Real Rights, Caselaw Evolutions Regarding the Abuse during the Possession and Exercise of a Real Right.* Athens-Thessaloniki: Sakkoulas editions, 2007.

Antoniou, A. *Examinership: A Missed Opportunity.* http://www.crigroup.com.cy/wp-content/uploads/2018/10/Examinership-A-missed-opportunity.pdf.

Artemis, P. & G. Erotokritou. *Cap 148, Civil Wrongs, Law and Case Law.* Nicosia, 2003.

Bevan, C. *Land Law.* Oxford University Press, 2018.

Bridge, M. *Personal Property Law.* 3rd ed. Calendon Law Series. Oxford University Press, 2002.

Burn, E.H. & J. Cartrwight. *Chesire and Burn's Modern Law of Property.* 17th ed. Oxford University Press, 2006.

Burn, E.H. & J. Cartwright. *Maudsley & Burn's Land Law Cases and Materials.* 9th ed. OUP, 2009.

Campbell, D. (ed.). *Neocleous's Introduction to Cyprus Law.* 2nd ed. Center for International Legal Studies, Yorkhill Law Publishing, 2009.

Cedric, B. *Land: The Law of Real Property.* 3rd ed. Old Bailey Press, 2003.

Chappelle, D. *Land Law.* 8th ed. Pearson Education, 2006.

Christodoulou, C. *The Insolvency Review.* 7th ed. Cyprus, December 2019. https://thelawreviews.co.uk/edition/the-insolvency-review-edition-7/1211464/cyprus. Last visited on 24 December 2019.

Christou, S. & S. Christofides. *Examinership: A Process of Saving Jobs while Taking Care of Creditors' Interests.* https://www.gzg.com.cy/media/filer_public/62/26/62264990-bf61-4068-838f-0579a4c35a39/examinership.pdf. July 2017.

Clarke, A. & P. Kohler. *Property Law, Commentary and Materials.* Cambridge University Press, 2005.

Dixon, M. *Modern Land Law.* 6th ed. Routledge-Cavendish, 2009.

Emilianides, A. *Family and Succession Law in Cyprus.* 6th ed. Wolters Kluwer, 2019.

French, D. *Mayson, French & Ryan on Company Law.* Oxford University Press, 2018–2019.

Georgiades, K. & K. Brandysova. *International Secured Transactions.* Chapter 11 Cyprus. https://www.neocleous.com. Last visited on 23 December 2019.

Gray, K. & S. Gray. *Elements of Land Law.* 5th ed. OUP, 2009.

Greville, H.H. & R. Harling Maudsley, *Hanbury and Maudsley Modern Equity.* 12th ed. Edited by Jill E. Martin. London: Stevens, 1985.

Selected Bibliography

Habdas, M. *Property and Trust Law in Poland*. Kluwer Law International, 2018.

Hatzimihail, N. 'Reconstructing Mixity: Sources of Law and Legal Method in Cyprus'. In *Mixed Legal Systems, East and West*, edited by Vernon Valentine Palmer, Mohamed Y. Mattar & Anna Koppel. Routledge, 2016.

Hatzinestoros, E. & G. Charalampous. *Cypriot Sale of Goods Law and Consumer Protection*. Nomiki Vivliothiki, 2016.

Hudson, A. *Equity and Trusts*. 4th ed. Cavendish Publishing 2005.

Ioannidis, A.P. *The Land and Survey Department: Jurisprudence and Land Registry Procedures*. Volume 2. Dorographics Ltd, 1998.

Ioannidis, A.P. *The Land Registry and Surveys Department, Legislation and Land Registry Procedures*. Volume 4. Nicosia, June 2006.

Ioannou, C. *Cypriot Land Law*. Nomiki Vivliothiki, 2014.

Ioannou, G. & A. Christophorou. *Amendments to Transfer and Mortgage of Immovable Property Law Introduced.*. October 2018.

Iordanou Theodoulou L., et al. *Lending and Taking Security in Cyprus: Overview*. https://uk.practicallaw.thomsonreuters.com/. Last visited on 23 December 2019.

Jougleux, P. *Elements of Cypriot Law of Obligations*. Athens-Thessaloniki: Sakkoulas Publications, 2011.

Kälin, H.C. *International Real Estate Handbook: Acquisition, Ownership and Sale of Real Estate, Residence, Tax and Inheritance Law*. John Wiley & Sons, 2005.

Karibali-Tsiptsiou, Y. *The Full Personal Easement of Habitation, Contribution to the Analysis of Easements*. Thessaloniki: Sakkoulas Publications, 1986.

Karibali-Tsiptsiou, Y. *Property and Trust Law – Greece*. International Encyclopaedia of Laws. Wolters Kluwer, Law & Business, 2012.

Knobel, I. 'Accession of Movables to Movables and Inaedificatio – South Africa and Some Common Law Countries'. *Journal of Contemporary Roman-Dutch Law* 74 (May 6, 2011): 296. https://ssrn.com/abstract=2016868.

Kombos, C. 'Le Droit de la necessité à Chypre'. In *La singularité de Chypre dans l'Union Européenne, Diversité des droits et des statuts*, edited by J. Rosseto & K. Joséphides. Paris: Mare & Martin, 2012.

Kombos, C. & S. Laulhé Shaelou. 'The Cypriot Constitution under the Impact of EU Law: An Asymmetrical Formation'. In *National Constitutions in European and Global Governance: Democracy, Rights, the Rule of Law*, edited by A. Albi & S. Bardutzky. The Hague: T.M.C. Asser Press, 2019.

Kombos, C. *The Doctrine of Necessity in Constitutional Law*. Athens: Sakkoulas Publications, 2015.

Konistis, T. *TENLAW: Tenancy Law and Housing Policy in Multi-level Europe: Tenant's Rights Brochure for CYPRUS*. National Report for Cyprus, Team Leader: Elena Bargelli, National Supervisor: Tatiani Eleni Synodinou. https://www.uni-bremen.de/fileadmin/user_upload/fachbereiche/fb6/fb6/Forschung/ZERP/TENLAW/Reports/CyprusReport_09052014.pdf Last visited on 20 December 2019.

Koukiadis, D. 'Legal Transplantation's Contribution to the Formation of Mixed Legal Systems, and the Paradigm of Cyprus' Legal System as a "Polyjural" System'. *Cyprus Law Review* 30 (Fall 2018) no. 2: 87–101.

Kountourisis, K. *Compulsory Grant of Way of Right* . Athens: P.N. Sakkoulas Publications, 1986.

Koutas, N. 'Real Property in Cyprus'. In *Studies on Cypriot Law*, edited by G. Shergides. Nicosia, 1992.

Kammitsi, L., President of Rent Control Court. *Lecture on Rent Control*. Limassol, 19 April 2007.

McFarlane, B., N. Hopkins & S. Nield. *Land Law, Text, Cases and Materials*. Oxford University Press, 2009.

Mangatchev, I.P. *Fiducia cum creditore contracta in EU*. https://www.academia.edu/3496659/Fiducia_cum_creditore_contracta_in_EU_law. Last visited on 23 December 2019.

Martínez Velencoso, L., S. Bailey & A. Pradi (eds). *Transfer of Immovables in European Private Law*. Cambridge University Press, 2017.

Mattei, U. *Basic Principles of Property Law: A Comparative Legal and Economic Introduction*. Greenwood Press, 2000.

Mowbray, J., et al. *Lewin on Trusts*. 17th ed. Sweet & Maxwell Ltd, 2000.

Neocleous, A. & D. Bevir. 'Legal History'. In *Introduction to Cyprus Law, Andreas Neocleous & Co*, edited by D. Campbell. Law Publishing, 2000.

Neocleous, E. & G. Chrysaphinis. 'Cyprus'. In *International Secured Transactions*. Thomson Reuters, 10/2015. https://www.neocleous.com.

Neocleous, E. & M. Kyriacou. *Multi-jurisdictional Guide 2011/12, Restructuring and Insolvency*. Andreas Neocleous & Co LLC, Practical Law Company, 2012. https://www.neocleous.com/publications/plc_restructuring_chapter_cyprus-pdf

Newsom, G.L. *Preston & Newscom's Restrictive Covenants Affecting Freehold Land, Property and Conveyancing Library*. 8th ed. London: Sweet & Maxwell, 1991.

Oakley, A.J., D.B. Parker & A.R. Mellows. *The Modern Law of Trusts*. 9th ed. Sweet & Maxwell, 2008.

Palmer, N. & A. Hudson. 'Improving Stolen Chattels'. In *Interests in Goods*, edited by N. Palmer & E. McKendrick. 2nd ed. LLP Reference Publishing, 1998.

Papandréou-Deterville, M.F. *Le droit anglais de biens*. L.G.D.J. 2004.

Papasteriou, D. *Land Law. Ownership*. Volume II. Athens-Thessaloniki: Sakkoulas Publications, 2008.

Papastylianos, C. 'The Cypriot Doctrine of Necessity within the Context of Emergency Discourse: How a Unique Emergency Shaped a Peculiar Type of Emergency Law'. *Cyprus Review* 30 (April 2018) no. 1: 113–144.

Paraskevas, C. *Cypriot Constitutional Law*. Nomiki Vivliothiki, 2015.

Piotr, S. 'Fiducia in an Emerging Economy'. In *Modern Studies in Property Law*, edited by Elizabeth Cooke. Volume 2. Hart Publishing, 2003.

Pogiatzis, I. 'Immovable Property Law'. *Cypriot Law Review* (July-December 1993).

Pogiatzis, I. 'Land Law'. In *Coprus de Jure Cyprii, Edition of the Board of Legal Studies*, Nicosia, 1988.

Pollock, F. & Wright, R. *An Essay on Possession in Common Law*. Oxford at the Clarendon Press, 1888.

Pollock and Mulla, *Indian Contract and Specific Relief Acts*. 9th ed. Bombay, N.M. Tripathi, 1972.

Pollock and Mulla. *Indian Contract and Specific Relief Acts*. 16th ed. Lexis Nexis, 2019.

Polyviou, P. *The Case of Ibrahim, the Doctrine of Necessity and the Republic of Cyprus*. Chryssafinis & Polyviou Publications, Nicosia, 2015.

Rahmatian, A. *A Comparison of German Movable Property Law and English Personal Property Law.* https://germanlawarchive.iuscomp.org/?p=340.

Shaelou, S., S. Stylianou & K. Anastasiou. 'National Report on the Transfer of Movables'. In *England and Wales, Ireland, Scotland, Cyprus*, edited by W. Faber & B. Lurger. Volume II. Selier European Law Publishers, 2009.

Sonti, I. *Contributions to Theory of Land Law.* Athens-Komotini: A. N. Sakkoulas Publications, 1986.

Sparks, P. *European Land Law.* Hart Publishing, 2007.

Stavrakis, A. *Granting a Way of Right under Sections 1012-1017 of Civil Code, Law & Economy.* P.N. Sakkoulas, 2009.

Symeonides, S.C. 'The Mixed Legal System of the Republic of Cyprus'. *Tulane Law Review* 78 (2003): 442.

Symeou, A. *The Protection of Property and Compulsory Acquisition of Property in Cyprus*. 2003.

Synodinou, T. *Land Law in Cyprus.* Athens-Thessaloniki: Sakkoulas Editions, 2011.

Synodinou, T. 'Real Property in Cyprus: In Search of an Identity'. *Jahreshefte der Internationalen Juristenvereinigung Osnabrück* (IJVO) 18 (2014).

Synodinou, T. 'The Land Registry in Cyprus: Between Formalism and Realism'. In *Grundbuchfunktionen im europäischen Rechtsvergleich (Functions of land registers in European Comparative Law Perspective)*, edited by A. Wudarski. Das Grundbuch im Europa des 21, Jahrhunderts. Berlin: Duncker & Humblot, 2016.

Synodinou, T. *Cypriot Private Law, Analysis by Law and Article.* Athens-Thessaloniki: Sakkoulas Publications, 2014.

Synodinou, T. 'Protection de la propriété à Chypre: cadre légal et frontières de l'acquis communautaire'. In *La singularité de Chypre dans l'Union Européenne, Diversité des droits et des statuts*, edited by J. Rosseto & K. Joséphides (Paris: Mare & Martin, 2012).

Synodinou, T. 'Copyright News from Cyprus'. *Revue Internationale du droit d'auteur* 261 (2019).

Tenekides, G. *La condition internationale de la République de Chypre.* Annuaire Français de Droit International, 1960.

Theofanopoulos, D. *System of Roman Law, Real Property Law*. Athens: M.I. Saliverou Publications, 1900.

Tornaritis, C. *The Evolution of the Law Relating to Land in Cyprus.* Nicosia, 1982.

Triantos, N. *Easements, Transcription, Land Registry.*Nomiki Vivliothiki, 2000.

Tsikkinis, L. *Land Law.* In *Neocleous's Introduction to Cyprus Law*, edited by D. Campbell. 2009.

Tsikkinis, L. 'Law of Succession'. In *Introduction to Cyprus Law, Andreas Neocleous & Co.* Yorkhill Law Publishing, 2000.

VerSteeg, R. *The Essentials of Greek and Roman Law.* Carolina Academic Press, 2010.

Vezouvios, C. & L. Tsikkinis. 'Cyprus'. In *ICLG, The International Comparative Legal Guide to: Real Estate, A Practical Cross-Border Insight to Real Estate Law*. 10th ed. London: Global Legal Group Ltd, 2015.

Worthington, S. *Personal Property Law Text and Materials.* Hart Publishing, 2000.

Yiallourou, S. *Enclaved Buyers: The Problem, Regulation and Constitutionality.* 2019. Available at: https://www.academia.edu/40671133.

Selected Bibliography

Table of Cases

Cypriot Case Law

A Pilottos Ltd et al. v. George Houghton et al., under the commercial name Sports Car Consultants (2007) 1 CLR 783
A. Gheorgiou v. K. Gheorgiou Andrea (1998) 1 D CLR 2311
A. P. Georgiades Ltd v. Space Bakery Plant & Equipment Ltd (2001) 1 CLR 916
Achilleos et al. v. Pittaras et al. (2012) 1 CLR 1590
Adamou v. Christophi (1974) 1 CLR 100
Administrative Court, DOMOPLEX LTD v. The Republic of Cyprus, Joined Cases Nos 889/2014 & 890/2014, 3 April 2019
Agapiou v. Panayiotou (1988) 1 CLR 257
Agathocleous Ltd v. Sofokleous (2000) 1C CLR 1953
Aggelidis and Filippou Ltd v. Spyros Colocassides Estates Ltd (1991) 1 CLR 327
Aggelidis v. Cooperative Credit Company of Palouriotisa (1997) 1C CLR 1771
Agrotis v. Electricity Authority (1981) 3 CLR 50
Ahmet HJ Hassan Dandelen v. Suleiman Ibrahim et al. (V4) (1898) 1 CLR 78
Ahmet Mulla Suleyman v. The Republic of Cyprus, No. 99/2005, 21 May 2007
Akama Theofanou et al. v. Ioannou Tsiakoli (1967) 1 CLR 206
Akil Hussein Arnaout v. Emine Hussein Zinouri, Civil Appeal No. 4012, 1953
Alexandrou v. Eleftheriou, No. 2043/2011, 22 June 2015
Ali Ibrahim Houssein Basma v. The Republic of Cyprus, No. 1353/2008, 3 September 2009
Alpan Furnishings Limited v. Savva Dimadi (1989) CLR 170
Alpha Bank Cyprus Ltd v. District Land Officer of Larnaca of the Department of Land and Surveys of the Ministry of Interior, Request for Appeal No. 24/2017, 8 March 2019
Alpha Bank Cyprus Ltd v. District Land Officer of Limassol, No. 53/16, 17 May 2017
Alpha Bank Ltd v. Director of the Department of Land and Surveys of Paphos, No. 71/16, 24 May 2017
Altan Salih Niazi v. The Republic of Cyprus through the Minister of Interior, No. 631/2005, 10 November 2006
Anastasiou v. Kyprianou et al. (2002) 1 CLR 1695
Anastassis Charalambous v. Alkis Demetriou (1961) 1 CLR 30

Table of Cases

Andreas Pericleous (Development) Ltd v. 1. Attorney General of the Republic, 2. Minister of Interior as Guardian of the Turkish Cypriot properties, 3. Director of Lands and Surveys, No. 627/2005, 18 December 2006
Andreou v. Chrysostomou (2006) 1B CLR 820
Angeli v. Lambi et al. (1963) 2 CLR 274
Antoniou Chrysostomou v. Christou Antoniou Frangou et al. (2000) 1 CLR 622
Apex Ltd v. Argyridou (1989) 1 CLR 265
Apollonio Private Hospital Ltd v. C & S American Heart Institute Ltd et al. (2011) 1(A) CLR 379
Archimandritis Sevastianos Stavrou v. Iera Moni Metamorfoseos, No. 110/2011, 7 February 2014.
Argiri v. Chrysostomou as an Administrator of the estate of Chrysanthos Chrysostomou (2006) 1 CLR 1362
Arif Moustafa v. Ministry of the Interior, No. 125/2004, 24 September 2004
Ashiotis et al. v. M Weiner et al. (1968) 1 CLR 43
Athanasi et al. v. Hadjimama et al. (1990) 1 CLR 208
Avgousti et al. v. Spyridou, Political Appeal No. 114/2012, 24 April 2018
Ayios Andronikos Development Co. Ltd v. The Republic of Cyprus through the Minister of Interior, the Director of Lands and Surveys and the Minister of Finance (1985) 3D CLR 2362
Ayoub v. Director of the Land Registry, No. 5165/2012, 20 November 2018
*Bank of Cyprus Plc v. ALENTIA LIMITED et al.***,** claim No. 4763/2013, 17 May 2019
Beaumont v. Papacleovoulou (2010) 1A CLR 525
Callia in his capacity as Receiver and Administrator of Pak Estates Limited and I Andri Georgiou (Coiffure) Limited v. 1. Georgiou 2. Andri Georgiou (Coiffure) Limited et al., No. 3587/10, 16 July 2010.
Cantounas v. Ioannis N. Patsalides General Entreprises Ltd, 2004 1C CLR 1876
Charalambous v. Aristo Developers Ltd (2009) 1 CLR 834
Charalampidis v. Konstantinou, Civil Appeal No. 85733 (1996) CLR
Chimonides v. Manglis (1967) 1 CLR 125
Christodoulou v. Chrysostomou (2006) 1B CLR 820
Christodoulou v. Eurika Ltd (2008) 1 CLR 1243
Christodoulou v. Minister of the Interior, as the Guardian of Turkish Cypriot Property through the Attorney General of the Republic, No. 331/2014, 29 July 2016
Christofi v. Kleanthous (2010) 1 CLR 1050
Christophorou et al. v. Bank of Cyprus Ltd (2003) 1B CLR 1205
Christophorou v. Vouria (1994) 1 CLR 624
Christophorou v. Christophorou (1998) 1 CLR 1551
Christos Agathocleous Ltd v. Sofocleous (2000) 1 CLR 1953
Christostomou Bros Company Ltd v. Theodorou Kapnisi, No. of Claim 1707/07, 9 January 2013
Christou Nicos Developments Ltd. v. Panagiotis Tofini (1998) 1 CLR 1990
Chrysanthou v. Pagkratiou (1998) 1B CLR 675
Chrysostomou Chalkousi & Sons v. Chalkousi & Sons (1978) 1 CLR 10
Chrysostomou v. Fragkou et al. (2000) 1 CLR 622

Chryssochou Bros v. 1. The Cyprus Telecommunications Authority 2. The Republic of Cyprus through the Council of Ministers (1966) 3 CLR 482
Clerides v. Stavrides (1998) 1 CLR 521
Constantinou v. Attorney General of the Republic (1997) 1 CLR 741
Constantinou v. Panayides (1984) 1 CLR 466
Constantinou v. Demosthenous (1992) 1 CLR 621
Constantinou as an Administrator of the estate of Stylianou v. Courides, No. 3011/08, 13 Mar h 2013
Crestar (overseas) Ltd et al. v. Visotskagia (2008) 1B CLR 942
Cyprus Cinema & Theatre Co. Ltd v. Karmiotis (1967) 1 CLR 42
Cyprus Tourism Organization v. Charilaou (1998) 1 CLR 607
D. Patiki v. A. G. Patiki and Co et al. (V20) (1954) 1 CLR 36
Demetriades v. The Republic (1974) 4 JSC 480
Diomidous et al. v. Diomidous et al., Political Appeal Nos 329/2011, 343/2011, 12 October 2017
Dionisiou v. Cyprus Bank Ltd, No. 450/12, 26 June 2019
Diplaros v. Nicola (1974) 1 CLR 198
Director of customs v. Pop life electric shops Ltd et al., Nicosia District Court, No. 4941/2008, 19 December 2014
Director of the Department of Land Registry v. Stavrou, Civil Appeal No. 156/2010, 24 March 2015
Director of the Land Registry v. Caracotou (2005) 1 CLR 99
Electricity Authority of Cyprus v. Milk and Ice Cream Zumaras Industry, No. 2734/15, 27 July 2017
Eliadis et al. v. Papakyriakou et al., Civil Appeal No. 220/2012, 27 November 2018
Ellinas v. Hajisolomou (1984) 1 CLR 225
Elliniki Trapeza Ltd and Trapeza Barkleys Plc v. Tsartelli (2003) 1 CLR 246
The Estate of the Deceased Osman Ahmed Pasha v. Mehmed Osman Pasha, 19 C.L.R. 226
Eystathiou v. Panayi (1992) 1B CLR 1297
Fezile Ahmet v. Republic of Cyprus, No. 1482/2010, 24 September 2012
Fili et al. v. The Republic of Cyprus et al. (1997) 4B CLR 1257
Flower, etc. v. Hadjiioannou, etc. (2008) 1B CLR 770
Fotiou v. Municipality of Larnaca (1997) 4 CLR 2815
Frostin Limited v. Bank of Cyprus Ltd, Request for Appeal No. 204/2016, District Court of Paphos, 14 November 2016
G. Spyropoulos Developments Ltd v. 1. Attorney General of the Republic, 2. Minister of Interior as Guardian of the Turkish Cypriot properties and 3. Director of Lands and Surveys, No. 626/2005, 4 October 2006.
Gavriilidi v. Hadjikyriakou et al. (1898) 4 CLR 84
Georghiades & Others v. Lambis (1976) 8 J.S.C. 1332
Georghiou v. Andrea (1998) 1(D) CLR 2311
Georghiou v. Hadjifessa (1970) 1 CLR 58
Georghiou v. Komodromou (1963) 2 CLR 221
Georgios Iraklidis & Sia Ltd et.al v. Director of the District Lands Office et.al, Application Appeal No. 10/99, 26 January 2001
Georgiou v. Argyrides (2012) 1 CLR185

Table of Cases

The Attorney General of the Republic v. The Water Board of Nicosia (1961) CLR 1
The Jerusalem and the East Mission Trust (Cyprus) v. Republic of Cyprus through 1. Council of Ministers 2. Minister of the Interior (1998) 4 CLR 598
The Lost Resort Ltd v. Municipality of Paphos, No. 1283/2016, 13 January 2017
The Republic of Cyprus through the Commissioner of Income Tax v. Charalambos Menelaou, 3 CLR 419, 11 May 1982
The Republic v. Demetriades (1977) JSC 2102
The Republic v. Sampson (1977) 2 CLR 1
Themistokleous v. Christodoulou (2010) 1 CLR 1177
Theodorou v. Hadjiantoni (1961) CLR 203
Thrasyvoulou v. Thrasyvoulou (1984) 1 CLR 411
Torgut Yashar as proxy of Yuksel Cemal Hudaverdi v. The Republic of Cyprus through the Director of Lands and Surveys, No. 454/2002, 16 September 2004
Tribunal of Limassol, Louimar Fisheries Lt v. 5 Oceans Food Ltd, No. 470/2008, 16 June 2014
Tsialis v. Hatziiandreou et al. (2000) 1(B) CLR 1250
Tsiamanta v. Tsiamanta (1990) 1 CLR 97526
Tsiartas et al. v. Alocay Holdings Ltd et al. (2010) 1 CLR 1523
Tsinki et al. v. The King's Advocate 10 CLR 55, 9 February 1914
Valana v. Elia (1983) 1 C.L.R 730
Venglis and The Electricity Authority (1965) 3 CLR 252
Voskou v. Hadjipetrou (1964) CLR 21
Vrahimi v. Kouloumbri (1992) 1 CLR 836
Yiangou Aradippioti v. Christos Kyriakou and others et al. (1971) 1 CLR 381
Zenon Efthimiadis Estates Ltd v. The Republic (2006) 3 CLR 166
Zinonas v. Pagkratiou (1998) 1 CLR 675

EU Case Law

Decision of the CJEU
Case C-420/07 *Meletios Apostolides v. David Charles Orams, Linda Elizabeth Orams*, Judgment of the Court (Grand Chamber) (2009), ECLI:EU:C:2009:271
European Court of Human Rights Case Law
ECHR, *Ali Kamil Karamanoglu and others v. Cyprus*, No. 49247 6 March 2012
ECHR, *Cyprus v. Turkey [GC]*, No. 25781/94, 10 May 2001
ECHR, *Demades v. Turkey*, No. 16219/90, 31 July 2003
ECHR, *Demopoulos et al. v. Turkey [GC]*, Nos 46113/99, 3843/02, 13751/02, 13466/03, 10200/04, 14163/04, 19993/04, 21819/04, 1 March 2010
ECHR, *Eugenia Michaelidou Developments Ltd and Michael Tymvios v. Turkey*, No. 16163/90, 31 July 2003
ECHR, *Mehmet Yilmaz v. Republic of Cyprus*, No. 4722/05, 28 August 2012
ECHR, *Loizidou v. Turkey* (Merits) No. 15318/89, 18 December 1996
ECHR, *Loizidou v. Turkey* (Preliminary Objections) No. 15318/89, 23 March 1995
ECHR, *Michael Tymvios v. Turkey*, No. 16163/90, 31 July 2003
ECHR, *Xenidis-Arestis v. Turkey*, No. 46347/99, 22 December 2005

Australian Case Law

Grant v. Australian Knitting Mills [1936] AC 85

Indian Case Law

R D Goyal and Anr v. Reliance Industries Ltd (2003) 1 SCC 81

UK Case Law

Ackroyd v. Smith [1850] 10 CB 164
Aldred's Case [1610] 9 Co Rep 57b
Baker v. Baker (1993) 25 HLR 408
Borden (UK) Ltd v. Scottish Timber Products Ltd [1981] Ch 25
Bridges v. Hawkesworth [1851] 21 LJQB 75, 15 Jur. 1079.
Copeland v. Greenhalf [1952] 1 All ER 809
Dalton v. Henry Angus & Co [1881] UKHL 1
D'Eyncourt v. Gregory [1866] LR 3 Eq 382
Elitestone Ltd v. Morris and Another [1997] 1 WLR 687
Elwes v. Brigg Gas co (1886) 33 ChD
Hannah v. Peel 1 K.B. 509 (1945)
Hatton v. Car Maintenance co Ltd [1915] 1 Ch 621
Hawkins v. Rutter [1892] 1 QB 668, D
Haywood v. Brunswick Permanent Benefit Building Society [1881] 8 QBD 403
Hunter v. Canary Wharf Ltd [1997] AC 655
IRC v. Electric Industries [1949] 1 All ER 120-6
Independent Trustee Services Limited v. GP Noble Trustees Limited & Others [2012] EWCA Civ 195
Keppel v. Bailey [1834] 2 My & K 517(1822-34), All ER Rep. 10
League Against Cruel Sports v. Scott [1985] 2 All ER 489
Leigh v. Taylor [1902] AC 157
Macmillan Inc v. Bishopsgate Investment Trust plc (No. 3) [1995] 1 WLR 978
Microbeads v. Vihurst Road Markings [1975] 1 WLR
Moody v. Steggles [1879] 12 Ch D 261
Pascoe v. Turner [1979] 2 All ER 945
Rangeley v. Midland Ry. Co. [1868] 3 Ch App 306
Re Diplock [1948] Ch 465
Re Ellenborough Park [1956] Ch 131
Re Peachdart Ltd [1984] Ch 131
Rhondda Cynon Taff County BC v. Watkins [2003] EWCA Civ 129, [2003] 1 WLR 1864
Roe v. Siddons [1888] 22 QBD 224
St Albans City and District Council v. International Computers Ltd [1996] 4 All ER 481
Taylor Fashions Ltd v. Liverpool Victoria Trustees Co [1981] 1 All ER 897
Thornborough v. Baker (1675) 36 ER 1000
Walsh v. Walsh et al. (1953) 1 All ER 1982
Waverley Borough Council v. Fletcher [1995] 4 All ER 756
Westdeutsche Landesbank Girozentrale v. Islington LBC [1996] AC 669
Winter Garden Theatre (London) Ltd v. Millennium Productions Ltd [1946] 1 All ER 678, 680

US Case Law

Table of Cases

Moore v. Regents of the University of California 51 Cal. 3d 120. 271 Cal. Rptr. 146; 793 P.2d 479

Index

The numbers here refer to paragraph numbers.

Index

Index

www.ingramcontent.com/pod-product-compliance
Lightning Source LLC
Chambersburg PA
CBHW071442230926
51846CB00001B/315
9789403527307